ADVENTURES IN THE SANTA FÉ TRADE
1844–1847

by

JAMES JOSIAH WEBB

edited by
RALPH P. BIEBER

D0752881

Introduction to the Bison Book Edition
by Mark L. Gardner

University of Nebraska Press
Lincoln and London

Introduction to the Bison Book Editon © 1995 by the University
of Nebraska Press
Manufactured in the United States of America

⊖ The paper in this book meets the minimum requirements of
American National Standard for Information Sciences—Permanence
of Paper for Printed Library Materials, ANSI z39.48-1984.

First Bison Book printing: 1995
Most recent printing indicated by the last digit below:
10   9   8   7   6   5   4   3   2   1

Library of Congress Cataloging-in-Publication Data
Webb, James Josiah, 1818–1869.
Adventures in the Santa Fe trade, 1844–1847 / by James Josiah Webb;
edited by Ralph P. Beiber.—Bison book ed.
p.   cm.
Originally published: Glendale, Calif.: A. H. Clark Co., 1931.
ISBN 0-8032-9772-6
1. Santa Fe Trail.   2. Chihuahua Trail.   3. Southwest, New—His-
tory—To 1848.   4. Webb, James Josiah, 1818–1869.   5. Mexico—
Commerce—History—19th century.   6. Frontier and pioneer life—
Mexico.   7. Frontier and pioneer life—Southwest, New.   I. Title.
F786.w36   1995
978'.02—dc20
94-43638   CIP

Reprinted from the original edition published in 1931 by the Arthur H.
Clark Company, Glendale, California

To the memory of
JAMES HENRY WEBB
Judge of the Superior Court of Connecticut
1914–1924

CONTENTS

ILLUSTRATIONS

INTRODUCTION TO THE BISON BOOK EDITION
Mark L. Gardner

"My preference is for the eyewitness," historian Bernard DeVoto once wrote, "for an intelligent eyewitness if he can be found but for any kind of eyewitness if intelligent ones are lacking."[1] James Josiah Webb is De-Voto's intelligent eyewitness. As a merchant on the Santa Fe and Chihuahua trails in the 1840s, Webb was a participant in the most celebrated international trade of the nineteenth-century West. He traveled to Santa Fe with merchandise when that city was still the capital of a Mexican province, when foreign goods had to be entered at a customs house, duties paid, and contraband either smuggled in or illegally entered with an inducement to the customs officers. Yet Webb was also one of the last to witness this feature of the "commerce of the prairies," for following in the wake of his Santa Fe–bound caravan in 1846 marched the Army of the West under Stephen Watts Kearny. War with Mexico had begun. Kearny's subsequent conquest of New Mexico brought an end to Mexican rule there, thus marking the close of an era, not only for the overland trade but for the entire Southwest.

Webb's *Adventures in the Santa Fe Trade, 1844–47* offers an inside look at the Santa Fe and Chihuahua trade on the eve of the Mexican War, as well as the complications and risks that that war caused for enterprising and determined American merchants such as Webb. His narrative is also interspersed with valuable observations on everyday life along the trail and in the Southwest during that transitional period. That Webb was able to record his vivid impressions with astounding accuracy decades after the events occurred is amazing and, for us, quite fortunate. Jack D. Rittenhouse, in his *The Santa Fe Trail: A Historical Bibliography,* wrote that Webb's memoirs are "Considered by many to be second only to the book by Josiah Gregg [*Commerce of the Prairies*] as a firsthand account by a major trader over the SFT [Santa Fe Trail]."[2] In my opinion, however, it stands second to none in many regards.

Webb came to know most of the characters, both prominent and obscure, Mexican and American, who played a role in the annals of the Santa Fe trade. But where some of these individuals are little more than footnotes in most narratives, Webb has a well-chosen anecdote or reminiscence that brings them to life.

Albert Speyer (also Speyers) is one personality who figures prominently in Webb's *Adventures*. He is generally remembered as the object of one of the greatest pursuits in the history of the West. This occurred shortly after the outbreak of the Mexican War when it was learned that Speyer's wagon train was carrying arms and ammunition intended for Chihuahua's governor. Two companies of U.S. dragoons sent by Kearny to halt the trader failed to overtake him. Webb, who likewise had a train in front of the Army of the West, provides some firsthand observations on this intriguing episode, but his narrative also reveals a man who was perhaps the smoothest entrepreneur (except maybe James Magoffin) who ever traveled the Trail. Time and again we see how Speyer, usually through the use of copious amounts of wine and some generous "gifts," is able to extricate himself from the most difficult situations, be they with Mexican officials or American.

Another individual about whom Webb provides much detail is Manuel Armijo, governor of the New Mexican province for many years. But unlike Speyer, Armijo is a figure who receives considerable coverage in the historical record, almost always in a negative light, and generally in relation to his "arbitrary" duty of $500 or more per wagon regardless of the contents. Webb's portrayal of the infamous governor, however, is a sympathetic one. Yes, Armijo had a per-wagon duty, Webb informs us, but if the governor had demanded the duties actually required by Mexican law the traders would have paid "from $1,800 to $2,500 the wagon load." "This was the foundation of the Santa Fe trade," Webb writes, "and the only advantage gained by introducing goods by the overland route for Chihuahua and the interior states of Mexico." According to Webb, Armijo's per-wagon duty in fact resulted in an increase in the trade.

There is much that is revealing in Webb's *Adventures* when it comes to the nature of the overland trade with Mexico. For one, Webb and his fellow American traders were, in his own words, "recognized and confessed contrabandists." American merchants, including Webb, spent a considerable amount of time devising ways to evade Mexican law, whether through smuggling or bribes. One comical individual in Webb's narrative, Nicholas Gentry, was commonly known by both the Americans and the Mexicans as "Old Contraband Gentry"! We also learn that the trade could at times be cutthroat. Webb relates how in 1844 one American firm was able to make an arrangement with the New Mexican governor giving them exclusive rights to retail goods in Santa Fe, thus cornering the market there. And in an episode demonstrating the rivalry between American and Mexican traders, Webb tells us that some American merchants acted together one year to reduce the competition from their Mexican counterparts by spreading rumors of an expedition of Texans organizing to raid Mexican caravans on the Trail.

During the Mexican War, business interests remained first and foremost with these prairie traders. Indeed, some saw the war as an opportunity to make additional profits on goods. And it is obvious from Webb's memoirs, as well as from the accounts of others, that they had few qualms about commercial intercourse with the enemy (the U.S. government in fact supported the continuation of the overland trade). But there were consequences and genuine risks associated with this quest for profits during wartime.

One evening in 1846, the caravan of Albert Speyer, which included the wagons of Webb and a partner, was halted by Mexican troops at Peñol in the State of Chihuahua. Speyer and Webb withheld from their American teamsters the information they learned, that they were all to become prisoners, fearing that their men would make a break for New Mexico during the night. They even directed the mules to be grazed far from their camp to prevent this. Webb's explanation for his and Speyer's actions is that had the teamsters escaped it "would have given us great trouble and imperiled our pecuniary interests."

Webb convinced the teamsters to surrender their arms the next day and traders and teamsters continued as prisoners to Chihuahua City. When Speyer and Webb did assist their teamsters to elude Mexican control (after having been allowed to proceed on their journey from Chihuahua sometime later), the men had to cross such unfamiliar country in an effort to reach U.S. forces at Monclova that several perished in the desert. The rest wandered back half-dead to the town of Guajuquilla (Jiménez). Had the merchants been able to disregard their "pecuniary interests" and given their men the opportunity to take their leave from Peñol, making a beeline for New Mexico, this tragedy might well have been averted.

The many expenses, delays, and anxiety that Webb experienced as a trader and, at times, prisoner, in wartime Mexico leaves one wondering how any profit could have resulted from this venture at all. Yet profits were made, by Webb and other merchants, too. It is only somewhat remarkable, then, that shortly after Webb's return to St. Louis in July 1847 he was eager to head back down the trail with wagons of merchandise. His reason: "there appeared to be a fine prospect for trade."

This "fine prospect for trade" would keep Webb's business interests in the Southwest for several years after the Mexican War. But the place that made his fortune was not to become his permanent home. Webb eventually left the trade for a large farm in his native Connecticut. The 1860 census for New Haven County lists James J. Webb as a forty-two-year-old farmer with real estate valued at $15,000 and a personal estate at $25,000.[3] When he died twenty-nine years later his estate was appraised at $53,249.35. Webb's Spring Glen Farm (215¼ acres), dwelling house and out buildings at Hamden, Connecticut, accounted for $43,000 of that total, reflecting a success as a farmer and dairyman that more than matched his earlier pursuit of Santa Fe trader.[4] Ironically, Webb's most historically valuable possessions were not listed in his estate inventory: his unfinished memoirs and mountains of correspondence and business records.

James Webb somehow managed to save nearly every invoice, letter, and account book generated by his seventeen years as a southwest trader, as well as his subsequent agricultural activities. Today these records constitute one of the greatest treasure troves of primary materials relating to the Santa Fe trade and pre–Civil War New Mexico known to exist. They are by far the most complete set of records documenting the business pursuits of one particular merchant, and, until recent years, have remained largely untapped. This archival legacy is split between three institutions. The Missouri Historical Society in St. Louis has the largest collection of Webb's business records as a Santa Fe trader, contained in eight document boxes of correspondence and over twenty bound volumes of letterbooks, purchase journals, and account books. In the Hamden Historical Society Library, Hamden, Connecticut, are two linear feet of manuscript materials pertaining to both Webb's career as a trader on the Santa Fe Trail and a Connecticut farmer. The smallest collection, though still valuable, resides at Southern Methodist University's DeGolyer Library, Dallas, Texas. It consists of forty-four items of correspondence between Webb and partner John M. Kingsbury.[5]

Among Webb's papers at the Missouri Historical Society is a 106-year-old manuscript of 248 pages. On these pages, actually stationery from Webb's Spring Glen Stock and Dairy Farm, are written in pencil the "adventures" that make up this book.[6] Historian Ralph Bieber (1894–1981) masterfully transcribed and edited these memoirs for publication by Arthur H. Clark Company, Glendale, California, in 1931. Printed in an edition of 1,252 copies, the book was the first volume in Clark's invaluable Southwest Historical Series, edited by Bieber and LeRoy Hafen. Bieber's informative annotations wonderfully supplement Webb's memoirs, in part because Bieber had Webb's business records at his disposal. Furthermore, Bieber's biographical sketches of many of the personalities mentioned by Webb are a model of scholarship decades later.

One individual who apparently knew Webb wrote that the old trader's "anecdotes of personal travel . . . while engaged in the mercantile business in Santa Fe would fill a volume of very interesting narrative."[7] As it turns out, this was a considerable understatement, for Webb's account of his activities for just three years in the trade does that. And while it is unfortunate that Webb was unable to complete his memoirs beyond 1847, scholars and those with an interest in the American Southwest and Mexico can still take pleasure in his *Adventures in the Santa Fe Trade* and be thankful that the University of Nebraska Press has made it available again. Perhaps more importantly, there is the promise of future volumes of scholarship on the Santa Fe trade that will be immeasurably enhanced by the insights provided in the priceless records that Webb and his family chose to preserve.

ADDITIONAL READING

Josiah Gregg's *Commerce of the Prairies*, first published in 1844 and reprinted numerous times since, is the standard work on the Santa Fe and Chihuahua trade during the Mexican period by a participant and is an excellent companion to Webb's *Adventures*. Webb is more candid in many respects than Gregg, but then again Webb had the advantage of writing his account many years after the fact and, perhaps intending his memoirs only for friends and family, did not have to worry about its reception among his fellow traders and the public.

For other firsthand accounts dealing with the experiences of overland merchants caught up in the Mexican War see Mark L. Gardner, ed., *Brothers on the Santa Fe and Chihuahua Trails: Edward James Glasgow and William Henry Glasgow, 1846–1848* (Niwot: University Press of Colorado, 1993), and Susan Magoffin's *Down the Santa Fe Trail and into Mexico: The Diary of Susan Shelby Magoffin, 1846–1847*, edited by Stella M. Drumm (1926; reprinted by the University of Nebraska Press).

The first extensive use of James J. Webb's overwhelming correspondence and business records in the collections cited above is *Trading in Santa Fe: John M. Kingsbury's Correspondence with James Josiah Webb, 1853–1861*, edited by Jane Lenz Elder and David J. Weber, forthcoming from Southern Methodist University Press.

Jack D. Rittenhouse's *The Santa Fe Trail: A Historical Bibliography*, cited above, contains over seven hundred entries of Trail literature and is an absolute must for the serious student. Also not to be overlooked is the quarterly of the Santa Fe Trail Association, *Wagon Tracks*, which contains the most current scholarship on the Trail as well as information on activities and events along its route (membership applications can be obtained by writing the Association at the Santa Fe Trail Center, R.R. 3, Larned, Kansas 67550).

Those who cannot resist striking out to retrace Webb's journeys and experience their own "adventures" should carry along Marc Simmons's *Following the Santa Fe Trail: A Guide for Modern Travelers* (Santa Fe: Ancient City Press, 1984) and Gregory Franzwa's *The Santa Fe Trail Revisited* (St. Louis: The Patrice Press, 1989) and *Maps of the Santa Fe Trail* (St. Louis: The Patrice Press, 1989).

NOTES

1. Bernard DeVoto, *The Year of Decision, 1846* (Boston: Little, Brown and Company, 1943), 523.

2. Jack D. Rittenhouse, *The Santa Fe Trail: A Historical Bibliography* (Albuquerque: University of New Mexico Press, 1971), 224.

3. Eighth U.S. Census for Connecticut, New Haven County, 309.

4. James J. Webb Probate Estate File, no. 28,722, New Haven District, Connecticut, in Connecticut State Archives, Hartford.

5. Peter Michel, Missouri Historical Society, to Mark L. Gardner, St. Louis, 11 January 1987; and MS 62-3962 and MS 92-1231 in *The National Union Catalog of Manuscript Collections,* volumes for 1962 and 1992, respectively.

6. Telephone conversation with Dina Young, Missouri Historical Society, 29 September 1994.

7. John H. Dickerman, as quoted in the Dana Collection, Vol. 76, 59A, New Haven Colony Historical Society, New Haven, Connecticut.

PREFACE

On January 15, 1888, James Josiah Webb, residing on his farm near New Haven, Connecticut, began to write the story of his adventures in the Santa Fé trade. He was then in his seventieth year. Though about three decades had passed since his return from the Far West, time had not dimmed his memory, nor lessened his interest in prairie life. After he had recorded but three years of his career, he succumbed to an attack of pneumonia, from which he died, March 22, 1889. His story remained unfinished. Still, because of its portrayal of important characters and events, it is published as a contribution to the history of the southwestern frontier.

The editor has reproduced the original manuscript with a few alterations. He has corrected spelling, punctuation, and paragraphing, and has changed capitalization to conform to the format of the publisher. He has made no attempt to revise sentences, alter grammar, or change word order. Additions have been made solely to clarify the meaning of the author, and these, with the exception of chapter headings, have been enclosed in brackets.

For aid given in the preparation of this work, the editor acknowledges his indebtedness to Mr. Paul Webb, attorney at law, New Haven, Connecticut; Mr. George A. Root, Kansas State Historical Society, Topeka; Miss Stella M. Drumm, librarian, Missouri Historical Society, St. Louis; Mr. Clarence E. Miller, assistant librarian, St. Louis Mercantile Library Association; and to Professors Richard F. Jones and George B. Marsh, of Washington University, St. Louis. The editor is also under deep obligation to his wife, who rendered constant assistance.

RALPH P. BIEBER

Washington University
St. Louis, Missouri
March 21, 1930

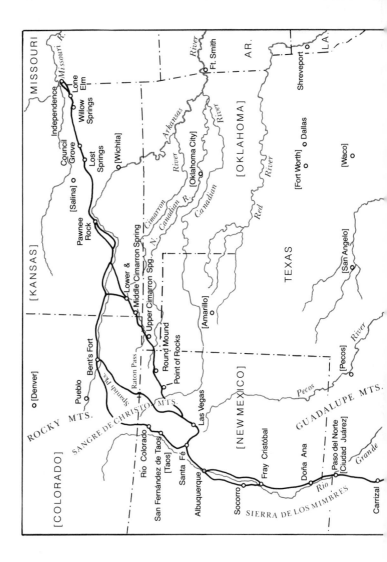

Trails traveled by James J. Webb, 1844–1847

(Present-day names and names of states created and of places settled since 1847 are in brackets.)

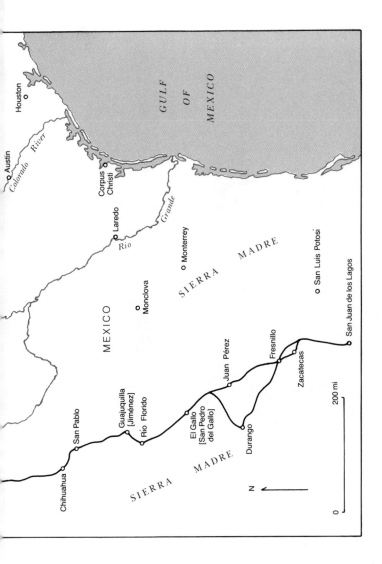

INTRODUCTION

INTRODUCTION

The story of the overland trade to Santa Fé has been a familiar subject to the American people for almost a century. Ever since 1844, when Dr. Josiah Gregg published the *Commerce of the Prairies*,[1] this story, with its stirring accounts of adventure, of hardship, and of financial profits and losses, with its strange tales of a quaint people and of quainter habitations in far-away New Mexico, presented to the general public the most alluring side of frontier life in the Far Southwest. Nor was this merely a popular subject; it was national and even international in importance. Many traders continued to cross the southwestern prairies for some thirty years after the publication of Gregg's book, yet none of them has published a chronicle of the later period of this important commerce. James Josiah Webb helps in some degree to fill this gap; for in the memoirs [2] here published he tells the story of his career as a Santa Fé trader from 1844 through the early part of the Mexican war. He paints a faithful picture of life on the old Santa Fé trail and in Mexico during a significant period in our westward expansion.

James Josiah Webb was born in Warren, Litchfield county, Connecticut, February 5, 1818. His father,

---

[1] Josiah Gregg, *Commerce of the Prairies* (New York, 1844). 2 vols.

[2] The original memoirs are in the possession of Mr. Paul Webb, of New Haven, Connecticut, a grandson of James Josiah Webb. There are two typewritten copies of the memoirs, one in the library of the Historical Society of New Mexico, and the other among the Webb manuscripts. The Webb manuscripts, of which Mr. Paul Webb is custodian, are the property of the heirs of James Henry Webb, the only child of James Josiah Webb.

Darius Webb, was a native of Stamford, Connecticut, and had removed to the little town of Warren in the western part of the state a few years before the birth of his son. James was educated in the district school and village academy of his native town. When he was sixteen years old, he left home and went to Rahway, New Jersey, where he secured employment as a clerk in the dry goods store of his uncle, George F. Webb. Three years later he obtained a similar position in a dry goods store, owned by another uncle, in New Haven, Connecticut. After a brief apprenticeship there, he returned to Rahway for a short time; and then, being of a restless nature, he decided to try his fortune in another part of the country, away from the influences of his native surroundings. His father approved of the decision and advanced him a thousand dollars for his first venture.[3]

In 1841, at the age of twenty-three, young Webb bade his friends and relatives good-bye, and with high hopes left New England for the "Sunny South." He located in Savannah, Georgia, where he made his début in the business world by establishing a clothing store under the name of James J. Webb and Company. He remained in this business for about two years; but at the end of that time, realizing that his hopes for success were not materializing, he closed his store and in the middle of January, 1843, left for St. Louis.[4] Like many

[3] The above account of Webb's early life is based upon a biographical sketch written by his son, James Henry Webb, in December, 1923. James Henry Webb was born in Santa Fé, New Mexico, December 22, 1854. When he was eight months old, his parents brought him east to Connecticut, where, in 1858, they established their residence at Hamden (near New Haven). Upon graduation from the Yale University Law School in 1877, he was admitted to the Connecticut Bar at New Haven, and there practiced law for almost forty years. In 1914 he was appointed to the Superior Court of Connecticut. He died at his home in Hamden, April 19, 1924.

[4] *Savannah* (Ga.) *Daily Republican*, Oct. 4, 26, 1841, Nov. 10, 1842.

other young men of his day, he had succumbed to the lure of the West. From Savannah he journeyed overland to Macon, Georgia, and thence to Mobile, Alabama, where he took a boat for New Orleans. After a short stay in that city he continued his journey by boat up the Mississippi river to St. Louis, arriving there in the latter part of February, 1843.[5]

St. Louis at that time was rapidly becoming the commercial metropolis of the West. It was the center of a great river traffic which extended from New Orleans to Fort Snelling, and from Pittsburg to Fort Union. In this thriving city it was not long before Webb was again engaged in business. This time he opened a dry goods store in partnership with a man by the name of Smith, the firm being known as Webb and Smith. The store was located at the corner of Third and Pine streets, a short distance from the levee. Webb and Smith's stock of goods consisted, among other things, of muslins, calicoes, linens, cotton hose, kid slippers, bonnets and bonnet ribbons, handkerchiefs, alpaca aprons, and silk mitts. "No trouble to show goods" was the trade slogan adopted by the firm.[6]

Webb remained in this business for about a year and a half, but without success. His funds gradually diminished; so that by July 1, 1844, after closing out his stock of dry goods, he possessed only about six hundred dollars of the capital which his father had advanced him when he left home. He decided to make another change, this time planning to go still farther west and engage in the overland trade with Santa Fé. He purchased an assortment of merchandise suitable for this trade, and

---

[5] Webb to Central Hotel (Macon, Ga.), Jan. 20, 1843, Webb MSS.; Webb to Mansion House (Mobile, Ala.), Feb. 3, 1843, *ibid.*; Webb to St. Charles Exchange Hotel (New Orleans), Feb. 7, 1843, *ibid.*

[6] *St. Louis Democrat*, Feb. 22, Mar. 5, May 23, 1844.

about the middle of July took passage on a Missouri river packet for Independence, Missouri, the starting point of the prairie journey.[7]

Webb was now twenty-six years of age. Towering over six feet in height, he was possessed of a powerful physique which was to stand him in good stead in the business in which he was about to engage. Undaunted by recent reverses, he entered upon his new venture with all the enthusiasm of youth. He had at last chosen the kind of business for which he was specially qualified, and from which after many years of hard work he was destined to reap a small fortune.

The Santa Fé trade, when Webb was about to make his first journey across the plains, had just been re-opened after having been closed for approximately six months. A number of regulations by the Mexican government in the early forties had hampered this traffic, and had finally brought it to an end altogether. The tariff of April 30, 1842, prohibited the importation of over fifty classes of articles, and forbade the exportation of gold and silver bullion, ore, or dust.[8] On August 7 of the following year Antonio López de Santa Anna, provisional-president of Mexico, issued a decree, which was to take effect forty-five days after its publication, declaring the custom-houses in Taos, New Mexico, and in Paso del Norte and Presidio del Norte, Chihuahua, closed to foreign commerce.[9] A week later another decree prohibited the importation of over two hundred classes of articles, and subjected to confisca-

---

[7] Webb, Daybook, 1844, Webb MSS.

[8] *House Ex. Docs.*, 27 cong., 3 sess., no. 29, pp. 224-227, 251.

[9] *Daily Missouri Republican* (St. Louis), Nov. 1, 1843; Gregg, *Commerce of the Prairies*, in *Early Western Travels, 1748-1846* (Reuben G. Thwaites, ed., Cleveland, 1905), xx, 236. Hereafter this edition of Gregg will be cited in the footnotes.

tion any such articles, already in the hands of merchants, which were not sold within twelve months.[10] Still another decree of September 23 of the same year forbade all foreigners from engaging in the retail business, except those naturalized in Mexico, or married to Mexicans, or residing with their families in Mexico.[11] Three days later a tariff was enacted imposing a duty of six per cent upon the value of all gold and silver coin exported from the country.[12]

These acts and decrees of the Mexican government met with considerable opposition in New Mexico, as well as in the United States. To those interested in the Santa Fé trade, the decree of August 7, 1843, was especially objectionable. Many inhabitants of New Mexico openly voiced their dissatisfaction with the termination of their commerce with the United States. American traders engaged in the overland traffic pronounced the decree of August 7 an unjust exercise of power by Santa Anna, and predicted a revolution in New Mexico if the custom-houses remained closed.[13] After receiving a number of protests from the United States government, Mexico altered its policy slightly. In March, 1844, President Santa Anna promised to modify the decree of the previous August 14; and in the latter part of the same month – on March 31 – he also revoked the decree of August 7, 1843, and declared the custom-houses in Taos, New Mexico, and in Paso del Norte and Presidio del Norte, Chihuahua, open to foreign commerce.[14]

---

[10] *Senate Ex. Docs.*, 28 cong., 1 sess., no. 1, pp. 36-38.

[11] *Ibid.*, pp. 31-32.

[12] *House Ex. Docs.*, 28 cong., 1 sess., no. 24, p. 113.

[13] Samuel Wethered to Manuel Álvarez, Mar. 27, 1844, Álvarez MSS., Historical Society of New Mexico; *Daily Missouri Republican*, Jan. 5, 13, 1844; Gregg, *op. cit.*, 236-237.

[14] *Senate Ex. Docs.*, 28 cong., 2 sess., no. 135, p. 171; *Daily Missouri Republican*, Dec. 27, 1843; Gregg, *op. cit.*, 236.

But the other restrictions remained in full force and limited the activities of the American merchants trading to Mexico.

Yet the traders who, together with Webb, had arrived at Independence in the latter part of July, 1844, were temporarily satisfied with the withdrawal of the decree of August 7, and hence made their preparations for departure with a light heart. Webb applied to Samuel C. Owens, the most prominent merchant in Independence, for an outfit on credit, and was treated "with that kindness and liberality which was his [Owens's] custom to extend to Santa Fé traders." [15] Owens furnished Webb with a wagon, four yoke of oxen, and some additional equipment. All the traders who were then in Independence agreed to rendezvous at Council Grove, and there to form a company before venturing out upon the plains.

Early in August, Webb and two other traders left Independence and traveled by easy stages to Council Grove, which they reached in about ten days. After a sufficient number of traders had arrived, a company was organized, and Samuel C. Owens was elected captain. Owens then appointed four sergeants of the guard, who organized the men to act as guards, leaving a cook from each mess free from such duties. Early one morning the caravan departed from Council Grove, every person in good health and spirits, and the greenhorns hoping to see the Indians.

The journey to Santa Fé was without incident, though the greenhorns had an opportunity to see a few Indians and large herds of buffalo. On account of sickness the company was seventy days in completing the

---

[15] When Webb's memoirs are used as a source of information, the editor considers it unnecessary to refer to them in the footnotes.

prairie journey, arriving at Santa Fé about October 20.[16] When the traders entered their goods at the custom-house, they learned that the non-retail decree and some of the other restrictive measures were still in force, and that, with the exception of Wethered and Caldwell who were good friends of the new governor, Martínez, they would not be permitted to retail.[17] Thereupon Webb and the Leitensdorfers began to do a small wholesale business; but not satisfied with the meager returns, they finally induced the governor to permit them to retail their goods in the country to the south of Santa Fé. After a three weeks' journey of about three hundred miles to the settlements along the Río Grande as far south as Socorro, Webb and Thomas Leitensdorfer returned to Santa Fé, having sold only four hundred dollars' worth of merchandise all-told. Some additional wholesale business was then transacted. Webb finally decided to leave New Mexico before all of his goods were disposed of, because this procedure would permit him to bring out another stock of merchandise the next year. On March 3, 1845, Webb, in company with a number of traders who had made the same decision as himself, left Santa Fé for "the States" and arrived in St. Louis in the latter part of April.[18]

Although Webb's first venture in the "commerce of the prairies" was not a financial success, he hoped for greater profits next time and decided to try again. While purchasing goods in St. Louis for his second trip,[19] he was fortunate in making the acquaintance of

[16] *Independence Journal* (Independence, Mo.), Oct. 3, 1844; *Daily Picayune* (New Orleans), Feb. 8, 1845.

[17] *Daily Missouri Republican*, Apr. 28, 1845.

[18] *Ibid.*

[19] *Weekly Reveille* (St. Louis), May 26, 1845.

George P. Doan, with whom he formed a partnership, the firm being known as Webb and Doan. Doan was the son of J. P. Doan, the senior member of the firm of Doan, King and Company, wholesale dry goods merchants, then located at 131 Main street, St. Louis.[20] With the additional credit extended by Doan, King and Company, Webb and his partner purchased sixty-three hundred dollars' worth of goods in St. Louis and transported them in two wagons from Independence to Santa Fé by the early part of September, 1845.[21] Before making an entry at the custom-house, Webb sold all of the goods and outfit to Mr. Norris Colburn, a well-known trader who had accompanied him across the plains. As a result of this transaction, Webb and Doan realized a net profit of about forty-five per cent. Feeling well-paid for the venture, both returned to St. Louis [22] and prepared to make a larger investment in the same business for the following year.

Shortly after his arrival in St. Louis, Webb felt prosperous enough to make a brief visit to his home in Warren, Connecticut. There he received a warm welcome, but found only a few of his former schoolmates and acquaintances, nearly all of them, like himself, having left home to try their fortunes in new fields. After a pleasant visit of about a month he left for St. Louis, traveling by way of Washington, D.C., in order to obtain a passport to Mexico. While in the capital city, he called upon the Secretary of State, James Buchanan, who, wrote Webb, "accosted me in a very pleasant and cordial manner," and who "very kindly asked me to remain awhile, as he wished to talk with

---

[20] *St. Louis Directory, 1845*, p. 51.
[21] Webb & Doan, Account of Goods as Baled, 1845, Webb MSS.
[22] *Weekly Reveille*, Jan. 5, 1846.

me about the country, its trade and resources; and I did so." As soon as he had made arrangements for obtaining his passport, he left Washington, and arrived in St. Louis early in April, 1846.

Within a short time after his arrival in St. Louis, Webb, with the aid of his partner, purchased merchandise that cost about $15,000,[23] more than double the amount they had taken out the year before. On May 9, 1846, with the four wagons that were necessary to transport these goods, Webb and Doan departed from Independence on what was destined to be the longest journey either had yet taken or would ever take while engaged in the Santa Fé trade.[24] The company of traders with whom they were traveling proceeded very rapidly and reached Santa Fé the latter part of June, about forty-five days from Independence.[25]

But before arriving at their destination, they received information of the outbreak of war between the United States and Mexico and of the proposed expedition of Colonel Stephen W. Kearny to New Mexico. This news disarranged all their plans; for, in view of the fact that they had to pay duties on their goods, they could not hope to compete successfully in New Mexico with the merchants accompanying the army of Colonel Kearny who would have their goods admitted free of duty. Hence Webb and Doan decided to take their merchandise south to Chihuahua in company with Albert Speyer, a Prussian Jew who was transporting, among other things, two wagon loads of arms and ammunition to the governor of Chihuahua.[26] At the last

[23] Webb & Doan, Daybook, 1846-1847, Webb MSS.
[24] *Weekly Reveille*, May 11, 1846; *Daily Missouri Republican*, May 21, 29, 1846.
[25] *Daily Missouri Republican*, June 25, July 3, 1846.
[26] *Ibid.*, Aug. 20, 1846.

moment Doan was temporarily incapacitated by an injury received after attending a *fandango* in Santa Fé; so Webb alone accompanied Speyer, with the understanding that Doan should follow as soon as he was able to do so.

Webb and Speyer traveled south with all possible speed, passing through Doña Ana and El Paso, and after several weeks reached the hacienda of Peñol, about forty miles north of the city of Chihuahua. There they had the misfortune to be taken prisoners by Mexican troops. Since the city of Chihuahua was in danger of being captured by the American forces in the near future, this delay again confronted them with the possibility of having to compete with goods imported free of duty. They therefore decided, in case they could obtain their release from the Mexican authorities, to proceed farther south into Mexico to the Fair of San Juan de los Lagos, where they might be able to dispose of their goods with some profit.

They were detained as prisoners for about a month and a half, a longer time than they had anticipated. Immediately after obtaining their freedom, they set out on their long journey through the states of Durango,[27] Zacatecas, Aguascalientes, and Jalisco, arriving at San Juan de los Lagos late in November, 1846. In that city, located about two hundred and fifty miles northwest of Mexico City and about fifteen hundred miles south of Santa Fé, Webb and Speyer sold most of their wares at the great annual fair which was held the first two weeks of December.[28] Doan arrived a few days before they were ready to depart, and

[27] George F. Ruxton, *Adventures in Mexico and the Rocky Mountains* (London, 1861), 109-110.

[28] Webb & Doan, Daybook, 1846-1847, Webb MSS.

accompanied Webb on his return journey as far as Chihuahua. There, after some delay, Webb again took charge of the wagons, and proceeded through El Paso and Santa Fé to Independence, where he arrived on July 13, 1847.[29]

Though the story of his adventures does not extend beyond 1847, Webb continued in the Santa Fé trade until the outbreak of the Civil war. In 1848 he invested for the firm of Webb and Doan about $30,000 in merchandise for New Mexico, half of which he obtained through the mercantile house of Doan, King and Company.[30] The late arrival of his partner from Chihuahua necessitated Webb's taking sole charge of the goods across the plains. This year, in addition to transacting a large business in Santa Fé, Webb again proceeded south to Chihuahua, where he disposed of over ten thousand dollars' worth of stock.[31]

When Webb returned to "the States" in the spring of 1849, he learned that George P. Doan, his partner for the past four years, was unwilling to continue in the Santa Fé business. This news confronted Webb with a new dilemma; for in the event of his inability to form another partnership, he would either have to abandon the business altogether or buy additional goods on his own credit. He determined to pursue the latter course, and purchased about twenty thousand dollars' worth of goods in St. Louis and transported them to Santa Fé.[32]

[29] *Weekly Reveille*, July 26, 1847; *Missouri Statesman* (Columbia, Mo.), July 23, 1847; Richard S. Elliott, *Notes Taken in Sixty Years* (St. Louis, 1883), 254-255.

[30] Webb & Doan, Invoices, 1848, Webb MSS.

[31] Webb & Doan, Chihuahua Daybook, 1848, Webb MSS.; Webb & Doan, Daybook, 1848, *ibid.*; *Santa Fé Republican* (Santa Fé, N. M.), May 23, June 8, 1848; *Daily Missouri Republican*, Mar. 21, 31, 1848; *Weekly Reveille*, Mar. 20, 1848.

[32] Webb, Journal, 1849, Webb MSS.; *Daily Missouri Republican*, May 29, June 30, Aug. 13, 1849.

There he remained during the summer and winter of 1849. Business was not quite as brisk as the year before, though some trade was carried on with the California emigrants who were passing through Santa Fé on their way to the gold fields.[33] Yet Webb still felt the need of a partner with additional capital, and so informed Doan, King and Company by letter in the latter part of November, 1849. In this letter he wrote: "I would prefer an honest poor man to a legally honest one with capital. Poverty is a stimulant at least to industry and economy, and the poor man will never be rich without the trial." [34]

By the latter part of 1849 Webb had been engaged in the Santa Fé trade almost six years. During that time he had thoroughly learned the details of the business and had gradually built up a profitable trade. His first lot of goods for New Mexico had cost about $1,200, but now he carried goods that cost him about $30,000. From an ordinary Santa Fé trader with a transient residence in New Mexico, he had become a prominent Santa Fé merchant with a permanent establishment there. Indeed, he had prospered beyond his fondest hopes, and could write in August, 1849, that he had "the largest store and premises in town." [35] With a good partner and additional capital, his business could be still further expanded and placed on an even firmer basis than it already was.

Nor was it long before Webb's hopes were realized; for in January, 1850, he was exceedingly fortunate in being able to form a partnership with a merchant in

[33] Webb, Daybook, 1849, Webb MSS.

[34] Webb to Doan, King & Co., Nov. 29, 1849, Letter Book, 1848-1849, Webb MSS.

[35] Webb to Doan, King & Co., Aug. 15, 1849, ibid.

Santa Fé who was his senior in business experience –
William Sluman Messervy. Messervy was a native of
Salem, Massachusetts. In 1834 he had migrated to St.
Louis, and five years later had started his career as a
Santa Fé trader.[36] He was a mature business man, possessed executive ability, and had sufficient capital to
invest in a growing concern of the type that Webb had
built up. Webb could not have made a better choice for
the success of his enterprise.

The new firm was known as Messervy and Webb, and
continued in business until February, 1854. It was
recognized as the leading mercantile house in Santa Fé.
Business had increased to such an extent that in 1851
between sixty and seventy wagons were required to
transport the merchandise of the firm across the plains.
With headquarters in Santa Fé, it carried on trade with
all parts of New Mexico. Business was transacted with
the native New Mexicans, with American merchants
and residents in New Mexico, with the Territorial government of New Mexico, and with the United States
government, which was establishing military posts in
the Southwest to protect the inhabitants against the
Indians. Messervy and Webb dealt in general merchandise, and disposed of it at wholesale as well as retail.
Messervy made purchasing trips to the East once a year,
while Webb remained in Santa Fé to attend to the sale
of the stock. The merchandise was usually shipped by
rail from the eastern cities to Pittsburg, and thence by
boat down the Ohio and up the Mississippi and Missouri rivers to Kansas City, where it was trans-shipped

[36] George P. Messervy, Biography of William Sluman Messervy, Mes-
servy MSS., George P. Messervy, New York City; *Daily Missouri Republican*,
May 11, 1840; *Daily Evening Gazette* (St. Louis), June 4, 1840; *Santa Fé
Weekly Gazette* (Santa Fé, N. M.), June 4, 1853.

to prairie schooners for the journey across the plains to New Mexico. Sometimes shipments were made by boat from Boston to Kansas City by way of New Orleans.[37]

While engaged in business with Webb, Messervy entered politics. On June 20, 1850, when New Mexico's "State" constitution was ratified by a popular vote, Messervy was elected the first delegate from New Mexico to the congress of the United States. As the National government never recognized this "State" government, Messervy had no opportunity to occupy the office to which he was elected. Yet he continued his interest in political affairs, and on April 8, 1853, was appointed Secretary of the Territory of New Mexico. In the early part of 1854 he also served as acting-governor of New Mexico in the absence of Governor David Meriwether. Messervy resigned his position as secretary in July, 1854.[38]

In the latter part of 1853, after a partnership with Webb of almost four years, Messervy decided to retire from business in the following year, and return to his home in Salem, Massachusetts.[39] Messervy's decision again left Webb without a partner. But this time the vacancy was soon filled; for in February, 1854, Webb associated himself with John M. Kingsbury, a native of Boston, Massachusetts, who had been the faithful clerk and bookkeeper of the firm of Messervy and Webb. It was not until June 1, 1855, that the articles of associa-

---

[37] Messervy & Webb, Daybook, 1851, Webb MSS.; Messervy & Webb, Invoices, 1852, *ibid.*; Messervy to Webb, Nov. 29, 30, 1853, Messervy Letters, *ibid.*; *Daily Missouri Republican*, May 19, 1851.

[38] Franklin Pierce, Commission to William S. Messervy, Apr. 8, 1853, Messervy MSS.; Messervy to Webb, Mar. 28, 1854, Messervy Letters, Webb MSS.; *Daily Missouri Republican*, Aug. 19, 1850; *Santa Fé Weekly Gazette*, June 4, 1853.

[39] Messervy to Webb, Sept. 29, Dec. 14, 1853, Messervy Letters, Webb MSS.

tion were formally drawn up organizing the new firm of Webb and Kingsbury, though in this document it was acknowledged that they had been doing business as partners without a written agreement since February 4, 1854.[40]

The firm of Webb and Kingsbury continued in business from February, 1854, until May, 1861. Though the amount of merchandise it carried in stock was not usually as large as the amount that had been carried by its predecessor, the new house handled a greater variety of wares, and firmly established its position as one of the leading mercantile establishments in Santa Fé. Goods that cost from $35,000 to $45,000 were annually bought in the East. Instead of carrying these goods from Kansas City to Santa Fé in their own wagons, Webb and Kingsbury entrusted their transportation to regular freighters. In 1857 and afterward two shipments of goods were made each year, one in the spring and another in the fall, the fall shipment being purchased for the most part in St. Louis. Webb and Kingsbury not only did business in all parts of New Mexico, but also in western Texas and northern Mexico.[41]

Webb now became interested in politics. In 1856 he was elected to the lower house of the New Mexico Assembly as one of the four representatives from the county of Santa Fé, and served with credit for one year.[42] But at the expiration of his term of office he decided, with Kingsbury's consent, to leave New Mexico permanently. For some time he had been planning to remove to his native state of Connecticut as soon as

[40] Webb & Kingsbury, Articles of Association, June 1, 1855, Webb MSS.

[41] Webb & Kingsbury, Invoices, 1854-1859, Webb MSS.; Webb & Kingsbury, Sales Books, 1854-1861, *ibid.*

[42] Webb to his wife, Sept. 7, 1856, Webb Letters, Webb MSS.

he could conveniently do so, and now that an opportunity presented itself, he was not long in taking advantage of it. It was agreed that Kingsbury should remain in Santa Fé in charge of the business of the firm, and that Webb should stay in the East to purchase goods and arrange for their transportation to Santa Fé. On August 1, 1857, with the best wishes of his friends, Webb departed from Santa Fé for Connecticut.[43] No purchases were made by Webb after 1859, because both he and Kingsbury, having accumulated sufficient capital for their immediate needs, decided to retire from business and close out their stock as soon as possible. It took over a year before this was accomplished, and it was not until May, 1861, that the firm of Webb and Kingsbury finally closed its business in Santa Fé.[44]

Webb thus brought to a successful conclusion his seventeen years' connection with the Santa Fé trade. During that time he had made eighteen journeys across the plains. He had started out in 1844 with a borrowed capital of about six hundred dollars, but by 1861 he had prospered to such an extent that he was able to retire from the business. He was one of those enterprising merchants in New Mexico who, with hundreds of miles of rolling prairie separating them from their base of supplies in the East, were the medium for the introduction of Anglo-american ideas and customs into a land which for two centuries and a half had been under the influences of an Hispanic-american civilization.

Webb retired from the Santa Fé trade at the age of forty-three. Eight years before – on December 1, 1853 – he had married Florilla Mansfield Slade, of Kent,

---

[43] *El Demócrata* (Santa Fé, N. M.), July 30, 1857.
[44] Webb & Kingsbury, Sales Book, 1857-1861, Webb MSS.

Litchfield county, Connecticut. In 1857, shortly after his return from New Mexico to act as buyer for the firm of Webb and Kingsbury, he had purchased the beautiful Vandenhuval estate in Hamden (near New Haven) Connecticut. To this estate, which he renamed "Spring Glen," Webb had removed with his wife and young son, James. In 1863 he was elected to the senate of the state of Connecticut. But politics was not his field, for soon after he returned to his estate he became enthusiastically interested in agriculture. Within a few years he transformed Spring Glen into a model stock and dairy farm. By study and experience he became very proficient as a farmer, and sometimes delivered lectures upon agricultural subjects before farmers' institutes throughout the state of Connecticut. In coöperation with Professors Johnson and Brewer, of Yale University, he was instrumental in securing the establishment of the Connecticut Agricultural Experiment Station at New Haven. Yet Webb never forgot the many years he had spent in the Santa Fé trade, and in later years was especially happy in relating his adventures in far-away New Mexico. He died at his home in Hamden, Connecticut, March 22, 1889.[45]

---

[45] James H. Webb, Biography of James Josiah Webb, Webb MSS.; Webb to Kingsbury, Nov. 21, 1853, Dec. 21, 1857, Jan. 4, 1858, Webb Letters, *ibid.*; *New Haven Evening Register* (New Haven, Conn.), Mar. 22, 1889; *New Haven Daily Morning Journal and Courier* (New Haven, Conn.), Mar. 23, 1889.

ACROSS THE PLAINS IN '44

ACROSS THE PLAINS IN '44

About July 1, 1844, after a business experience in St. Louis, Missouri, of a year and a half, I found myself with six hundred dollars [46] left from a borrowed capital of one thousand dollars, and out of business and ready for any adventure that offered employment and a reasonable prospect of future profit. Messrs. Eugene [47] and Thomas Leitensdorfer [48] and Mr. [Norris] Colburn [49] had just arrived [50] from Santa Fé, and after conversation with them I concluded to try my credit

[46] On July 9, 1844, Webb had $665 in cash. Webb, Daybook, 1844, Webb MSS.

[47] Eugene Leitensdorfer, a native of Carondelet (now a part of St. Louis), Missouri, began his career as a Santa Fé trader in 1830. On July 31, 1846, Colonel Stephen W. Kearny, then at Bent's Fort in command of the "Army of the West," sent him on a secret mission "with important business in the direction of Taos." On the following September 22, after the occupation of New Mexico by the United States troops, Kearny appointed him auditor of public accounts for that territory. From 1844 to 1848 Eugene Leitensdorfer, Thomas Leitensdorfer, and Joab Houghton transacted business in Santa Fé under the name of E. Leitensdorfer & Co. Though this firm went bankrupt in December, 1848, Eugene again engaged in the Santa Fé trade in the early fifties. Eugene Leitensdorfer to Secretary of War, June 7, 1846, MS., Index to Letters Received, Secretary of War's Files, War Department; Stephen W. Kearny, Special Order No. 2, July 31, 1846, MS., Adjutant-general's Office, War Department; Santa Fé Republican, Feb. 12, 1848; Daily Missouri Republican, Oct. 22, 1836, Feb. 13, 1849; St. Joseph Gazette (St. Joseph, Mo.), July 17, 1850; Walter B. Stevens, Centennial History of Missouri (St. Louis, 1921), ii, 550; Benjamin M. Read, Illustrated History of New Mexico (Santa Fé, 1912), 439.

[48] Thomas Leitensdorfer was a brother of Eugene Leitensdorfer.

[49] Norris Colburn, a resident of St. Louis, was a brother-in-law of Eugene and Thomas Leitensdorfer. Weekly Reveille, Apr. 19, 1847.

[50] Norris Colburn arrived in St. Louis on January 11, 1844. Eugene and Thomas Leitensdorfer appear to have returned to St. Louis on June 21, 1844. Daily Missouri Republican, Jan. 13, June 22, 1844.

and see what I could do towards buying an outfit. With the assistance of Mr. [Eugene] Leitensdorfer in selecting goods and obtaining credit for a part, I bought about twelve hundred dollars' worth of goods, and left St. Louis about the fifteenth for Independence, with money enough to pay my freight and passage up the river and hotel [51] bill at Independence.[52]

[I] applied to Colonel S. C. Owens [53] for an outfit on credit, and was met with that kindness and liberality which was his custom to extend to Santa Fé traders. He used to furnish wagons, teams, provisions, and general outfit on credit, and send his nephew, 'Ki Harrison,

[51] Webb stayed at the Independence House, a tavern owned by F. F. Hansford. Webb, Daybook, 1844, Webb MSS.; *Weston Journal* (Weston, Mo.), Mar. 1, 1845; *Daily Missouri Republican*, Apr. 28, 1845.

[52] Founded on the edge of the frontier in 1827, Independence shortly thereafter became the main starting and outfitting point for those who traveled across the plains and mountains of the Far West. It was a very busy place during the spring and summer, when its merchants sold outfits and supplies to numerous caravans bound for New Mexico, California, and Oregon. It had a population of about seven hundred in 1844. *Missouri Intelligencer and Boon's Lick Advertiser* (Fayette, Mo.), June 14, 1827; *Lexington Express* (Lexington, Mo.), Feb. 18, 1845; Gregg, *op. cit.*, xix, 188-189.

[53] Samuel Combs Owens was born in Green county, Kentucky, in 1800, and migrated to Franklin county, Missouri, about 1818. There, at the age of twenty-two, he was elected to the lower house of the State legislature. Later he moved farther west to Jackson county, Missouri, where he helped to found the town of Independence. He was the first treasurer, and the second clerk of the circuit court, of Jackson county, retaining the latter office for about fifteen years. He was manager of James Aull's general store in Independence from 1827 to 1831, and of its successor, J. & R. Aull, from 1831 to 1836. In the latter year he and Robert Aull purchased the house of J. & R. Aull in Independence, and continued the business under the name of Samuel C. Owens & Co. When this firm was dissolved in 1844, Owens became sole owner of the establishment. The general stores which he managed or owned were the most popular resorts for those who purchased outfits for the trade to New Mexico. Sue Adair Owens, Statement, Nov. 5, 1928; Samuel R. Phillips to R. P. Bieber, Dec. 27, 1928; Missouri, *House Journal*, 2 Gen. Assem., p. 3; *Independence Journal*, Sept. 12, 1844; *History of Jackson County, Missouri* (Union Historical Co., Kansas City, 1881) 179, 182, 636; "Letters of James and Robert Aull," (Bieber, ed.), Missouri Historical Society, *Collections*, v, 289-293.

SAMUEL COMBS OWENS
From a daguerreotype

with a few goods; but his [Owens's] main business was to look after Uncle Nick (Nicholas Gentry) [54] and the new traders whom he outfitted, and if they were found gambling or dissipating, he wanted his money there [?] – if they attended to business and conducted themselves properly as business men, he wanted his pay in Independence. He furnished me a wagon [that] cost $100, four yoke of oxen [that] cost $28 per yoke, and other advances to [the] amount of about $100. While outfitting, Wethered [55] and Caldwell, [56] and Louis D. Sheets, [57] and Saucer arrived and commenced outfitting for the trip. Judge Joab Houghton [58] became a partner

[54] Nicholas Gentry traded in New Mexico at least as early as 1829. *Missouri Intelligencer and Boon's Lick Advertiser* (Fayette, Mo.), May 8, 1829.

[55] Samuel Wethered, a resident of Baltimore, Maryland, was engaged in the Santa Fé trade at least as early as 1839, and continued in the business until the early fifties. From 1844 to 1847 he was associated with Thomas J. Caldwell, the firm being known as Wethered & Caldwell. Owens & Aull, Daybook, 1846-1847, MS., Lexington Historical Society, Lexington, Mo.; *Santa Fé Weekly Gazette*, Aug. 6, 1853; Gregg, *op. cit.*, xx, 204-205.

[56] Thomas J. Caldwell was a native of Baltimore, Maryland, and was engaged in the commerce with New Mexico at least as early as 1840. He was the junior member of the firm of Wethered & Caldwell. During the early part of the Mexican war he served as interpreter in Colonel Alexander W. Doniphan's regiment of Missouri Mounted volunteers. American Merchants in Santa Fé to Manuel Álvarez, Dec. 8, 1840, Álvarez MSS., Benjamin M. Read Collection, Santa Fé; M. B. Edwards, Journal of an Expedition to New Mexico and the Southern Provinces, 1846-1847, MS., Missouri Historical Society; *Daily Missouri Republican*, Mar. 30, 1847.

[57] Louis D. Sheets appears to have continued in the Santa Fé trade after 1844. In 1851 he was appointed prefect and probate judge of Santa Fé county, New Mexico, and in the following year became auditor of public accounts for the territory. From 1854 to 1855 he was clerk of the Supreme Court of New Mexico. *Daily Missouri Republican*, Apr. 4, Aug. 28, 1851, Oct. 27, 1855; Hubert H. Bancroft, *History of Arizona and New Mexico, 1530-1888* (*Works of H. H. Bancroft*, xvii, San Francisco, 1889), 631.

[58] Joab Houghton, a native of the state of New York, made his first trading expedition to New Mexico in 1843. From 1844 to 1848 he was a member of the firm of E. Leitensdorfer & Co. In 1846 he was appointed one of the three justices of the Supreme Court of New Mexico. During the fifties he

of E. Leitensdorfer at Independence and went out with him. Colonel Owens was also fitting up a train, and it was agreed that we should rendezvous at Council Grove.

Leitensdorfer, Sheets, and myself started early in August, and arrived at Council Grove [59] in ten or twelve days and took possession of some bark lodges left by the Kaw Indians on their return from their spring buffalo hunt. In about a week Colonel Owens came up with Wethered and Caldwell, C. C. Branham,[60] Uncle Nick, and Saucer. The train was made up as follows: Colonel Owens, 8 mule teams; Wethered and Caldwell, 3 mule teams; N. Gentry, 2 ox teams; E. Leitensdorfer and Company, 4 ox teams; C. C. Bran-

practiced law in Santa Fé. After serving as register of the land office in Santa Fé from 1861 to 1868, and as associate justice of the Supreme Court of New Mexico from 1865 to 1869, he resumed his practice of law in Santa Fé. In 1874 he moved to Las Vegas, New Mexico, where he died, January 31, 1876. *House Reports*, 36 cong., 1 sess., no. 321, p. 175; *New Mexico Reports*, i, 36-37, v, 3; *Weekly New Mexican* (Santa Fé), Feb. 8, 1876; Bancroft, *History of Arizona and New Mexico*, 426, 704, 720; Ralph E. Twitchell, *Leading Facts of New Mexican History* (Cedar Rapids, 1912), ii, 272.

[59] Council Grove, one of the most important landmarks on the Santa Fé trail, was located at the present site of Council Grove, Morris county, Kansas, about one hundred and fifty miles southwest of Independence. In 1844 it was uninhabited by white men, and was nothing more than a strip of woodland extending some distance along both banks of the Neosho river. It was customary for Santa Fé traders to travel in separate parties from western Missouri to Council Grove, and there to organize themselves into a company for protection against the Indians while journeying across the prairies. At this point, too, the traders procured hard wood for wagon repairs. Here, in August, 1825, three commissioners, authorized by the United States government to survey a road from western Missouri to New Mexico, held a council with the Great and Little Osage, and named the spot "Council Grove." The name was then "carved in large and legible characters on the trunk of a venerable White Oak tree that stood and flourished near the entrance" of the tent in which the council with the Indians was held. *Western Journal*, v, 178-179; Gregg, *op. cit.*, xix, 196-201; Kansas State Historical Society, *Eighteenth Biennial Report* (Topeka, 1913), 111, 118.

[60] Christopher C. Branham, of Platte City, Missouri. W. M. Paxton, *Annals of Platte County, Missouri* (Kansas City, 1897), 56.

ham, 3 ox teams; L. D. Sheets, 1 ox team; Saucer, 1 ox team; and myself, 1 ox team of four pairs – all the others six pairs of cattle to the team, and mule teams five pairs. John Tulles, Sénécal, Leblanc, B. Pruett, and another gentleman named Langelier in search of health, accompanied us. The train was made up of 23 wagons, 140 mules, 80 yoke of oxen, and 40 men.[61]

The next day we held an election, by ballot, for captain. Colonel Owens was elected, and he appointed four sergeants of the guard, who drew lots for choice of men; and the guard organized, leaving a cook for each mess free from guard duty. This being the last place where we could procure hard wood for repairs of wagons, one day was spent in cutting and slinging timber under the wagons and preparing for an early start the next morning. As soon as possible after daylight we "catched up" and drove out, every person in camp in good health and spirits, and we greenhorns hoping we should see the Indians.

[We] passed Diamond spring,[62] where we partook of mint juleps and passed a vote of thanks to the public benefactors who some years before had transported and set out some mint roots at the spring which by this time had increased to a bountiful supply for all trains pass-

[61] In a letter dated "Caches, Arkansas river, 9th September, 1844," Samuel C. Owens wrote that "an organization of the company took place at the Farther Coon creek, at which place we found that we mustered sixty men and thirty-four wagons, with two dearborns." *Daily Missouri Republican*, Oct. 10, 1844. It is probable that additional traders joined the company after leaving Council Grove, thus necessitating a second organization.

[62] Diamond spring, which still flows, is located about four miles north of the present village of Diamond Springs, Morris county, Kansas. It was discovered on August 11, 1825, by Benjamin Jones, a hunter employed by the government commissioners engaged in surveying the Santa Fé trail. One of the commissioners, George C. Sibley, named it "The Diamond of the Plain," but it later became known as "Diamond spring." *Western Journal*, v, 180-181; Kansas State Historical Society, *Eighteenth Biennial Report*, 111, 118.

ing. [We] passed Lost spring to Cottonwood [creek] without adventure, except a delay of half a day at Mud creek, where we mired down, "doubled out," cut grass to bridge and fill, and had the usual experience at that place. Uncle Nick said Mud creek was no name for it; it was the devil's hind quarters. At Plumb Buttes we saw the first buffalo, an old bull which we killed and took the best cuts – sirloin, tenderloin, hump ribs, marrow bones, marrow guts, etc. – and proceeded to camp. There a fight was predicted by Uncle Nick, as he had never known it to fail that the first buffalo meat would create a fight in camp. My after-experience taught me that as a rule he was correct; but I have known a few honorable exceptions.

The next day we proceeded to Big Bend, where many took their first wash since leaving the Grove; thence to Pawnee Rock,[63] where we camped, and Sheets and myself went a hunting – two greenhorns hunting buffalo. The old ones in derision asked us for the horns, hoofs, etc., and agreed to eat them if we would kill a buffalo and bring them in. We said nothing but thought as they were so plenty it would be no trick at all. So we started southward towards the breaks of the Arkansas,

---

[63] Pawnee Rock, according to Wislizenus, "is a yellow sandstone, overlaid and surrounded by ferruginous sandstone and the scoriaceous rock." A. Wislizenus, *Memoir of a Tour to Northern Mexico, Connected with Col. Doniphan's Expedition, in 1846 and 1847* (Washington, 1848), 10. Gregg stated: "It is situated at the projecting point of a ridge, and upon its surface are furrowed, in uncouth but legible characters, numerous dates, and the names of various travellers who have chanced to pass that way." Gregg, *op. cit.*, xix, 211. Pawnee Rock is located near the present village of Pawnee Rock, Barton county, Kansas. Though portions of it have been used for building material, much of the original rock still remains. A granite monument, erected by several women's clubs of the state of Kansas, now stands on top of the rock. Kansas State Historical Society, *Eighteenth Biennial Report*, 87-88, 112; Henry Inman, *The Old Santa Fé Trail* (Topeka, 1916), 404-405.

and a tramp of an hour or so brought us to an arroyo; and looking up it, [we] saw a bualo walking leisurely down on the opposite bank. We concluded to secrete ourselves under the bank and wait his approach. I took the direction of affairs and told Sheets we would cock our guns, keep cool, and wait till he got directly opposite to us, so we could have a fair shot. We would show them that greenhorns could get meat, for those chaps should have nothing but what they asked for – horns and hoofs. I was to give the word to fire by saying, "Ready! One, two, three!" and we were both to fire at the word "three." When he arrived at the desired point, I gave the word according to program. We both fired, and the buffalo gives [gave] a few jump[s] and ran off in the awkward, limping, hog-style of the animal towards the trail. We followed, sure we had wounded him, and that he must soon lie down and die. But he kept limping on until he got a mile or so away, when we saw two men after him on horseback who soon ran up to him and with one shot brought him down.

Thomas Leitensdorfer and another hunter had got him ready for skinning when we arrived on the ground to claim the tongue as our trophy, having given him the first shot. They claimed that he was not wounded at all, but the skinning would prove whether there was more than one ball in him, and we could wait and satisfy ourselves who was correct. We watched closely and could see but the single ball hole, and skinning down the other side, Tom took out the ball and asked if either of us could claim it. Neither of us could, and we walked off, satisfied that we had both missed him and must have had a spasm of back ague at the moment of firing. We returned to camp unmitigated greenhorns, and without providing the desired feast for our friends.

Traveling on to Walnut creek,[64] we found plenty of buffalo, and the hunters brought in a good supply of good cow meat. Thence onward we were scarcely out of sight of buffalo for many days.

After crossing Ash creek, I thought I would try my luck alone. So mounting my mule, I struck off southward and traveled as cautiously as I knew how, but somehow could not avoid raising the game. But after some hours [I] saw a band of buffalo walking leisurely in a path and strung out in single file for a quarter of a mile or so, moving eastward. I thought I could approach near enough to get a shot at some of the last of the herd, and hobbled my mule and approached them as fast as I could by running, creeping, and then crawling, until pretty well wearied out. I found the game were by their course increasing the distance from me and I must shoot them or miss getting a shot. So I got in position to shoot and was raising my gun to fire, when I heard a heavy trampling over the ground directly behind me; and looking around, [I] saw another band raised by the moving train or hunters, and running at full speed to join the herd I was about to shoot at and in direct line to where I lay. I lowered my gun and in the excitement of the moment thus reasoned:

"If I lie still, they will surely run over me; if [I] get up and run, they will run after me."

At this stage of the discussion reasoning ceased, and legs decided the question. I ran two or three rods, the running herd at the same time turning from their course and increasing their speed for several rods and [then] stopped and turned their heads to see what the trouble was. I stood perfectly still for a moment, when

---

[64] This is an error. The traders crossed Walnut creek before coming to Pawnee Rock.

the other herd also stopped and turned their heads towards me, and, as I concluded, meditating whether to charge me or run. So formidable *apparent* danger I never [before] encountered. Every bushy head in both herds [was turned] directly towards me, and so near I could see their glaring eyes, sharp horns, and vicious appearance. I dropped in the grass and crawled away as carefully as I had formerly approached them. After a few moments they turned their heads and *walked* off on their course. I crawled to my mule, mounted, and started for camp, and calm reflection convinced me that I had been badly scared, and if any of the old hunters had seen me, I should be the subject of their jokes for the balance of the trip. After I had killed one or two buffalo, the joke was too good to keep, and I told [it] on myself.

The second day after, we arrived at Pawnee Fork,[65] and, as the crossing was very difficult, we concluded to turn out, repair the road, and prepare for crossing the next morning. The east bank must be from twenty to thirty feet above the water and very steep – so much so, that we were compelled to lock both hind wheels, hitch a yoke of good wheelers to the hind axle, and all the men that can be used to advantage to assist in holding back and prevent the wagon from turning over. Even with all these precautions, accidents frequently happen, and the descent is so rapid the teams get doubled up and oxen run over.

The next morning we began crossing; and when the wagons were about half across, one of Wethered's wagons turned over into the stream. The west bank was steep but not so high as the east one. Yet we had to double teams to get out and make a short and very difficult turn up the stream; so the wagon fell into deep

---

[65] Pawnee Fork is now called Pawnee river.

water, and bottom up. All hands took to the water and in two or three hours succeeded in getting dry goods and wagon to camp on the opposite bank. The next two days were spent in opening the goods, and spreading them on the ground to dry, repacking, and loading up. Two of the best hunters were sent out to kill meat and brought in a large amount, a part of which was jerked and hung around the wagons to dry.

Leaving Pawnee Fork, we took the Coon creek or dry route,[66] with no water, except occasionally at Far Ash creek (four miles), and twenty-five miles to Big Coon creek, which we reached without accident or adventure. The next day I began to feel as though my nerves and courage would stand the strain of another trial to kill a buffalo. This time, notwithstanding the warnings of the old hunters of the danger from Indians, I resolved to go afoot and alone. Walking ahead of the train a mile or so, and most of the time off the road, [I] saw many buffalo but did not succeed in finding a good chance to approach game until near sundown, when I saw a herd quietly grazing and a good chance to get within gunshot. Crawling carefully, I was just about to shoot, when they raised their heads as if alarmed; then as coolly as possible for me, I selected a cow and fired. The report raised the band to a run up the ravine, and while [they were] passing, I reloaded and took my chances at one on the run. The one first wounded was lying as if mortally wounded, and I flattered myself I had two fat cows near camp. The train was approach-

[66] At Pawnee river the trail forked, one branch following close to the north bank of the Arkansas river, and the other running from four to ten miles northwest of the river. The latter was sometimes known as the dry route and was the one taken by Webb and his companions. It again joined the river route some distance east of where Dodge City, Kansas, is now located. Kansas State Historical Society, *Eighteenth Biennial Report*, 112, 120.

ing over the hill, and both raised, following the herd
but evidently badly wounded. I followed cautiously for
a mile or more, when one of them began to fail and
about two miles from where I shot her lay down and
died.

The triumph and joy of killing the first buffalo after
one or two ridiculous failures, no one can realize who
has not experienced it. I must take the tongue to con-
vince the camp that I had at last got meat; but that
would not satisfy them that a greenhorn could kill a
cow by fair hunting and approach. They won't come
for the meat unless I take a sample; so I took the
tongue and a good fat piece of loin and started for
camp.

[I] arrived and found all had got through supper
and were talking about sending out to find the lost
greenhorn. I went to our mess and asked for assistance
to dress and bring in the meat. In reply they said it was
probably some old bull unable to get out of my way and
not worth the trouble. A look at the tongue was not
entirely convincing; so I showed the piece of sirloin,
which was satisfactory proof of the quality of the meat.
But there was still a doubt whether I could return to it
in the night. At last I prevailed upon them to make the
trial, and we found it after a long walk, dressed it, and
returned to camp.

Some time after ten o'clock I was taking a lunch
(having eaten nothing since breakfast), when Colonel
Owens came around and asked if we could furnish a
man from our mess to sit up with a man who needed
watchers.

"What is the matter?" [we asked]. "Who is sick?
How many do you want?"

"Well, two or three will do. If more are required,

you can call. Webb has killed a buffalo cow, and I fear
he will become so excited over it that he will get beside
himself and keep the whole camp awake all night. I
want someone to look after him and talk on other subjects until he gets quieted down, so it will be safe to
leave him alone."

From this [point] to the Arkansas river we passed
without adventure, scarcely ever out of sight of buffalo
to the crossing. About ten miles below the crossing we
met two Shawnee Indians, who had the year before
gone out with Mr. Albert Speyer [67] (the excited man
of Black Friday who bid "164 for a million more"),
and had spent the winter in the mountains trapping.
These were the only persons, white men or Indians,
seen by the people with the train after leaving the state
line till arriving at the New Mexican settlements, [a
distance of] seven hundred and fifty miles.

The crossing of the Arkansas [68] was looked forward

[67] Albert Speyer, an enterprising Santa Fé trader, was a native of Prus-
sia. He migrated to the United States and made his home in New York City.
Engaging in the "commerce of the prairies" at least as early as 1843, he
continued in this business until about 1848. Later he returned to New York
City and became a gold broker. On September 23 and 24, 1869, he purchased
about thirty-five million dollars' worth of gold for Jay Gould, James Fisk,
Jr., and their associates, and on the latter date ("Black Friday"), after a
rapid decline in the price of that metal, was deserted by them, thus ruining
his business. In 1846 a traveler who saw Speyer in Independence, Missouri,
described him as follows: "There, do you see that small, spare man [Speyer],
with a wirey figure and thin, sharp visage, him with the sallow complexion
and dark moustache. You perceive what a keen, clean set eye he has got,
and a nose so aquiline that he might pass for a woman. The firm compression of his thin lips, indicate a strong determination of purpose. He is a man
of great energy of character – nothing daunts his courageous spirit." Alfred
S. Waugh, Desultory Wanderings, 1845-1846, p. 118, MS., Missouri Historical
Society. See also Ebenezer W. Pomeroy to Albert Speyer, Oct. 17, 1848, Aull
MSS., Lexington Historical Society, Lexington, Mo.; House Reports, 41 cong.,
2 sess., no. 31, pp. 63-73; Daily Picayune, Mar. 22, 1848; Wislizenus, op. cit.,
5.

[68] The Arkansas crossing, sometimes known as the Cimarrón crossing,

to with much solicitude, as at best it was attended with a good deal of risk and labor. The stream is about a third to half a mile wide, with a rapid current and quicksand bottom – the channel shifting from day to day, forming holes and bars, making necessary much crooking and turning in the stream to avoid miring down so the water would not reach the bottoms of the wagons and wet the goods. I have two or three times had to raise the load by placing timbers on the bolsters as high as we dare and avoid the risk of the shaking off or turning over the loads. Uncle Nick, who had made many trips before this, said that on one or two occasions he found the water so high that they could find no place to ford, and had selected a wagon body best fitted for the purpose, caulked it as well as they could, and (stretching raw buffalo skins on the outside) made a boat or scow to ferry over. This is no small job to ferry across such a stream seventy-five to one hundred tons of freight, delaying a train sometimes a week or ten days, and under an expense of eighty dollars to one hundred dollars a day.

We found the river in fair fordable condition and crossed in one day by doubling teams, with twelve yoke of oxen to each wagon, with three or four drivers to a wagon, and plenty of men to walk beside the wagon to lift at the sides in case of danger of turning over, or to roll at the wheels in case of danger of miring down. The current is so rapid and the quicksand so treacherous that a wagon shakes and rattles by the sand washing from under the wheels as much as it would going over the worst cobblestone pavement. And if the team stops for a very few minutes, it will settle so deep that it is with the greatest difficulty it can be got out.

The next day was spent in greasing up and making repairs, cooking, and resting teams, preparatory to entering the *jornada*, or journey of fifty miles without water, and by the couriers who go ahead to Santa Fé to make arrangements for renting stores and bargaining about introduction of goods, and duties to be paid.

The duties charged by Governor Armijo [69] for several years previously had been five hundred dollars per wagon load,[70] and many goods contraband under the Mexican tariff were admitted by him and no examination made. This was the foundation of the Santa Fé trade, and the only advantage gained by introducing goods by the overland route for Chihuahua and the interior states of Mexico. The legal tariff on legal goods would amount to from $1,800 to $2,500 the wagon load; introduction duties and the inter-state

[69] Manuel Armijo, a native of New Mexico, was of humble birth. In his youth he was employed as a shepherd. Though poor, he was ambitious; and by 1822, despite his lowly origin, he had become a man of some prominence in the town of Albuquerque. Thereafter his rise was rapid. He was thrice governor of New Mexico, serving during the years 1827-1829, 1837-1844, and 1845-1846. Besides achieving political success, he was also a prominent merchant and invested extensively in the Santa Fé trade. W. W. H. Davis, *El Gringo; or, New Mexico and Her People* (New York, 1857), 362; Lansing B. Bloom, "New Mexico under Mexican Administration, 1821-1846," *Old Santa Fé*, i, 29, 45, 162, 168, 256, 266, ii, 15-16, 31, 168, 249.

[70] This charge was an arbitrary one, but as Webb and other adventurers testified, it eventually became an advantage to many Santa Fé traders. If Governor Armijo had strictly enforced the Mexican tariff laws, collecting the legal duties and prohibiting the introduction of contraband, the Santa Fé trade would have declined rapidly. Charles Bent to Manuel Álvarez, Mar. 22, 1841, Álvarez MSS., Benjamin M. Read Collection, Santa Fé; Samuel Wethered to Manuel Álvarez, Mar. 27, 1844, Álvarez MSS., Historical Society of New Mexico; *St. Joseph Gazette*, Nov. 7, 1845.

tariff, or *consumos*[71] duties, one-third the *arancel*,[72] or import duties, *on all goods sold*, in each state.

As our whole interests were not under the protection of law, but subject to the will of one man, and being recognized and confessed contrabandists, it was necessary for the traders to start early and take a long and rapid journey ahead and see how the land lay. Colonel Owens being the leading merchant in Independence and having control of the outfitting trade for Mexicans as well as Americans, and Governor Armijo having sent a train to "the States" for goods for several years, felt safe to remain with the train and depend upon reports of other traders of any change of rulers or rates of duty. When talking over matters who should go ahead, Eugene Leitensdorfer and Thomas Caldwell, who had been in the country several years and knew the officials well and understood the language thoroughly, were selected to represent the interests of all the traders in the necessary negotiations; but it was thought safer to have three or four more in the company in case of an encounter with Indians. I was very anxious to go, but had doubts about being accepted, as I was a greenhorn and had never had my courage tested by the approach of Indians. But [I] asked the privilege of joining them and was permitted to do so, to my extreme satisfaction. I had bought a mule of Leitensdorfer for thirty-five dollars, and she had not proven as good as we expected; so I had some doubts of her being able to stand the trip, but concluded to risk her, hoping to be

---

[71] Consumption duty, or excise tax. "It supplies the place of a direct tax for the support of the departmental government," wrote Gregg. Gregg, *op. cit.*, xx, 149.

[72] Tariff.

able to exchange [her] for another at Bent's Fort in case she failed me.

So when the train left the river by the Cimarrón route,[73] we re-crossed the river and started on our trip ahead by way of Bent's Fort and Taos to Santa Fé. The custom of small parties traveling in the Indian country is to start at dusk, making ten or fifteen miles travel, and before arriving near the proposed camping place, to leave the road and travel a mile or two in the prairie until a hiding place is found, or such a place as will afford passable feed for the animals, and as secure as possible from discovery from any considerable distance. The party was made up by Eugene Leitensdorfer, Thomas Leitensdorfer, Thomas Caldwell, Sénécal, and myself. The outfit for these trips was very limited. Of course [there was] a good supply of powder and ball, one pair of Mackinaw blankets, with a supply of coffee, sugar, crackers or bread, and jerked buffalo meat, sometimes salt and always tobacco – would dispense with either article of food rather than tobacco.

I think we were five days to Bent's Fort,[74] and saw no Indians until we got to within a few miles of Big Timber,[75] about twenty or twenty-five miles below the fort. We left the road and turned to the river bottom and camped. Before lying down, E. Leitensdorfer went to

[73] The Cimarrón route left the Arkansas river at the Cimarrón crossing, and proceeded southwest through what is now southwestern Kansas, southeastern Colorado, northwestern Oklahoma, and northeastern New Mexico. It was the shortest route to Santa Fé, and was used by most caravans after about 1834. Gregg, *op. cit.*, xx, 91-92.

[74] Webb and his companions left the Cimarrón crossing on September 13, and arrived at Bent's Fort on September 17. *Weekly Reveille*, Nov. 4, 1844.

[75] Big Timber was located in the present Bent county, Colorado. In 1853 Beckwith described it as "a section of the river of about twenty-four miles in length, on the islands and banks of which more than the usual amount of cotton-wood grows." *House Ex. Docs.*, 33 cong., 2 sess., no. 91, p. 27.

the river for a drink of water, and was about to return to camp when he heard a dog bark across the river; and on taking a careful look, [he] saw an Indian village of some twenty lodges on the opposite bank. [He] reported the fact in camp, and it was thought prudent (although we presumed they were Cheyenne and there would be little or no danger if we had camped there in the day time) to saddle up and leave, which we did as expeditiously and quietly as possible, crossing the trail and traveling in the prairie for several miles and camped for the night. The next day we arrived at the fort [76] and met a hospitable reception and took one day's good rest.

My mule was much jaded and nearly given out, and we were all convinced she could not carry me through; so I must either remain at the fort, delay the company in the journey, go on foot, or get another mule. They had no mules to spare, but recognizing the strait I was in, finally concluded that Marcellin St. Vrain [77] had a good pacing mule which he would part with on no con-

[76] Bent's Fort, sometimes called Fort William, was one of the most important trading posts in the Far West. It was the headquarters of Bent, St. Vrain & Co., widely known as Indian traders, trappers, and Santa Fé traders. It was quite likely built of Santiago silt loam or San Joaquín black adobe, soils which are in the immediate vicinity and which are especially adapted to adobe construction. The fort was situated near the north bank of the Arkansas river in what is now the eastern part of Otero county, Colorado. Its construction probably occurred about 1833. In August, 1849, William Bent, possibly fearing an attack by hostile Indians, destroyed the fort. A granite monument now marks its site. Bureau of Soils (United States Department of Agriculture), *Soil Map of Colorado, Rocky Ford Sheet* (1902); United States Department of Agriculture, *Field Operations of the Bureau of Soils, 1902*, pp. 754-757; United States Geological Survey, *Colorado, Las Animas Sheet* (1893); *Official Correspondence of James S. Calhoun* (Annie H. Abel, ed., Washington, 1915), 42; *Daily Missouri Republican*, June 29, Oct. 2, Dec. 18, 1849; George B. Grinnell, "Bent's Old Fort and its Builders," Kansas State Historical Society, *Collections*, xv, 82.

[77] Marcellin St. Vrain, a brother of Ceran St. Vrain, was born at Spanish Lake (near St. Louis), Missouri, October 14, 1815. He died in Ralls county,

dition; but she was so tricky and headstrong that he had given up riding her and [had] turned her over to his squaw, who could do anything with her and ride her anywhere she desired. He said [that] he feared he should sometime attempt to ride her away, and she would either refuse to leave, or if she left and he wanted to dismount for any purpose, she would be sure to get away from him, and he was afraid he should in his anger shoot her. He had her brought up, and she was just what I should have most desired except [for] her tricks. He was showing her to me and describing her ways when she took a notion to join the herd. He called on the bystanders to assist in holding her, and three strong men took hold of the lariat but made no impression, and she went off. I traded, however, and agreed to pay him twenty dollars when I got the money. Before leaving, he brought a pair of fetters and tied [them] to my saddle and told me how to manage her:

"When you want to dismount if near a tree, tie her to the tree before dismounting, then put on the side-hopples and turn her loose. If no tree is near, tie her to another mule and pursue the same course." On leaving, he said, "Now don't forget, if that mule gets away from you this side of the mountains, you may look for her at Bent's Fort; if on the other side, not till you get to Taos."

I named her "Dolly Spanker," and she proved just as he told me, very naughty, but very wise, easy riding, fleet of foot, and never tired. I became very much attached to [her] and crossed the plains several times with her and had no other riding mule. In 1848 she was sent with the herd, on arrival at Santa Fé, to Agua Fría to pasture. A few days after, my herder Antonio came up and informed me that Dolly was missing and he feared she had been stolen. I saw nor heard nothing of her until February, 1850, when I crossed the plaza to the store of St. Vrain and McCarty and saw a mule hitched to a post which looked familiar; and on examination I recognized my old pet and companion, Dolly Spanker. Colonel St. Vrain [78] was in the store, and I called him out to look at her. And on calling his attention to the time I got her of his brother and the reason of his parting with her, he recognized her and admitted my claim. He said he had had her about a year and a half, and Bransford, his wagon master, had used her as his favorite riding mule. He was fitting out for his partner to go to "the States" for goods, and Bransford wanted me to allow him to ride her in and turn [her]

[78] Ceran St. Vrain, a prominent western pioneer, was born at Spanish Lake (near St. Louis), Missouri, in 1798. He came to New Mexico at least as early as 1826, when he participated in a trapping expedition to the Gila river. During the next few years he engaged in the fur trade and in the Santa Fé trade and in 1830 joined with Charles Bent to found the firm of Bent & St. Vrain, the predecessor of Bent, St. Vrain & Co. Though appointed United States consul at Santa Fé on May 12, 1834, he never entered upon the duties of his office. During the fifties and sixties, after the dissolution of Bent, St. Vrain & Co., he was primarily interested in the Santa Fé trade and in flour milling. He died at Mora, New Mexico, October 28, 1870. "Mr. St. Vrain was a gentleman in the true sense of the term," wrote Garrard, "his French descent imparting an exquisite, indefinable degree of politeness, and, combined with the frankness of an ingenuous mountain man, made him an amiable fellow traveler." Lewis H. Garrard, *Wah-To-Yah, and the Taos Trail* (Cincinnati, 1850), 7. See also Douglas, Genealogy of the Family of De Lassus and St. Vrain, MS., Missouri Historical Society; B. Davis to T. B. Catron, Oct. 18, 1913, MS., Benjamin M. Read Collection, Santa Fé; *New Mexican*, Sept. 16, 23, 1864; *Daily Missouri Republican*, Mar. 22, 1850, Mar. 2, 1854; L. Bradford Prince, *Concise History of New Mexico* (Cedar Rapids, 1914), 154; Thomas M. Marshall, "St. Vrain's Expedition to the Gila in 1826," *Southwestern Historical Quarterly*, xix, 251-260; Grinnell, *op. cit.*, 50, 88.

over to Mr. A. G. Boone [79] for me when I should conclude to go in, and I unfortunately gave my consent. She was stolen by the Pawnee at Big Bend, an account of which circumstance will appear in a trip further on.

This is a long story about a mule, but Dolly with all her naughtiness was an animal I loved. She never failed me from weariness, carried me as fast as it ever became necessary to ride, and as easy as the rocking of a cradle, through many long and weary journeys, and under the protection of a kind Providence through dangers seen and unseen. And I cannot do less in giving this account of my journeyings than pay this affectionate and merited tribute to her memory.

From the fort we traveled up the north side of the river about fifteen miles and crossed, thence without trail or track, taking the Wet mountain as a guiding point to the Huérfano river, aiming to strike it below the canyon, in which we were successful. [We] crossed the river and on our way up overtook a party of Mexicans on their return from a trading expedition with the Indians. E. Leitensdorfer began complaining of illness, and we concluded to travel with them for a time, hoping we should soon be able to leave them and travel more rapidly. The next day he was so ill that we were compelled to lie by a day for rest. [We] camped in a beautiful grove of cottonwoods at the foot of the mountains, where he had a good "shake," and being without a doctor or medicine, the prospect of a rapid journey was rather discouraging. We cut two poles and prepared a litter by tying a rope to the small ends and hanging [it] across the saddle and letting the other

[79] Albert G. Boone, a merchant of Westport, Missouri. *Santa Fé Gazette*, Jan. 1, 1853.

ends [of the poles] drag; and weaving lariats across behind the mule and spreading blankets over for a bed, thus forming a very easy and comfortable litter. Where the path was too narrow to permit its passage, the litter was doubled up and dragged, the sick man riding his mule.

The scenery from many points of observation I will not attempt to describe. It would be beyond my power to do so if I were to attempt it. I can only say it is beautiful – grand – perhaps sublime would not be extravagant. I think it has been painted by one of the greatest artists, Bierstadt; if not the same, it is very like it. I think he calls it the St. Louis pass. We used to call it the Huérfano pass.[80] The difference in name leads me to doubt whether it is the same. I never saw the painting but once, and was then sure [that] that was the original of the picture.

Mr. Leitensdorfer's continued illness compelled us to travel by short journeys across the mountains and down the valley on the west side of the mountains to Río Colorado, the first settlement. One day we camped on the Río Culebra [81] (a small stream running from the mountains into the Río Grande), and in the early afternoon saw three men approaching camp at a brisk gallop, each with a led horse. They dismounted, unsaddled, and in a few minutes had a fire kindled, and the coffeepot over the fire. They were soon recognized as

---

[80] Webb refers to the Sangre de Cristo pass, which is on the boundary line between the present Huérfano and Costilla counties, Colorado. This pass had been used by travelers and traders ever since Spanish days. Today an abandoned road leads through the pass. "An Anonymous Description of New Mexico, 1818" (Alfred B. Thomas, ed.), *Southwestern Historical Quarterly*, xxxiii, 50-74; Ralph H. Brown, "Colorado Mountain Passes," *Colorado Magazine*, vi, 233-234, 237.

[81] Río Culebra, now called Culebra creek, is in Costilla county, Colorado.

old mountain men and acquaintances of several of the party – Kit Carson,[82] Lucien Maxwell,[83] and Timothy Goodale.[84] As soon as they got dinner cooking (coffee boiling, a prairie dog dressed and opened out on a stick before the fire), Carson and Maxwell came to our camp. This was my first interview with these three celebrities. It was very short, and I can remember noth-

[82] Christopher Carson was born in Kentucky in December, 1809, and later moved to Missouri. In 1826 he ran away from home and journeyed with a caravan of traders bound for Santa Fé. Employed as teamster, cook, or interpreter, he traveled through New Mexico and Chihuahua until the spring of 1829, when, at the age of nineteen, he joined a party of trappers at Taos, New Mexico. Residing at Taos, he continued to hunt and trap in all parts of the Far West until 1842. In that year he guided John C. Frémont on his first journey of exploration to the Rocky mountains. He acted as hunter and guide on Frémont's second journey of exploration in 1843 and 1844; and again accompanied Frémont on his third expedition in 1845 and 1846. Thereafter, at various times, he served the United States government in the capacity of guide, despatch bearer, and Indian agent, and also enlisted in the Union army during the Civil war. He died at Fort Lyon, Colorado, May 23, 1868. Elias Brevoort, a frontiersman who knew Carson intimately, described him as follows: "Personally he was mild, [with a] rather effeminate voice, but when he spoke his voice was one that would draw the attention of all; everybody would stop to listen. His language was forcible, slow and pointed, using the fewest words possible. He talked but little. . . He was a very cautious man, which sometimes made people accuse him of cowardice; he was very superstitious. . . More latterly he wouldn't start a trip on Friday." Elias Brevoort, The Santa Fé Trail, MS., Bancroft Library. See also Dewitt C. Peters, *Kit Carson's Wild West* (New York, 1880) ; Edwin L. Sabin, *Kit Carson Days, 1809-1868* (Chicago, 1914).

[83] Lucien B. Maxwell was born in Kaskaskia, Illinois, in 1818, and in the thirties migrated to Taos, New Mexico. In the early forties he was employed at Fort St. Vrain, a trading post on the South Platte river. He served as hunter on Frémont's first expedition in 1842, and accompanied Frémont's third expedition in 1845 and 1846. He was an intimate friend of Kit Carson. He died at Fort Sumner, New Mexico, July 25, 1875. *Senate Ex. Docs.*, 28 cong., 2 sess., no. 174, pp. 9, 31 ; Twitchell, *Leading Facts of New Mexican History*, ii, 415-416; Sabin, *Kit Carson Days*, 238, 344, 644-645.

[84] Timothy Goodale trapped in the Far West probably as early as 1839, and in the fifties was employed as a guide by the United States government. *House Ex. Docs.*, 35 cong., 1 sess., no. 2, pp. 455-481; *Daily Missouri Republican*, July 8, 1856; Randolph B. Marcy, *Thirty Years of Army Life on the Border* (New York, 1866), 404.

ing of the interview except that they left Pueblo [85] that morning and expected to reach Taos that night. They soon left, ate their dinner, saddled their horses, caught their led horses, and were off, Kit galloping up to the trail rope, or lariat, of his horse and, stooping in his saddle, picked it up and was off without breaking a gallop, giving us this word of caution:

"Look out for your har, boys! The Ute are plenty about here."

Thomas Caldwell, becoming dissatisfied with our slow rate of travel, left with them and went on to Santa Fé.

We were about a day and a half getting to Río Colorado,[86] where I took my first meal in a New Mexican house. It was a simple meal after a fast of thirty-six hours. I do think it was the best they had and prepared for company – baked pumpkin, wheat *gordos*, and *atole*.[87] The *gordos* are prepared by grinding the wheat

[85] An early settlement on the site of the modern Pueblo, Colorado. This settlement was made in the fall of 1842. In July of the following year John C. Frémont described it as a place "where a number of mountaineers, who had married Spanish women in the valley of Taos, had collected together, and occupied themselves in farming, carrying on at the same time a desultory Indian trade." He stated that these mountaineers were "principally Americans." *Senate Ex. Docs.*, 28 cong., 2 sess., no. 174, p. 116. See also T. D. Bonner, *The Life and Adventures of James P. Beckwourth* (Charles G. Leland, ed., London, 1892), 383; Wilbur F. Stone, "Early Pueblo and the Men Who Made It," *Colorado Magazine*, vi, 199-210.

[86] Río Colorado was first settled in 1816. *Annals of Congress*, 15 cong., 1 sess., vol. ii, p. 1962.

[87] A thick gruel made of corn flour, somewhat similar to mush. Gregg wrote: "A sort of thin mush, called *atole*, made of Indian meal, is another article of diet [in Mexico], the preparation of which is from the aborigines; and such is its nationality, that in the North it is frequently called *el café de los Mexicanos* (the coffee of the Mexicans). How general soever the use of coffee among the Americans may appear, that of *atole* is still more so among the lower classes of Mexicans. They virtually 'breakfast, dine and sup' upon it." Gregg, *op. cit.*, xix, 293.

on the *metate*,[88] wetting the meal with water sufficient to pat it into cakes about the size and rather thicker than our buckwheat cakes, and baking them on a flat stone without the addition of soda or yeast and frequently without salt.

Eugene asked if they could not get a chicken and make him some soup. "Yes, sir," [they replied]. "But we have no money to buy it."

He gave the hostess some money, and she went out with her *tinaja* (water jar) on her head and soon returned with the *tinaja* of water on her head, an old hen in one hand, some onions in the other; and these, when cooked, made the soup, without the addition of any further ingredient except salt. We all ate of it and at the time called it good. And I have since seen the time when I would [have] been glad to get a very little even of that.

We remained here the rest of the day, and next morning started for Turley's Mill and Distillery,[89] about six miles [distant] and across a spur of the mountain. We met with [a] warm and cordial reception, and [were] entertained with that hospitality universal among the American residents in New Mexico at that time on the arrival of the gringos (strangers), especially countrymen, at their houses. Our bill of fare was the usual dishes of *chile colorado*,[90] beans, *atole, tortillas*,[91] etc.,

---

[88] "A hollowed oblong stone, used as a grinding-machine," according to Gregg. *Ibid.*, 290.

[89] Turley's Mill and Distillery was located a short distance east of the present village of Arroyo Hondo, Taos county, New Mexico. Its proprietor was Simeon Turley, who came to New Mexico at least as early as 1827. Turley was killed and his establishment destroyed during the Taos Revolt of 1847. *Missouri Intelligencer* (Fayette, Mo.), May 24, 1827; Ruxton, *op. cit.*, 204-205, 234-238.

[90] Red pepper. Davis described *chile colorado* as "a compound of red peppers and dried buffalo meat stewed together, flaming like the crater of

Americanized by the addition of bacon, ham, coffee, and bread. Mr. Turley had a pen of some fifteen or twenty hogs, which he fed from the mill and distillery, and raised pork enough for his own family. But there was no market for hog products outside of his own wants. This was the only place where [I] ever saw hogs kept in any numbers either in New or Old Mexico; and during my fifteen years' residence and travels over New Mexico and through the states of Chihuahua, Durango, Zacatecas, and Aguascalientes, I never saw fifty hogs in all, besides what I saw at this place.

We remained here a couple of days, and although Eugene was still very weak, we went to Taos[92] and stopped at the house of Mr. Charles Beaubien.[93] He

Vesuvius." Davis, *El Gringo*, 360. *Chile colorado*, according to Garrard, was "a compound of red-pepper pods and other spicy ingredients." Garrard, *Wah-To-Yah*, 200. When American traders and travelers stated that they ate *chile colorado*, they may have meant *chile con carne*.

[91] A thin cake made of corn – a species of corn bread. Gregg gave the following description of the making of *tortillas*: "The corn is boiled in water with a little lime: and when it has been sufficiently softened, so as to strip it of its skin, it is ground into paste upon the *metate*, and formed into a thin cake. This is afterwards spread on a small sheet of iron or copper, called *comal* (*comalli*, by the Indians), and placed over the fire, where, in less than three minutes, it is baked and ready for use. The thinness of the *tortilla* is always a great test of skill in the maker, and much rivalry ensues in the art of preparation." Gregg, *op. cit.*, xix, 290.

[92] San Fernández de Taos – the present village of Taos, Taos county, New Mexico. Taos, an adobe town situated in a beautiful valley, had a population of about seven hundred in 1844. It was the official port of entry for New Mexico, though the custom-house was located at Santa Fé. Formerly many of its residents had been engaged in the fur trade of the Far Southwest; but now that business was declining in importance. It was the home of such famous mountaineers as Kit Carson, Charles Bent, Ceran St. Vrain, Lucien Maxwell, and Charles Beaubien. *House Ex. Docs.*, 30 cong., 1 sess., no. 41, pp. 456-457, 478; Bloom, "New Mexico under Mexican Administration," *Old Santa Fé*, ii, 122-123; Joseph J. Hill, "Ewing Young in the Fur Trade of the Far Southwest, 1822-1834," *Oregon Historical Quarterly*, xxiv, 22-23, 27, 29.

[93] Charles Beaubien was born at Three Rivers, Quebec, about 1801. He came to New Mexico in the early twenties, made his home at Taos, and

was a Canadian Frenchman who had settled in that country many years before, married a Mexican woman, and had a family of daughters, one of whom was about that time or soon after married to Mr. Lucien Maxwell. Mr. Beaubien was one of three proprietors of the Mexican Grant at the Rayado, and afterwards known as the Maxwell Grant.[94] It was not settled upon until some years after the acquisition of New Mexico by the United States,[95] on account of the industrious habits, enterprising character, and philanthropic principles of the Apache and Ute Indians. Devilish Poor Lo! Mrs. Maxwell inherited Mr. Beaubien's claim and sold it to an English company for one hundred thousand dollars; and I have heard that, since passing into the hands of the confidence men, the bonded and other indebtedness amounted to between five and six millions. I have no doubt I could at this time and for several years afterwards have bought the entire claim for less than ten thousand dollars.

Eugene was still too ill to travel, and being in good quarters it was thought best that Tom and myself should go out and meet the train. There was much

became a Mexican citizen. In 1846 General Stephen W. Kearny appointed him one of the three justices of the Supreme Court of New Mexico. He died at Taos, February 10, 1864. *House Reports*, 36 cong., 1 sess., no. 321, p. 248; *Daily Missouri Republican*, Feb. 10, 1861; Ralph E. Twitchell, *History of the Military Occupation of the Territory of New Mexico from 1846 to 1851* (Denver, 1909), 267-269.

[94] On January 11, 1841, Manuel Armijo, governor of New Mexico, granted to Charles Beaubien and Guadalupe Miranda a tract of land, most of which was within the present limits of Colfax county, New Mexico. In 1843 Beaubien established the first settlement on this grant at Cimarrón creek; in 1845 Carson and others, the second; and in 1849 Maxwell, the third at Rayado creek. Later, when Maxwell became sole proprietor, this became known as the Maxwell Grant. *House Reports*, 36 cong., 1 sess., no. 321, pp. 245-257; LeRoy R. Hafen, "Mexican Land Grants in Colorado," *Colorado Magazine*, iv, 85, 89.

[95] This is an error. Consult previous footnote.

uncertainty what course the authorities would pursue about admitting contraband goods, as Governor Armijo had been deposed and General Martínez [96] from the low country appointed in his place; and [the latter] was on his way to Santa Fé to assume the office. As there was nothing to be done until his arrival, we concluded to hurry on and trust to luck.

After [a] two or three days' stay in Taos we secured the services of Manuel Lefevre as guide and started across the mountains without road or trail in the direction of the crossing of Red river. The first night was spent in the mountains, not daring to make a fire for fear of attracting the attention of some good Indian, who would, if in his power to do so, show his christian sympathy and Indian generosity by taking our hair. Or if he thought the personal risk of hurting our feelings in that way too great, he would at least attempt to appropriate our mules as objects of comfort and convenience to himself and squaw. . . After passing the night among the spruces and aspens in chilly dreaminess, we left camp at daylight and descended the mountain into a valley, where we surprised a prairie dog village. And I succeeded in killing one, which we took to our noon rest, where we dined on prairie dog and coffee without salt or sugar. In the afternoon we got to the foot of the mountain and camped but a short distance from the road leading to the Ratón mountain and Bent's Fort.

[We] slept supperless and started at daylight, as we supposed on the plain. But shortly, to our great sur-

96 Mariano Martínez de Lejanza was appointed governor of New Mexico on March 30, 1844, and entered upon the duties of his office on the following April 29. Bloom, "New Mexico under Mexican Administration," *Old Santa Fé*, ii, 168.

prise, we came to a bluff which at first appeared impossible to descend, but by this time we had learned to "never give up" but try. The mesa must be at least three hundred feet higher than the plain below, and we descended at an agle of nearly or quite forty-five degrees over a débris of trap rock formed by ages of decay and crumbling, with no vegetation, path, or track. And every moment it seemed as if we should, and the mules must, stumble and fall, [and] go rolling and tumbling over the rocks to the bottom. In some places [where] there would be a perpendicular descent of four or five feet from one rock to another, we would jump down, give our mules their time and plenty of rope. And after a thoughtful and intelligent survey of the distance and landing place, [they] would make the jump and land upon all fours, their feet sometimes so close together that it seemed as though within a space not larger than a half bushel measure. After long and patient effort we landed on the plain below without accident to man or mule.

Today the scene appears as vivid and real as if the occurrence had taken place but yesterday; and calm reflection leads me to doubt which manifested the most caution, courage, and intelligence, the men or the mules. Dolly Spanker here scored a long point.

After a short rest we proceeded on our journey, and it was not long before we discovered a band of antelope. Mr. Lefevre said he would kill one for dinner. I had my doubts, but he started off and, in full view of us, approached the band and brought one down at the first shot. We skinned the animal and took the liver and meat, cutting it up so we could each take his portion on his mule tied to his saddle-skirt. Soon after, [we] struck the wagon road in the valley about midway between the Red river and the Point of Rocks.[97] Coming to a pool of water, we camped for a meal. [We] dined on antelope meat, liver, and coffee, and had a feast. Traveled but three or four miles further, we camped for the night with good water, plenty of grass, and a secluded camp. [We] rested well and arose early next morning, refreshed and happy.

At early dawn we started on the trail to meet the train. [We] passed the Point of Rocks [98] and Willow creek and met the wagons between there and Whetstone Branch. [We] were received with many cheers and "how de's," and the afternoon was spent (while traveling) with an account of the adventures of each party during our separation. Colonel Owens and some others had left the train a few days before and gone on to Santa Fé. The cattle of Leitensdorfer were rather tired and poor, and Houghton thought Tom had better go to the settlements for a few yoke of fresh cattle. They had a cold and sleety storm at Sand creek which was very trying on the animals; and two or three died in camp, [including] one of mine, leaving me with three yoke and an odd steer for change. But in order to have as few loads as possible, the wagons had been loaded so as to leave each owner with a kitchen wagon, in which were stowed the provisions, bedding, clothing, etc. The goods in my wagon were distributed in those of Leitensdorfer and Houghton, and the wagon used as a kitchen wagon for the mess. The train had found buffalo nearly all the

[97] They reached the Cimarrón route in the eastern part of the present Colfax county, New Mexico.

[98] In 1846 Wislizenus wrote: "Point of Rocks itself is a mass of large blocks of sienite, towering to the height of several hundred feet. A clear mountain spring comes out of the rock." Wislizenus, *op. cit.*, 15.

way from the Arkansas to Round Mound [99] and had plenty of fresh and jerked meat; but the antelope was very acceptable to them for a change.

The next day, not far from the Point of Rocks, I thought I would take another hunt. The old hunters told me I need not expect to see buffalo, and it was of no use for me to hunt antelope. But Dolly was recommended as having sufficient speed to run on [down] a fat bull, and I wanted to try her. [I] struck off south, and after two or three miles travel saw an old bull grazing and concluded to try my hand in the race. After riding cautiously, sufficiently near as I thought to commence the run, I called Dolly to the gallop and found she knew her business better than I did. She did not spend her strength at the first dash, but gradually increasing her speed until she came within a dozen or twenty rods, when she let out and was soon alongside and sufficiently near for me to shoot, yet carefully and persistently refusing to approach near enough to be in danger of getting horned if he should turn upon her. Finding she would run no nearer, I concluded to fire as we were. [I] fired one shot, when he made a dash for her; but she was looking out for the danger which I was too much excited to comprehend and shoved off some distance till he turned again on his course, when she renewed the pursuit and again ran alongside of him. I gave him another shot, and at the discharge of the gun she again shoved off to a safe distance. The last shot proved to be a good one, and he stopped and shook his head and soon lay down, Dolly and I at a safe distance

---

[99] Round Mound, probably identical with the present Mt. Clayton, Union county, New Mexico, was "a beautiful round-topped cone" rising to a height of over six hundred feet above the prairie. It was "formed of a brown, decomposed basaltic rock." *Ibid.*, 15, 136; Gregg, *op cit.*, xix, 241; *Old Santa Fé*, iii, 284-285.

looking on. And while doing so, I reloaded my gun – a double-barreled shotgun carrying an ounce ball.

By the time I had loaded, the buffalo was dead, and I was then in a puzzle what to do. Dolly made no objections to going as near to the dead bull as I pleased, but I was afraid to dismount lest she might take a notion to leave me and go to the train. I wanted the tongue and concluded to risk her. I rode up and dismounted, and Dolly remained perfectly quiet and contented until I tied her to a leg. [I] took out the tongue, when I thought I would prove what the hunters had often told me: that you could not get a ball to penetrate the skull of a bull after he was three years old on account of the thickness of the skull and skin and the long matted hair on the forehead. I stepped to within a short distance, so the muzzle of my gun was not more than six or eight feet from his head, and shot him directly between the eyes. On examination I found where the ball struck, but there was no indentation and the skin was not broken.

Satisfied with my hunt and the result, I returned to camp. The old traders said they had not seen or heard of a buffalo being killed so near the settlements for many years, and I never have seen buffalo since within sixty or eighty miles, and never but once within one hundred. The train had found buffalo sufficient to supply the camp with fresh meat constantly for between three hundred and three hundred and fifty miles. I have several times crossed without seeing buffalo on the route for more than fifty to eighty miles.

We expected to meet the soldiers at Río Colorado,[100] as it had been the custom to send out a guard to that point to keep watch and see that no goods were sent off

---

[100] Red river. They crossed this river near the present village of Taylor, Colfax county, New Mexico.

to other points. But on account of the change of governors, I presume, we did [not] meet any soldiers until
somewhere near the Wagon Mound, and then but a
small escort. Preparations and changes had been made
(in season) to enter the settlements in such condition
as not to render any further changes necessary.

We traveled on, crossing Red river, Ocate,[101] and
[on] to Wagon Mound,[102] where we met Tom with fresh
cattle; thence to Río Moro,[103] where there were two
houses – one an adobe house with two rooms near the
crossing, occupied by an American, named George Carter, and his housekeeper. About a mile and a half above
[there was] a dugout, or cellar, dug in the ground and
poles laid across, covered with grass and earth – only
one room, and occupied by an Englishman named Bonney. I think he had a wife or housekeeper and three or
four children, the eldest a son, I should think, fourteen
or sixteen years old.[104] These were the only houses
nearer than Las Vegas or El Moro, sixteen or eighteen
miles distant.

Next morning [we] started early and crossed Sapello,[105] and thence over the mesa to Las Vegas, where we
arrived in good season and camped in the meadow in

101 Ocate creek.

102 Wagon Mound is at the present town of Wagon Mound, Mora county,
New Mexico.

103 Now called Mora river.

104 In the summer of 1843 George Carter and James Bonney settled at
the Mora river on a tract of land which, on March 29 of that year, Governor
Manuel Armijo had granted to John Scolly, William T. Smith, James M.
Giddings, Gabriel Allen, George H. Estes, Agustín Durán, Gregorio Tru-
jillo, Mateo Sandoval, Ignacio Ortiz, Vicente López, and Francisco Romero.
Later this grant was known as the Scolly Grant. *House Reports*, 36 cong.,
1 sess., no. 321, pp. 162-182; *House Ex. Docs.*, 30 cong., 1 sess., no. 41, pp.
25, 443.

105 Sapello creek, now called Sapello river.

the valley of the Gallinas [106] (at the foot of the mesa and a mile or so from the town). Our camp was visited, as usual, by a numerous delegation of men, women, and children, who [came] from curiosity, to meet acquaintances, and to sell such articles in the way of provisions as they had to dispose of. Our men were very anxious to indulge in the luxuries of raised bread, eggs, onions, etc., which afforded them a lively market.

Wethered's mule herder, Old Ramon, an old resident of the town, met many acquaintances and seemed very proud and happy to get among his people once more, as he had gone in with them the fall before, and it was now October; so he had been nearly or quite a year absent. He had bought a good many articles of utility and fancy, spending all his wages; among other things a nice double-barreled gun, of which he was very proud, kept in first rate order, and showed his people with much pride. During the night or early in the morning he somehow lost sight of it for a moment, and it was stolen from him. I don't think I ever saw a more grieved or madder man than he. He ran all about the camp, and when he came across a Mexican would inquire if they had seen anyone or suspected anyone of having stolen it. At last he gave up the hope of finding it, and vented his indignation and contempt for his people very freely:

"Here I have been among the gringos and heretics for a year, working hard but kindly treated, well fed and well paid, and spent my wages for such things as I could not get in my country and such as I most desired. And the first night spent among my people (and they calling themselves christians), [they] steal everything

---

[106] Río Gallinas, now called Gallinas river.

they can lay their hands [on] – more than half my savings. What am I to think of my people and their christianity?"

Father Lliba, the priest of San Miguel parish, called at camp the evening before and took supper with Wethered and Caldwell. They had a good supper, with a good supply of liquors for the entertainment of their reverend guest, of which he partook quite freely and became rather hilarious. On leaving camp, he mounted his pony and rode around the camp at the fastest run of his horse (two or three times), and coming to the road leading to town, struck off on it, raising his hat with a grand flouish, [and] gave us the parting *"Adiós!* Goodbye! Go to hell!" and went off satisfied and happy.

The next day we passed through Las Vegas,[107] at that time but a small town of not more than three or four hundred inhabitants, and no Americans either there or in Tecolote and but one in San Miguel – Don Thomas Rowland. The road through the mountains was the worst imaginable, to be called a road, no labor being expended to keep it in repair except such as was done by the traders to make it possible to get along. Tecolote hill was a place always looked forward to with dread and apprehension. The best we could do by throwing [was to throw] out loose stones, and doubling [double] teams to twelve yoke of oxen to the wagon. It

---

107 Las Vegas, founded in 1835, had grown to be a town of over one hundred houses by 1846. In the latter year Abert described it as follows: "There was a large open space in the middle of the town; the streets run north and south, east and west; the houses are built of 'adobes.' The 'azoteas,' or roofs, have just enough inclination to turn the rain, and the walls of the houses, which are continued up one foot above the roof, are pierced for this purpose. Through the midst of the town there was a large 'acequia,' or canal, for the purpose of supplying the town with water, and of irrigating the fields." *House Ex. Docs.*, 30 cong., 1 sess., no. 41, p. 444. See also Wislizenus, *op. cit.*, 17.

was a very hard day's work to get up with a train of twenty or twenty-five wagons and camp a mile or two from the summit.

At San Miguel [we] met Colonel Owens, Squire Collins,[108] and, I think, Anthony Thomas, who came out to meet us. I well remember the squire and his appearance. He was then advanced in years [109] (but brisk and quick in all his motions as a young man of twenty-five), [and] dressed in [a] well-worn broadcloth suit (but neat and clean without a particle of stain or dirt) and an old-fashioned plaid camlet cloak. I think his was the last one I ever saw of the genuine old style. They traveled with us (I think) one day and returned to Santa Fé.

From San Miguel to Santa Fé we were compelled to graze our cattle morning and evening and corral them during the night, on account of the timber and their liability to wander off in the woods or be stolen by Mexicans or Indians.

I was on camp guard one night some three or four miles from old Pecos, and while sitting on a water keg before the camp fire, I felt something tickling on my

108 James L. Collins, usually known as Squire Collins, was a justice of the peace in Franklin, Missouri, in 1824. Later he moved to Boonville, Missouri. In 1827 he made his first journey to New Mexico as a trader. He continued in the Santa Fé trade until the early part of the Mexican war, when, in January, 1847, he was appointed interpreter and despatch bearer for Colonel Alexander W. Doniphan's regiment of Missouri Mounted volunteers. In the fifties and sixties he was the principal owner of the *Santa Fé Gazette*, and during most of that time was also its editor. From 1857 to 1863 he likewise served New Mexico in the capacity of Superintendent of Indian Affairs. Edwards, Journal of an Expedition to New Mexico, MS., Missouri Historical Society; *Senate Reports*, 39 cong., 1 sess., no. 156, p. 330; *Missouri Intelligencer* (Franklin, Mo.), Aug. 14, 1824; *Missouri Intelligencer* (Fayette, Mo.), May 24, 1827; *Daily Missouri Republican*, Nov. 13, 14, 1851; *Santa Fé Weekly Gazette*, Feb. 16, 23, 1856; Douglas C. McMurtrie, "The History of Early Printing in New Mexico," *New Mexico Historical Review*, iv, 398-404.

109 This is an error.

legs between the ankle and knee. [I] gave a scratch and went on smoking. Pretty soon the trouble was renewed, and again – and then again. At last I thought I would look and see what was the matter. On rolling up my drawers and turning down my stockings, I was surprised to find my leg covered with crawling – well, *lice!* I was mortified and afraid that if found out I should become the laughing-stock of the whole camp; so I concluded my best way would be to acknowledge the coon in [the] best and shortest way I could and have it over with. I threw myself flat upon the ground and caught hold of a wagon wheel with both hands and holloed, "Help! Murder!" at the top of my voice.

Those near-by came to me, and Samuel Wethered holloed from the other side of the corral to know what the matter was.

"Run here quick, Sam, the lice are carrying me off. What *shall* I do?"

"Go to bed and stop your noise. There is no danger. I have been lousy ever since I crossed the Arkansas."

I afterwards found it was a common complaint prevailing all over the territory, with but here and there only an exception.

The next day [we] passed the old Pecos, ruins of a Pueblo Indian village, which had become so reduced in numbers that they were unable to keep their irrigating ditches in repair, and other necessary community labor, to support themselves in comfort, and had abandoned the home of their fathers and joined the pueblo Jemez. The time of this abandonment I never heard, but many years must have passed as the church was nearly in ruins – the walls and tower with a very small portion of the roof only remaining. The migration was made with great formality, the sacred fire not being allowed to become extinguished, but was kept burning and borne upon the shoulders of the old men who had formerly had charge of it and [who had] directed the ceremonious worship of the Indians in the *estufa*.[110] The Pueblo Indians are good Catholics, each having a church and paying the parish priest his tithes and firstlings and the legal fees for marrying, baptizing, and burying. Yet in each pueblo the ancient mode of worship was maintained in the *estufa* in all its forms as handed down by tradition, and seldom or ever was a Mexican permitted to enter the *estufa* even to gratify curiosity, much less to be present during the performance of any religious ceremonies...

But a few miles from here we enter the big canyon, where the road winds and turns, crossing steep pitches and ravines, over rocks, and around boulders, making short and difficult turns, with double teams to make an ascent. At other places the turns are so short that only two or three yoke of cattle can be allowed to pull the load, from danger of turning over into the ravine. One of these difficult passes we called the "S," which required all the skill of the best drivers to get around. And often wagons would be turned over with all the precautions we could use. Six or eight miles a day was considered good traveling.

From the big canyon we cross[ed] a spur of the mountain, not very high but very steep and rough; so it was necessary to "double" to get up. Thence through heavy pine timber and by a very rough and winding road to Arroyo Hondo, six miles from Santa Fé, where we camped for the night and made preparations to enter the long-sought end of our journey.

---

[110] Council chamber.

The men here wash their faces and hands, and those possessed of that luxury would don a clean shirt. But those having no spare clothes would content themselves with fixing up shirts and trousers by substituting splinters for buttons and tying a handkerchief around their necks in such a way that it would cover the holes in their shirts as much as possible. But the most important preparation for the drivers was to put on new and broad crackers, so as to be able to announce their arrival by the cracking of their whips, which would nearly equal the reports made by the firing of so many pistols.

The next morning we started at early dawn [and] arrived on the *loma* [111] overlooking the town about ten o'clock. The custom-house officers, Don Agustín Durán [112] and Don [José Antonio] Chávez, [113] met us and escorted us to the custom-house, where we were compelled, contrary to the custom under the administration of Governor Armijo, to unload and have our goods undergo inspection. [114] Armijo had permitted the traders to unload their goods in their stores, and had allowed the introduction of all goods suitable for the

[111] Hill.

[112] Agustín Durán was *Interventor de Rentas*, or Treasurer. Bloom, "New Mexico under Mexican Administration," *Old Santa Fé*, ii, 223, 243.

[113] José Antonio Chávez was chosen *Jefe Superior de Hacienda*, or collector of the customs, April 22, 1839. Though Governor Martínez usurped Chávez's powers after April 29, 1844, the latter continued to perform some of the duties of his office. *Ibid.*, 132, 223, 231-232, 243.

[114] During Governor Martínez's administration such inspections, when made, were a mere formality. In fact, inspections at the custom-house, as in Armijo's administration, were usually dispensed with. "The wagons were unloaded in the houses of private parties," according to Chávez. Martínez, like Armijo, didn't collect the legal revenues upon imported goods, nor did he prohibit the introduction of contraband. Martínez's policy in regard to the Santa Fé trade was similar to Armijo's, except that the former levied a slightly higher duty on each wagon load of goods. *Ibid.*, 231-232; *Daily Missouri Republican*, Dec. 5, 1844.

market of New Mexico except clothing, boots and shoes, tobacco, and some other goods which were manufactured in the low country and would interfere with that trade.

The duties demanded by the new governor, Martínez, were seven hundred and fifty dollars a wagon load,[115] and [the goods] must go through the customhouse with the formality of inspection. Several parties had candlewick, powder, tobacco, sadirons, etc., in small quantities, and there was much apprehension lest they should be confiscated. There was a good deal of chaffering and *diligencia*[116] about getting our goods through, and several days spent before anything was decided on. Uncle Nick was known among the traders and authorities as "Old Contraband Gentry," as he had been permitted for several years to enter one or two loads of tobacco at a nominal duty. Governor Armijo said he was an old veteran in the trade, clever and poor, and always gambled off the proceeds, taking no money out of the country; and therefore the small amount of contraband business he did was a benefit rather than an injury, and he would allow him special terms.

Uncle Nick was now on the anxious seat with the rest of us, and called on the governor one day with another party (but who could not speak Spanish), depending upon Don Guadalupe Miranda,[117] private secretary to Governor Martínez, who, he understood,

---

[115] In 1844 most traders paid between five and six hundred dollars for each wagon load of goods brought into New Mexico from the United States. Solomon P. Sublette to William L. Sublette, Oct. 20, 1844, Sublette MSS., Missouri Historical Society; *Daily Missouri Republican*, Dec. 5, 1844; Bloom, "New Mexico under Mexican Administration," *Old Santa Fé*, ii, 232.

[116] Diligence, or industry.

[117] Guadalupe Miranda was secretary of the government of the Department of New Mexico. Bloom, "New Mexico under Mexican Administration," *Old Santa Fé*, ii, 145.

could speak English, but now refused to do so and insisted that he did not understand it. After vain endeavors to make him understand English or even his broken Spanish, Uncle Nick in disgust turned to his companion and said,

"Let's go. We can do no business. This damned rascally fool can't interpret what I want to say."

And on being expostulated with by his companion for expressing himself so loud, and in his [Miranda's] presence, [he] replied,

"That damned fool can't understand English, and has no idea that I am talking about him."

He could understand very well, as I found from after-acquaintance with him.[118]

After about a week's negotiation an order was issued by the governor releasing our goods [119] from the custom-house, but with an accompanying order that Americans would not be permitted to retail goods in Santa Fé, except Messrs. Wethered and Caldwell, who, in consequence of their loss sustained by having their load of goods damaged at Pawnee Fork, might retail. Thomas Caldwell had made the acquaintance of Martínez in Chihuahua, and they were on intimate and confidential terms, which enabled him to corner the

---

[118] Miranda appears to have been a linguist. Read, *Illustrated History of New Mexico*, 534-535.

[119] Webb's stock of goods consisted of dry goods, notions, and hardware. The dry goods, which were the largest item, included: black cloth; striped, plaid, and black and white calicoes; white cambric; cotton, pongee, silk, fancy, and blue plaid handkerchiefs; bleached, and plaid muslins; blue, and brown drillings; bleached sheeting; red pongee; bonnet ribbons; plaid silk shawls; women's white cotton hose; hickory shirts; and satin jeans. Among the notions were: cotton thread, black sewing silk, hooks and eyes, ivory combs, coat buttons, plain, and gilded vest buttons, needles, "London pins," and suspenders. Brass nails, iron spoons, scissors, pocket knives, butcher knives, saw files, padlocks, tacks, hoes, and spades comprised most of the hardware. Webb, Invoices, 1844, Webb MSS.

retail trade in Santa Fé for that year. But this, like many another corner, reverted on one of the parties. This was a successful trip. And the next year they made another probably equally successful and returned in the spring of 1846, Mr. Wethered coming east for goods, leaving Caldwell to get up the outfit and buy some goods in St. Louis (leaving funds for the payment with him); and on his return to St. Louis, [Wethered] found Caldwell had left for Arkansas, taking the funds with him. So neither corners nor defalcations belong entirely to the present enlightened and advanced civilization, although I am willing to admit that the present generation has made wonderful advances in these accomplished modes of financiering.

Governor Armijo and leading politicians in Mexico used a more direct and honest term for such proceedings. They called it "making *diligencia*," or "finesse," for legal stealing. To illustrate: Governor Armijo admitted goods by the wagon load, receiving nominal duties; and of these goods but comparatively few went to the low country. Previous to his administration the General government had been compelled to send considerable sums to support the government in the territory, but by means of the duties received from the increase of trade through the course pursued by him, he never called upon the General government for a dollar. True, he would send trains of his own to "the States," and introduce goods (I presume paying no duties) and pay off the soldiers in goods with a small portion of money, thus making a profit for himself and a saving to the government. And the soldiers were regularly paid, and at least as well as the uncertain and frequently reduced pay in the low country.

During the winter of 1844 and 1845 Armijo visited

Santa Fé, and occupied quarters in a house, a little front room of which was occupied by B. Pruett as a store. The door between the store and the room of Governor Armijo was one of the old-fashioned affairs, swinging upon a stud, or post, fitted into holes in the upper and lower doorsills, thus swinging without iron hinges or latch and of course leaving large cracks [on] each side. Governor Martínez made a formal call upon him [Armijo], and Pruett had the curiosity to listen to the conversation. After the usual formalities and while partaking of their wine, Governor Armijo asked Governor Martínez why General Santa Anna had superseded him in the office of governor, and stated in justification of his course how he had maintained the government in New Mexico without calling on the National treasury for aid.

"Well," replied Martínez, "Santa Anna told me he wanted, and would make, a change here. The administration of affairs had become exceedingly corrupt. There had been stealing in every department, from the governor to the lowest subordinate officer."

"True," said Armijo, "the custom-house officers have no doubt stolen. They demand fees and perquisites from the merchants introducing goods to which they are not legally entitled. And my secretary also avails himself of his opportunities. I have also stolen a good deal by permitting this indirect and illegal trade. And in fact, if you call it stealing, I have been stealing all my official life and have got the money in my pocket to show for it. But I don't see how he has mended matters by sending you here, for I know your history and have known your course for years. You, poor devil, have been stealing all your life, and today haven't got a dollar. Which is the smartest man, and which is the best fitted to administer an economical government in New Mexico?"

I cannot forbear, while on this subject, describing an interview I had with Governor Armijo in 1846. The firm of Webb and Doan had four wagons well loaded with a well assorted stock, and the duties amounted to quite a sum for us. We had bought a pair of horses on the line for which we paid one hundred and seventy-five dollars. Governor Armijo's brother, Juan, went out with several wagons in the same train and knew the price we paid and admired them very much; [he] thought quite likely his brother, the governor, would want to buy. We took good care of them, and at Arroyo Hondo I had them well groomed, the harness and ambulance put in good shape, and drove into the city. On arriving at the plaza, instead of driving direct to the custom-house at the east end of the Palace,[120] I drove down the south side and around in front of the Palace, and called the officer in attendance to examine my carriage to see that all was right and I was not a contraband. He allowed me to pass on without an examination, and I drove around the east and south side to the corral of E. Leitensdorfer and Company and turned out.

In a short time a messenger from the governor came over and said he wanted to see me. I immediately went over and met a very kind and fatherly reception from him. And after a little conversation he told me he wanted to buy the sorrels, and asked my price. I told him that I hardly knew what to ask, but thought they ought to fetch about nine hundred dollars.

---

[120] The Palace of the Governors. This was the governor's residence, though it also contained a number of government offices.

"Why, young man, what are you talking about? I mean those sorrels you bought on the line for one hundred and seventy-five dollars. You surely cannot ask nine hundred dollars for them?"

"Yes, they are a very fine pair of horses, and it is a great deal of trouble and risk to get them here; and more than that, you are asking very high duties."

"Pay the tariff then, and I will give your price for the horses."

"It would be better to give you the goods."

"Now, young man, answer me honest. How many wagons did you have at Palo Blanco, or Whetsone Branch, or any other place this side the Cimarrón?"

"Now, General, your brother has told you all about it. He knows, as well as he knows what we paid for the horses. We had four wagons heavily loaded and a kitchen wagon with some goods in it, which, on nearing the settlements, we put into the large wagons, making as heavy loads as we could haul through the mountains." [121]

"Well, young man, I will be liberal with you. You know that the legal duties on your goods would amount to $1,800 to $2,000 a wagon load, and I allow you to enter them at seven hundred and fifty dollars a wagon, and if you want to take them to Chihuahua or any interior market, I give you the manifest for them and certify that all import duties have been paid. Now this,

---

[121] In order to reduce their import duties, traders were accustomed to enter Santa Fé with a minimum number of wagons. Thus Charles Bent, writing from Taos on November 12, 1844, informed Manuel Álvarez that his brother, George Bent, was on the way to Santa Fé with eight wagons, but that he "intended to leave two or three before he got to the Mora." He continued: "You had better not mention that you have heard from the waggons for fear that an escort might be sent out before he leaves theas waggons." Charles Bent to Manuel Álvarez, Nov. 12, 1844, Álvarez MSS., Benjamin M. Read Collection, Santa Fé.

young man, is stealing, but we do all the stealing and divide with you, giving you much the largest share of booty. I will give you the duties on one load of goods for the sorrels, and you must pay seven hundred and fifty dollars [122] a load for the balance."

How would our people have named such an operation? I think they would have appropriated the horses and called it a shrewd financial operation, and claimed to be smart above their fellows. And more than probable their claim would be rewarded with an office in some savings bank, or some religious or philanthropic society as financial manager; and if the fraud was ever discovered, [they] would throw the whole blame upon the shoulders of the second parties.

Well, were we smugglers? Were we guilty of any fraud? We entered the country with our goods and paid the duties demanded by the legal authorities according to a custom prevailing for years, which had become recognized as law by the authorities throughout the country, without any misrepresentation, prevarication, or deceit. And if there was fraud or evasion, the governor never shirked the responsibility or attempted to throw it on the shoulders of others.

From a long acquaintance with him, and from the representations of other traders who had a more intimate acquaintance with him, I am satisfied the American opinion of him, derived from the manner of his obtaining the position of governor and [from] the account of him given by Kendall in his *Expedition*,[123] is

[122] This is an error. Webb paid five hundred dollars for the importation of each of three wagon loads of goods, being permitted to enter the fourth free of duty. Thus Armijo paid Webb only five hundred dollars for the horses. Webb & Doan, Daybook, 1846-1847, Webb MSS.

[123] See George W. Kendall, *Narrative of an Expedition across the Great Southwestern Prairies, From Texas to Santa Fé* (London, 1845), i, 369-385.

unjust. He was naturally irritable and sometimes over-bearing, but allowance should be made for his early opportunities. He was emphatically a self-made man, and rose from the position of pastor, or sheep herder, to that of governor by his own energies, without aid, counsel, or even sympathy from those in higher position. He learned his letters, while herding sheep in the prairies, from a Catholic primer. And his first efforts in arithmetic were from some rudimentary book, and learning to make the figures and do the sums by selecting a soft stone such as he could pick up in the prairie or coal from the camp fire, and doing his ciphering upon the knees of his buckskin breeches. And it was not until he had gained a position in which he could *command* respect that he gained the aid and sympathy of those who were born in a higher walk of life and had opportunities of superior instruction.

The arrest and execution of the persons executed as spies of the Texas expedition was in consequence of information given by an American who resided in the territory several years before and for many years after, who was very clever and tolerably well liked by Americans and Mexicans, but such an inveterate babbler that we could seldom trust him; always, like others of his class, ready to tell all he knew, and generally a good deal more, frequently doing us material injury when intending only to gratify his propensity for vain babbling.

A VENTURE IN THE SANTA FÉ
TRADE

A VENTURE IN THE SANTA FÉ TRADE

My first arrival in Santa Fé [124] was in October [125] after a journey of seventy days, which at that time was not considered a specially long trip. My first impressions I can but imperfectly describe after the lapse of so long a time – forty years – but I well remember that there was nothing to induce me to entertain a desire to become a resident or to continue in the trade except as an adventurer and the possible advantages the trade might afford of bettering my fortune. The people were nearly all in extreme poverty, and there were absolutely none who could be classed as wealthy except by comparison. The Pinos and Ortizes were considered the *ricos*, and those most respected as leaders in society and political influence; but idleness, gambling, and the Indians had made such inroads upon their means and influence that there was but little left except the repu-

---

[124] Santa Fé, the capital of New Mexico, was founded by Governor Pedro de Peralta some time between 1610 and 1614. Although an important northern outpost of the Spanish Empire in America, it was isolated and sluggish, unlike the lively mining towns to the south. It had a population of about three thousand in 1844. Like other New Mexican towns, its houses were one story high and built of adobes, or large mud bricks dried in the sun. To many Americans entering Santa Fé for the first time, this method of construction gave the town the appearance of a group of brickkilns. *House Ex. Docs.*, 30 cong., 1 sess., no. 41, p. 34; Herbert E. Bolton, *The Spanish Borderlands* (New Haven, 1921), 177-187; George P. Hammond, *Don Juan de Oñate and the Founding of New Mexico* (Santa Fé, 1927), 180; Lansing B. Bloom, "When was Santa Fé Founded?" *New Mexico Historical Review*, iv, 188-194; Gregg, *op. cit.*, xix, 253, 283.

[125] About October 20. *Daily Picayune*, Feb. 8, 1845.

tation of honorable descent from a wealthy and distinguished ancestry. The houses were nearly all old and dilapidated, the streets narrow and filthy, and the people, when in best attire, not half dressed.[126] And even those who could occasionally afford a new and expensive dress, would make it up in such a way that it would appear extravagantly ridiculous.

There were but a very few houses north of the Palace on the street now called Palace avenue. Don Agustín Durán, Don Félix García, Don Antonio Sena y Baca, and James Conklin [127] and one or two others lived not far from where the Presbyterian church now stands and had quite grand houses for the time; and some of them [had] two or three acres cultivated in corn, beans, and red peppers, and a few apricot trees, the only fruit then raised in the town. There were three residences on Palace avenue, extending from the corner of Washington street towards the *ciénaga*,[128] in one of which we quartered for a few days when we first arrived, and where I afterwards lived a year with my family, owned by Don Juan Sena. The northeast corner of the plaza was the government storehouse, or *lóndiga*,[129] devoted in ancient times to the storage of corn by [the] government to sell to the poor and improvident in time of necessity, but this year used as a government warehouse

[126] Compare Kendall, *op. cit.*, i, 338-340; Bloom, "New Mexico under Mexican Administration," *Old Santa Fé*, ii, 230.

[127] James Conklin was one of the first Anglo-americans to settle in New Mexico. He was born in Canada about 1800, and at an early age removed to St. Louis. In 1825 he journeyed to New Mexico, and lived there until his death in 1883. J. H. Watts, Santa Fé Affairs, MS., Bancroft Library; *Senate Reports*, 39 cong., 2 sess., no. 156, p. 336; Prince, *Concise History of New Mexico*, 154; Twitchell, *Leading Facts of New Mexican History*, ii, 102.

[128] Marsh, or meadow, on the east side of Santa Fé. Ralph E. Twitchell, *Old Santa Fé* (Santa Fé, 1925), 52.

[129] *Alhóndiga*, or public granary.

to store our goods while being examined by the custom-house officers. From thence south was nearly all government offices, except the southeast corner, which was a store occupied by Don Juan Sena as agent of Don José Chávez. This was the second best store in town (Mr. John Scolly having the best), and floored with plank – the only plank floor in New Mexico, except a store in Taos built by Mr. — Branch, and, I think, perhaps Mr. [Simeon] Turley, at Turley's Mill, had one or two rooms floored with plank. On the southeast corner was the residence of one of the Pinos and only one or two stores, or *tendajones*,[130] till you came to the corner of the street leading to Río Chiquito,[131] where [there] was a store about fifteen feet square which was rented and occupied by Messrs. Leitensdorfer and Company, with several back rooms for storage and housekeeping.

Here I spent my first winter in New Mexico (messing with them), having a French-canadian cook, with a dry goods box for a table, brown domestic tucked over for a tablecloth, and our prairie camp kettles, tin cups, iron spoons, and butcher knives for cooking and table furniture. We had one glass tumbler which was used to mix our drinks in – which was usually eggnog compounded of one egg, a little sugar, and water, [and] an allowance of *aguardiente*[132] compatible to the taste of the drinker – and a Spanish grammar placed on the top of the tumbler and held firmly by the thumbs and fingers and shaken till the egg was well beaten and the beverage thoroughly mixed, when we would drink to

---

[130] Small rickety shops.

[131] "A small stream which used to flow down the present Water Street." Twitchell, *Old Santa Fé*, 329.

[132] Brandy.

the health of our associates or far-away friends and pass the tumbler to the next claimant.

There was an old church [133] about the center of the block on the south side of the plaza which had not been occupied as a place of worship for many years; and after the organization of the Territorial government, [it] was opened by the authorities and fitted up for a courthouse. When [it was] nearly finished and ready for occupancy, the claim was set up that it was Church property, and it was a sacrilege to devote it to such a purpose.

"How can we come into these sacred precincts as litigants or witnesses and try our cases or give testimony, standing upon the graves of our fathers?" said the Mexicans.

And with due regard for the delicacy of their feelings, and in obedience to the demands of Bishop Lamy,[134] the plan was abandoned, and the property turned over to the Church.[135] It was shortly after [136] sold to Don Simon Delgado and fitted up for a store, where he kept an assorted stock of dry goods, groceries, and

---

[133] *La castrense*, or the military chapel, built in the form of a cross, was erected some time between 1717 and 1722. It was probably abandoned as a place of worship in the decade prior to Webb's arrival in Santa Fé. Twitchell, *Old Santa Fé*, 50; "*Barreiro's Ojeada Sobre Nuevo Mexico*" (Lansing B. Bloom, ed.), *New Mexico Historical Review*, iii, 85; W. H. H. Allison, "Santa Fé as it Appeared during the Winter of the Years 1837 and 1838," *Old Santa Fé*, ii, 177; W. H. H. Allison, "Santa Fé in 1846," *ibid.*, ii, 395.

[134] Most Rev. John B. Lamy was born at Lempdes, France, October 11, 1814. At the age of twenty-five he came to the United States. In 1851 he removed to New Mexico, and resided there until his death, February 14, 1888. Twitchell, *Old Santa Fé*, 329.

[135] Governor James S. Calhoun transferred the military chapel to the Church in the latter part of August, 1851. Thereafter it was again used as a place of worship. "The Official Correspondence of James S. Calhoun" (Abel, ed.), 406-412; Twitchell, *The History of the Military Occupation of the Territory of New Mexico*, 223; Davis, *El Gringo*, 166, 175.

[136] In 1859. *Daily Missouri Republican*, Mar. 26, 1859.

liquors, and disposed of them for cash, as he found customers among the poor or needy. I presume the bones rest in peace and quiet, as the transfer was made by the Church for a valuable consideration instead of being appropriated by the government and devoted to secular uses.

The west side of the plaza was nearly all residences. Near the center was the post-office, where a mail sometimes arrived from the south, and also the *estanquillo*,[137] where the government sold a limited amount of cigars and tobacco. There were but few houses on the *loma* south of the river. The principal one was owned and occupied by "Old Taosenian"; and he used to give a *fandango* once or more a week, according to the number of strangers visiting the city and the demand for amusement.

A Mexican *fandango* [138] in those days was a curiosity. The *sala*, or dancing hall, [was] from twenty to thirty

---

[137] A shop licensed to sell cigars.

[138] In New Mexico a *fandango* was not a particular type of dance, but any ordinary assembly where dancing was the principal amusement. A *baile*, or ball, was a *fandango* attended chiefly by the better classes. Sometimes there was no clear distinction between a *baile* and a *fandango*. Gregg, *op. cit.*, xx, 35-36; Davis, *El Gringo*, 315. An American gave the following description of a *baile*, or *fandango*, in Santa Fé in 1839: "All dances or balls in Santa Fé are called *Fandangos*, at least by the Americans. Scrupulously republican in their amusements as well as their dealings, the Mexicans never exact a charge for admission into the ball room. There is generally an extra apartment where sweet-breads, Pasa whiskey, and wine are sold at double prices, and this is the landlord's or landlady's remuneration for the use of the ball room. . . In the whole town there is but one house that has a boarded floor. . . This apartment with the boarded floor is the fashionable ball room, although the *señoras* entertain a decided predilection for the native soil on the ground of old use. In compliment to the American strangers then in Santa Fé, Governor Armijo gave a ball in this grand boarded saloon during our visit. All the beauty and fashion attended, and also all the rabble, for, true to their republican principles, none can be refused admission. The night was warm, the windows were open, the Americans threw down their hats carelessly, and the Spaniards walked off with them cautiously. The Governor's

feet long, and fifteen to eighteen feet wide, with some-times benches on the sides (but frequently without seats of any kind) and packed full, only leaving suffi-cient space through the center for the couples to waltz through, up and down. When the dance began, the men would place themselves in line on one side, and when the line was complete, the women would begin to rise and take their positions opposite the men, almost always in regular order without manifesting any choice of partners; and when the numbers were equal, the music would strike up and the dance proceed.

I have witnessed some most ludicrous scenes at these *fandangos*. It was not anything uncommon or surpris-ing to see the most elaborately dressed and aristocratic woman at the ball dancing with a peon dressed only in his shirt and trousers open from the hip down, with very wide and full drawers underneath, and frequently barefoot, but usually with moccasins. And such dis-parity of ages! On one occasion I saw at a ball given by Governor Armijo an old man of eighty or over dancing with a child not over eight or ten. I could not help the reflection that it was a dance of the cradle and the grave. They do literally dance from the cradle to the grave. And I have never seen anything lascivious or [any] want of decorum and self-respect in any woman in a

lady, Señora Armijo, led off the dance with one of the young American guests. . . The only music is a guitar and violin, and the same instruments are used for sacred music in the churches. Although there is little of ele-gance in their dances, yet about them there is a wildness and novelty truly enchanting to such young enthusiasts as we were. With all this unrestrained freedom of manners, they seldom quarrel, and the harmony of an evening's amusement is seldom broken unless by some imprudent conduct of the Amer-icans themselves. Scarcely an evening of the week passes without a *fandango* in one part or other of the town, and the same faces will be seen at every one. It would seem as if the people could not exist without the waltz." *Daily Evening Gazette*, Feb. 20, 1840.

fandango, whatever might be her reputation for virtue outside. I have known of disorders and serious brawls in *fandangos*, but it was almost invariably where Americans and whiskey were found in profusion.

The only Americans then residing permanently in Santa Fé were James Conklin, James M. Giddings,[139] and another whose name I don't recollect – these were married and settled. James L. Collins, Anthony Thomas, and Ennis J. Vaughn [140] were there most of the time, but did not consider that their residence. John Scolly [141] an Irishman, Don Manuel Álvarez [142] a Spaniard, and an old French doctor living with Scolly, and W. T.

---

[139] James M. Giddings was born in Kentucky about 1812, and first engaged in the Santa Fé trade in 1835. Five years later he removed to Santa Fé, where he continued in business until 1853. In that year he established a ranch on the Pecos river near the present town of Fort Sumner, De Baca county, New Mexico. This ranch was one of the first – if not the first– in that part of the territory. There Giddings raised cattle, sheep, horses, and mules, all of which, he declared, kept "in good condition all winter without hay, from natural pasturage." He was still living on his ranch in June, 1865. *Senate Reports*, 39 cong., 2 sess., no. 156, pp. 342-343; *Daily Missouri Republican*, Dec. 28, 1853; J. P. Dunn, Jr., *Massacres of the Mountains* (New York, 1886), 467.

[140] Ennis J. Vaughn, a native of Kentucky, migrated to Missouri when quite young. He came to New Mexico at least as early as 1833, and lived there until his death, May 15, 1854. "Integrity, honor, truth, and courage" were the qualities which, according to the *Santa Fé Weekly Gazette*, "endeared him to all who knew him best." *Daily Missouri Republican*, June 28, 1854. See also *House Ex. Docs.*, 30 cong., 1 sess., no. 41, p. 483.

[141] John Scolly came to New Mexico in the thirties and opened a store in Santa Fé, where he built up a profitable business. In 1843 he became one of the principal proprietors of the land grant on the Mora river which was later known as the Scolly Grant. There he established a ranch, though he continued to reside in Santa Fé until his death, April 11, 1847. *House Reports*, 36 cong., 1 sess., no. 321, pp. 162-182; *Weekly Reveille*, June 7, 1847; Read, *Illustrated History of New Mexico*, 411-414.

[142] Manuel Álvarez was born in Spain about 1794. He left his native land in 1818, and in the following year came to Mexico. In 1824 he journeyed from Missouri to New Mexico and began his career as a Santa Fé trader. Opening a store in Santa Fé, he continued in business there for over thirty years, building up one of the largest mercantile establishments in New

Smith [143] a clerk for him [Scolly] are the only foreigners I now remember of finding in the city on my arrival.

The Frenchman was very poor and living upon the bounty of Mr. Scolly. Several years before, the Mexicans broke into his store and robbed him of what little he had, beat him severely, and left him for dead. When found, he was much maimed and had his jaw broken at the point of the chin, which never got well. The fracture was so loose that he always wore a piece of sheet tied over his lower incisors to keep the jaw in place to masticate his food or even to talk intelligibly.

I forgot to say, while speaking of the Pinos and the Ortizes, that Don [Pedro Bautista] Pino,[144] the father

Mexico. He was appointed United States consul at Santa Fé on March 21, 1839. Though never receiving an exequator from the Mexican government, he performed some of the duties of his office, 1839-1841, being permitted to do so through "an extension of courtesy" by the governor of New Mexico. He was appointed commercial agent of the United States at Santa Fé, March 18, 1846, but received his commission after General Kearny's entrance into Santa Fé. On June 20, 1850, when New Mexico's "State" constitution was ratified by a popular vote, he was elected lieutenant-governor of New Mexico; and, in the absence of Governor Henry Connelly, Álvarez served for a time as acting-governor. He died in Santa Fé, July 5, 1856. Manuel Álvarez to Manuel Armijo, Aug. 21, 1839, Memorandum Book of Manuel Álvarez, MS., Historical Society of New Mexico; Guadalupe Miranda to Manuel Álvarez, Sept. 22, 1841, Álvarez MSS., Benjamin M. Read Collection, Santa Fé; Manuel Álvarez to the congress of the United States, Feb., 1842, Álvarez MSS., ibid.; B. Davis to T. B. Catron, Oct. 18, 1913, MS., ibid.; Daily Missouri Republican, July 8, Aug. 23, 1850, Aug. 29, 1856; Santa Fé Weekly Gazette, Oct. 4, 1856; Read, Illustrated History of New Mexico, 395-402; Lansing B. Bloom, "Ledgers of a Santa Fé Trader," El Palacio, xiv, 133-136.

143 William T. Smith was living in Santa Fé at least as early as 1840. Three years later he became one of the proprietors of the land grant on the Mora river. In 1845 he formed a partnership with Norris Colburn, the firm being known as Colburn & Smith. American Merchants in Santa Fé to Manuel Álvarez, Dec. 8, 1840, Álvarez MSS., Benjamin M. Read Collection, Santa Fé; House Reports, 36 cong., 1 sess., no. 321, pp. 162-182; Weekly Reveille, Jan. 6, 1846.

144 Pedro Bautista Pino was the only delegate New Mexico ever had in

of Don Miguel and Don Facundo Pino, was much beloved and honored by the early traders, having proved a true and trusted friend to them in all their business and social relations, and one on whom they could rely for counsel and assistance in all dealings with the authorities. Mr. Vaughn often spoke of him with the highest respect and admiration, and to illustrate the esteem in which he was held by the Americans, delighted in relating a dream of an old trader who was quite a wag and related by him the day after the funeral of his old friend. It was the habit to close the stores from twelve till two every day for dinner and siesta, and the Americans would meet at one of their places of business to talk over various matters and have a social chat. This wag came in one day, and Mr. Pino's death coming up as the subject of conversation, he said he had a very peculiar dream the night before, and it had made such an impression on his mind [that] he must be excused for relating it.

"I dreamed," said he, "that I died, and was transported directly to the gates of Paradise. On arriving, I knocked at the door and was admitted by St. Peter in person, and invited into the anteroom for examination. There were many ahead of me, and among them Mr. Pino. When his turn came, St. Peter asked his name and where he was from. He replied:

" 'My name is [Pedro Bautista] Pino, from New Mexico.'

" 'How dare you attempt such a trick upon me?' said St. Peter. 'You are a fraud and an imposter. There is no such a place on earth as New Mexico. Go to your place, where you will find plenty of company of your kind.'

the Spanish Cortes. He was elected to that position, August 11, 1810. Bancroft, *History of Arizona and New Mexico*, 287-288.

"Mr. Pino gently reminded him that there was such a place, that he had just arrived from there, and [that] if he had a map handy, he would show it to him – in the mountains truly, and far distant from any other christian population. St. Peter took him to a map, where he showed him New Mexico plainly laid down and the location of many christian churches. St. Peter looked astonished and confounded that there should be such a place and he not know it, but finally excused himself by saying that on reflection his mistake was not so singular after all, as he was the first person that ever came from there, and this was the first occasion he had ever had to refer to it on the map – then very blandly opened the door and allowed him to pass in without further questioning."

The day after our arrival the ox teams of nearly all the train were sold to Mr. Bonney, who followed us in from the crossing of Moro river for the purpose of buying or taking them to the prairie to herd. Several of us preferred to sell rather than take the risk of having them herded through the winter. We sold our oxen for seven dollars a yoke, and Mr. Scolly loaned Bonney the money to pay for most of them.

After about a week we were permitted to withdraw our goods from the custom-house, but were not permitted to sell at retail. The change of administration and the apprehension of the Mexicans that there would be a demand for forced loans, impaired confidence to such an extent that those able to buy and willing to do so ordinarily, chose rather to plead poverty, and would only buy in limited quantities and on credit, for fear of exciting the cupidity of the new governor. We were consequently compelled to store our goods and wait for something to turn up.

I stored my goods with E. Leitensdorfer and Company and authorized them to sell as they had opportunity, allowing them a commission of ten per cent. The prospect of my bettering my fortunes by this adventure was by no means encouraging. And with nothing to do and not understanding the language, I concluded that rather than give way to despondency, I would keep a good heart, avail myself of every opportunity offering to see the country, and satisfy myself whether the country afforded any encouragement for a continuance in the trade.

A look at the resources of the country was not encouraging. The only products, beyond the immediate needs of the people, were wool (which would not pay transportation), a few furs, a very few deerskins, and the products of the gold mines, which did not amount to more than $200,000 a year when in bonanza, and very seldom to anything near that amount. Another resource of the country was from the proceeds of sheep driven to the low country in large flocks (amounting to from 50,000 to 100,000 a year), the proceeds from which would be in the hands of a very few of the *ricos*.[145] And the only chance I could see of getting any portion of it was from the little that might be in the hands of a very few who might want to start a little store and had not yet got in the way of going to "the States" for goods, or [who] might indulge in the national propensity of gambling and thus put some portion of it into general circulation.

The system of peonage, or voluntary servitude, was a fixed institution. The wages of the laborers was only from three to six dollars a month, and a ration to the

---

[145] Rich. Consult Gregg, *op. cit.*, xix, 304, 323; *"Barreiro's Ojeada Sobre Nuevo Mexico"* (Bloom, ed.), *New Mexico Historical Review*, iii, 147.

laborer only. From this he would have to support his family and pay the dues to the priest for marrying, baptizing, and burial of seven dollars and upwards, according to the ability and ambition of the individual desiring the services. An inflexible rule with the priests was: no money, no marrying; no money, [no] baptizing; no money, no burying. Or as they put it: *no haya dinero, no hay casamiento; no haya dinero, no hay bautismo; no haya dinero, no hay entierro.* As a consequence the poor were extremely so, and without hope of bettering their condition. The priesthood [was] corrupt, vicious, and improvident. Is it strange, then, that with such a heartless, demoralized, and utterly impious, yet very religious, priesthood, the people in such abject poverty could see no merit in virtue or honesty?

In a conversation with Dr. Connolly [146] some years after the establishment of the Territorial government, and after his marriage to the widow Chávez, he was boasting of the improved condition of his servants under his liberal management. He had raised the wages of his shepherds from two and three, to four and six,

---

[146] Dr. Henry Connelly was born in Virginia, and moved to Kentucky at an early age. In 1824 he made his first journey from Missouri to New Mexico and engaged in the Santa Fé trade. Later he opened a place of business in Chihuahua, where he resided for about twenty years. Shortly after the Mexican war he returned to New Mexico and made his home on a ranch near Peralta. He was elected governor of the "state" of New Mexico on June 20, 1850, but, owing to his absence from New Mexico and to the abortive nature of this government, he never entered upon the duties of his office. Continuing in business, he established stores at Santa Fé, Las Vegas, Albuquerque, and Peralta. In 1861 Abraham Lincoln appointed him governor of the territory of New Mexico, an office which he filled with credit until his death in July, 1866. *Senate Reports*, 39 cong., 2 sess., no. 156, p. 332; *Missouri Intelligencer* (Franklin, Mo.), June 5, 1824; *Daily Missouri Republican*, July 8, 1849, Aug. 19, 1850; William E. Connelley, *Doniphan's Expedition and the Conquest of New Mexico and California* (Topeka, 1907), 276-282; Davis, *El Gringo*, 356.

dollars a month, and the peons on the hacienda to six and eight, and teamsters with his wagon train to ten; and some of the best and most industrious laborers he had allowed to work a portion of the land on shares. And he flattered himself that he was treating them with great generosity and kindness, and was doing more to improve the condition of his servants than any of his neighbors.

"Well, doctor," [I said], "how many servants have you on your hacienda?"

"Big and little, 108."

"Well, I suppose you furnish them all [with] work through the winter?"

"Oh no. The crops are all gathered and stored, and I have no further work for them until time to plant the [?]."

"Of course they have a good store of corn and other provisions laid up for the winter?"

"Not an ear – not a thing."

"But how are they to live with nothing in store, and nothing to do to earn a living?"

He saw the point, and laughingly replied, *"Steal from Otero."*

"And how are Otero's servants to live, who you said were not as well cared for as yours?"

"Oh, they will steal from me – if they have the chance. It is considered dishonorable to steal from the master, but neighborly stealing is no disgrace."

This was the condition of the laboring classes of old New Mexico, and in view of the example set by the religious fathers, and their entire dependence upon their masters, is it strange [that] they were, as John Randolph very truly but uncharitably called them, "a blanketed nation of prostitutes and thieves?" Let us withhold our denunciations until we in imagination have put ourselves in their places, and ask ourselves what we would do. We can and ought to thank God that in mercy He placed us [in] a christian land under a free and liberal government, and under pious and moral teachings, where honest labor is liberally rewarded and there is no necessity of resorting to immoral or dishonest practices to live in comfort and decency. Let us watch and pray lest we be led astray by false doctrines of religious and political teachers, and fall into a like condition or entail it upon posterity.

After remaining in Santa Fé a week or two, Mr. Scolly was about sending his clerk, Mr. Smith, to the plains for some cattle he had on the range, and I asked the privilege of going with him. We went across the mountains from Pecos to Upper Tecolote, and thence to his ranch not far from Moro town, and found the herd in a valley between the Moro and Bonney's, where the herders had a temporary corral and *jacal* [147] made of bushes laid upon poles supported by crotches driven into the ground, where the herders boarded and lodged and made cheese. The curd was prepared in the usual way with rennet, and set in small kettles and earthen water-vessels; and when in proper condition, tied in a cloth and pressed by placing it upon a flat rock and a heavy stone laid upon it. We were invited to eat of it and found it very good, for the time and place, but not by any means what I had been accustomed to eat as cheese at home. We had about thirty head driven into the corral, where they were to remain until the next morning, when we were to start for Santa Fé. The

147 Hut.

herders said they had company, or visitors, from the Moro who had come out to gather *piñones*,[148] and they would be in at night.

When bedtime came, Smith was about to spread his blankets outside, when I expostulated for preparing to sleep outside when we could sleep under shelter. He said there would be a houseful, but if I could stand it, he could, and we would try it; but [he] feared I would repent my rashness before morning. I insisted, and we spread our blankets and laid down and soon fell asleep. But it was not long before the visitors commenced coming in, and several times on partially awaking I found myself so crowded that I could not move without disturbing a neighbor; and on further awaking to the situation, found that I could not get out without walking over several sleepers, and that my blankets were not only furnishing bedding for myself but [for] numerous others. So there was no way but to lie still and rest as well as I could.

At daylight I awoke and took a look of the sleepers. The *jacal* was *full* – packed so thick [that] it was impossible to count them or distinguish who was which, or myself from my bedfellow – men, women, and children piled in promiscuously regardless of sex, age, or nationality. As soon as I could pick my way out, I seated myself on a stone and determined to count (so far as possible) the number of lodgers, and as I remember, it was, I know, over twenty, and, I think, nearer thirty. Smith found several acquaintances, and the people had a good deal of fun, he told me, inquiring how the stranger enjoyed his lodgings among so many bedfellows.

---

148 Pine kernels.

After an early breakfast we started with the cattle, and one or two herders assisted us for a few miles, when we went on alone by a path but little traveled and over mountains and across ravines which it seemed impossible to pass with a drove of cattle, and nearly so on mule back. But we got along without losing an animal, and made very good time considering the difficulties and intricacies of the way.

Arriving in Santa Fé, we commenced to butcher and care for the meat. The cattle were shot down in the corral and bled and skinned where they fell, and cut up, laying upon the skin the paunches taken out, and a small incision made to empty the contents; then turned inside out and washed, and then re-turned and laid away until the tallow was rendered, when it was poured into the paunches after cooling sufficiently so they could be filled to nearly their original capacity. The fore quarters were hung under the portal, where they would keep without salt or other care until warm weather the next summer, if desired. The meat from the hind quarters was jerked by cutting [it] in strips from four to six inches wide, and then sliced to about half an inch thick and hung on ropes of rawhide in the open courtyard in the sun to dry.

Mr. Scolly used to slaughter from fifty to seventy-five head of cattle each fall, and dispose of the meat in quarters or jerked, as he found a market; and the tallow was sold and used for cooking purposes the same as we use lard – a part, perhaps, made into candles. I don't recollect of ever eating any salted, or even corned, beef in any part of Mexico during my fifteen years' residence in the country.

While hunting the cattle at the ranch, we saw two

men coming from the prairie who from a distance appeared like traders, and waited their approach. When they came up, they proved to be Mr. Albert Speyer with a servant. Mr. Speyer informed us that he came in for mules; that he had encountered a very severe storm of sleet and rain on the Cimarrón not far from Willow Bar,[149] and had lost a good many mules, and was going to Moro to see what he could do towards getting assistance to bring in the train. We informed him that Colonel Owens was still in Santa Fé, but was making arrangements to leave in a few days for Chihuahua.

After a short conversation we separated, and on our arrival in Santa Fé found him there. He had bought Colonel Owens's whole outfit – goods, wagons, and teams – and was fitting up to leave with a part of the wagons and all the mules, which, with the few he had bought at Moro, would enable him to move his train. We here learned that he had lost over seventy-five mules in one night of the storm.[150] He said that Connelly and Glasgow [151] must have suffered from the same

---

[149] Willow Bar was in the northeastern part of the present Cimarrón county, Oklahoma. *Old Santa Fé*, iii, 284.

[150] In September, 1844, Albert Speyer left Independence with twenty-five wagon loads of merchandise for the Santa Fé trade. One night, while encamped on the Cimarrón river near Willow Bar, he was overtaken by a snowstorm. His mules "crowded all around a little fire which he had kindled, but the cold was so intense that most of them died the same night; and others, in a state of starvation, commenced eating the ears of the dead ones." In later years it was customary for traders who camped near this place to amuse themselves by arranging and rearranging the disjointed skeletons of the mules. "When I last saw them," wrote one traveler, "the leg-bones were laid in rows, having been placed with great regularity, while the skulls formed a ghastly circle upon the ground." George D. Brewerton, "In the Buffalo Country," *Harper's New Monthly Magazine*, xxv, 457-458. See also *Daily Missouri Republican*, Mar. 6, 1845; Wislizenus, *op. cit.*, 13-14.

[151] Edward James Glasgow was born in Belleville, Illinois, June 7, 1820.

storm, as they would be ready to leave Independence but a few days after him, and must have been not far off. Dr. Connelly arrived before he left and reported that he had suffered about an equal loss with Mr. Speyer and would be compelled to go to the Río Abajo [152] to get sufficient mules to bring in his train.

The Americans were all (with the exception of Wethered and Caldwell, who had got a corner on the Santa Fé trade) much disappointed in the expectation of realizing large profits.[153] They had expected an unusually good trade, as the Mexicans had been deterred from going to "the States" for goods by apprehensions of privateers from Texas preying upon the "commerce of the prairies" under the plea of war between the two nations; and [also by apprehensions of] robbers from the frontier, as the proprietor of one train (Mr. Chávez) had been murdered and the train robbed by Dr. Prefontaine and his gang from Westport, Missouri,

In July, 1840, he was appointed United States consul at Guaymas, Mexico. Three years later he went into business in Chihuahua and became the partner of Dr. Henry Connelly. In March, 1846, Glasgow was appointed commercial agent of the United States at Chihuahua, a position which he resigned, October 23, 1848. Thereafter he engaged in business in St. Louis, where he died, December 7, 1908. Julian K. Glasgow, Statement, Jan., 1927; *Daily Missouri Republican*, Jan. 13, 1844; *Encyclopedia of the History of St. Louis* (William Hyde and Howard L. Conard, editors, New York, 1899), ii, 900.

[152] "The settlements *up the river* from the capital are collectively known as *Río-Arriba*, and those *down the river* as *Río-Abajo*." Gregg, *op. cit.*, xix, 284.

[153] Four caravans arrived at Santa Fé from Independence in 1844. They were in charge of Samuel C. Owens, Albert Speyer, Connelly & Glasgow, and Bent, St. Vrain & Co. George R. Gibson, editor of the *Independence Journal*, estimated that these caravans consisted of ninety-two wagons, one hundred and sixty men, seven hundred and eighty mules, and sixty oxen, and carried merchandise that cost about $200,000. Gibson based his estimate upon information obtained from prominent Santa Fé traders. *Independence Journal*, Sept. 12, 19, Oct. 24, 1844; George R. Gibson to Charles Gibson, Oct. 22, 1873, Gibson MSS., Missouri Historical Society.

ARRIVAL OF THE CARAVAN AT SANTA FÉ
From Josiah Gregg, *Commerce of the Prairies*, New York, 1844

the year previous.[154] But the order prohibiting retailing in Santa Fé, and the losses of teams and consequent delay largely increased the expenses of the Chihuahua traders [and] left but a small margin of profits.

I think the traders had some hand in deterring the Mexicans from going in for goods by exaggerating the danger and reporting rumors of a large expedition from Texas being organized for the purpose of making a raid upon the prairies and taking every Mexican train that should attempt to cross the plains that year. I am led to this belief by the knowledge of such a report being started at a meeting of the traders at the rooms of Leitensdorfer and Company after the arrival of Speyer and Connelly with their trains. Their house was the headquarters for all American traders for social and business conversation, and [for] plans for promoting their general interests. Mr. Charles Bent[155] arrived from the fort about this time and reported that Colonel

---

154 In April, 1843, Antonio José Chávez, a New Mexican trader who was traveling from Santa Fé to Independence, was robbed and murdered near the Santa Fé trail at a point which is within the present limits of Rice county, Kansas. The deed was perpetrated by John McDaniel and his band of western Missourians, most of whom were subsequently tried for murder and larceny. Of the eight convicted of murder, John McDaniel and Joseph Brown alone were executed. The others – Dr. Joseph R. DePrefontaine, David McDaniel, Thomas Towson, Nathaniel H. Morton, John A. McCormack, and William J. Harris – were pardoned by the president of the United States. *Daily Missouri Republican*, Sept. 26, 1843, Apr. 29, Aug. 17, Oct. 23, 1844; Gregg, *op. cit.*, xx, 227-229.

155 Charles Bent, well known throughout the West, was born in Charleston, Virginia (now West Virginia), November 11, 1799. He removed to St. Louis in 1806. As early as 1823 he traveled to the headwaters of the Missouri river in the employ of the St. Louis Missouri Fur Company. Making his first journey to New Mexico in 1829, he engaged in the Santa Fé trade, and shortly afterward settled at Taos. He was one of the founders of the firm of Bent & St. Vrain, the predecessor of Bent, St. Vrain & Co. General Stephen W. Kearny appointed him governor of New Mexico on September 22, 1846. On the following January 19, during the Taos Revolt, he was assassinated. *Missouri Intelligencer and Boon's Lick Advertiser* (Fayette,

Warfield [156] had been there that fall and assured him that there would be a large body of Texas rangers on the plains, and that all trains which could be identified with Mexican interests by any evidence real or presumptive would be taken, regardless of any claims of proprietorship; and as Leitensdorfer was a long time resident of the country and from his intimate and confidential relations with the Mexicans, it would be very risky even for him to bring but a limited amount, as it was known that his means were limited, and if he should attempt to bring more than five or six wagons, it would be considered as sufficient evidence that he was allowing the use of his name to cover Mexican interests. Therefore it would be more prudent for him to remain in the country the next year and allow some of them to supply him what goods he needed, which they would contract to do for a small commission. Eugene told me he thought they were trying to play it rather fine; but the plan was well laid, and if there was a probability of the present order prohibiting Americans from retailing continuing in force, it might be an inducement to accept the proposal in order to give force to the plot.

After remaining a few days in Santa Fé, business being very dull, Leitensdorfer and Company thought of trying an adventure to the Río Abajo; and consulting

---

Mo.), July 17, 1829; *Daily Missouri Republican*, Feb. 27, 1847; Allen H. Bent, *The Bent Family in America* (Boston, 1900), 121; "Diary of James Kennerly, 1823-1826" (Edgar B. Wesley, ed.), Missouri Historical Society, *Collections*, vi, 69; Grinnell, *op. cit.*, 29; Bancroft, *History of Arizona and New Mexico*, 426, 432.

[156] On August 16, 1842, the republic of Texas commissioned Colonel Charles A. Warfield to commit certain acts of hostility against New Mexico and its trade. For an account of Warfield's activities, see William C. Binkley, *The Expansionist Movement in Texas, 1836-1850* (Berkeley, 1925), 106-116.

the governor, found they might get permission to retail goods anywhere outside of Santa Fé. So they selected a stock of goods and packed [it] for transportation on pack mules. I thought I might see the country at least, and possibly find some place where I could dispose of my goods, and concluded to join the expedition.

Thomas Leitensdorfer and myself, with each a riding mule and an extra mule for the two Mexicans, and three pack mules left by way of the *bajada* for Peña Blanca,[157] where we hoped to begin a trade. But after staying one day and selling but two or three dollars' worth, we concluded to move on to Algodones, where our success was not much better. Thence [we traveled] on through the settlements along the river to Albuquerque,[158] where we crossed the river and [where] a circumstance occurred which showed me the force of habit among men, accustomed to going constantly armed and traveling in a dangerous country, in their care to keep their arms in good order and their powder dry. Tom went down the bank first, the pack mules to follow, and I was to go in last and drive. He told the dismounted Mexican to jump up behind the pack of one of the mules and ride across. But either misunderstanding or thinking best to mount behind Tom, he did so and they traveled in the stream till the water came up to the saddle-skirts, and the mule miring in the quicksand began struggling to extricate himself, throwing the Mexican into the water behind him and Tom over his head. The Mexican was thoroughly ducked,

---

[157] For an account of Peña Blanca, see Paul A. F. Walter, "Peña Blanca and the Early Inhabitants of the Santa Fé Valley," *El Palacio*, iii, 17-41.

[158] Albuquerque, originally named San Francisco Xavier de Alburquerque, was founded in February, 1706. "*Noticias que da Juan Candelaria Vecino de Esta Villa de San Francisco Xauier de Alburquerque*" (Isidor Armijo, translator), *New Mexico Historical Review*, iv, 274-275.

and all I could see of Tom for a moment was his arm holding his rifle above the water. Rising and blowing the water from his mouth and nose, and wiping his face, his first words were:

"No you don't! You don't wet my rifle unless the water is over my head!"

We traveled down the river to Socorro, stopping at all the towns along the route [and] making some sales in each town. [We] spent two or three days in Socorro, and started for home one cold windy morning.

And after traveling two or three [hours?], Tom proposed we should stop and rest awhile, make a fire and warm ourselves, and take a smoke. I supposed he would, of course, select a sheltered place under the hills, where there was plenty of brush to make a fire, and rest ourselves comfortably out of the wind; but he stopped on the bank of the river where the wind had full sweep. We had a few words about camping in such a place, but I was a greenhorn and any suggestions from me about choosing a camp were treated with contempt. We unpacked the mules and made a fire to leeward of the goods. I thought I would have a good fire, and commenced breaking limbs from a fallen cottonwood tree which had been thrown down by the caving of the bank. Tom thought we had fire enough; and I wanted a good one as there was plenty of wood. He kept expostulating, and I kept piling on the wood.

All at once he jumped up and seizing a keg of powder, said, "If you are going to blow us all up, I will help you and have the affair over with."

"Throw it in, Tom, and let us have a lively fire and get warm."

"Do you banter me?"

"Yes, Tom, I banter you; go it."

I watched his eye closely to see the direction, whether in or over the fire, knowing full well he would accept the challenge, when he gave it a throw through the blaze of the fire (and as close to the ground as he dare without the chance of its stopping in the fire) directly in the direction of my feet.

I stepped aside and let it pass, and laughing, said, "There, Tom, I knew you would not let it stop in the fire."

"Well, I would, but these Mexicans couldn't understand, and I did not want to blow them up. Now let us both be sensible and sit down and smoke."

There were no further words about it, but we were ever after fast and confidential friends, and he never again called me a greenhorn.

That night he gave me his confidence, and explained the reason for his always choosing Fournia to accompany him whenever he went hunting or was called to leave the train in hunting stray animals. He said Fournia was jealous of him (but without reason), and shot at him from the window of [a] house while passing one night, but he never let on that he suspected him of it. And when he was making preparations to leave Carondelet, Fournia applied for employment; but a friend had cautioned him not to employ him, as he had threatened to kill him on some hunting expedition.

Tom immediately went to his house and hired him, as he said, "Just to show him he was not smart enough to do it."

I do think Tom enjoyed his triumph more than he would the making of a thousand dollars. I always considered Thomas Leitensdorfer as a brave, honest, and trusted friend in any emergency, and I remember him with the highest respect and affection.

We arrived in Santa Fé after an absence of about three weeks, having traveled three hundred miles and sold between three hundred and fifty and four hundred dollars' worth of goods. I had seen now all the principal settlements, and after a thorough calculation of the resources of the country, I could not see much inducement to continue in the trade. But what could I do? My goods were unsold, and I owed for a part of them, which with my outfit would amount to about a thousand dollars. There was nothing to do but wait and see what would turn up.

Albert Speyer had arrived from the plains with his train and was about to leave for Chihuahua. About the first news from him was that the Navajo Indians had attacked him at Fray Cristóbal and run off one hundred and fifty mules, leaving him unable to move his train, and necessitating the purchase of a third set of teams. Connelly and Glasgow were expected in two or three days, and George P. Doan [159] was waiting the arrival of Glasgow, with whom he had been intimate in St. Louis, desiring to accompany him to Chihuahua. He had come to Bent's Fort with their train, and after a short stay there, came to Santa Fé with Mr. Charles Bent.

He [Doan] had been presented with an old rifle by Messrs. Bent, St. Vrain and Company, and wished me to trade with him for a double-barreled shotgun I had. The trade proposed was not very enticing, but in con-

---

[159] George P. Doan, a resident of St. Louis, was born in the British West Indies. His father, J. Parker Doan, was the senior member of the firm of Doan, King & Co., wholesale dry goods merchants of St. Louis. Though a lawyer by profession, George P. Doan also clerked in his father's store. From 1845 to 1848 he was Webb's partner in the Santa Fé trade. *Weekly Reveille*, Jan. 4, 1847; *St. Louis Directory, 1848*, p. 72.

sideration of his anxiety for the trade and the history
of the rifle (given me [him?] by Mr. Bent), I finally
accommodated him by an even swap, and have never
regretted it. Many years before, a trapper employed
by the American Fur Company had taken it on a trapping expedition in the Blackfeet country. The Indians
killed him and took his gun. Years after, Messrs. Bent,
St. Vrain and Company sent an expedition to that
nation on a trapping and trading trip, and traded for the
old rifle. At the fort it was re-stocked (full length), and
altered from flint-lock to percussion, and kept at the
fort for a target rifle for several years. In 1846 I had it
newly grooved, half stocked, and [added] a new lock
and breech pin, and have carried it in all my travels in
the trade except my last trip. In 1849 a man from Boonville, Missouri, on his way to California, came into the
store when I was cleaning it up, and on looking at it,
said:

"My father made that gun. There are his initials. It
must be very old, for he has been dead many years and
did no work of that kind for many of the last years of
his life. He made all his guns by hammering out the
barrels by hand, and boring them and creasing them
in the same way."

This is the history of my old and trusty friend, companion, and bedfellow, who never went back on me –
"Old Blackfoot" – the name it was known by at the fort
and which I have always retained.

Everything continued in the same dull routine in
our mess – waiting and hoping, no business, no news
from "the States," and nothing particularly interesting
or exciting until early in February, [when] a mail arrived bringing news of the presidential election which

took place the November previous. It was news, and oh, *such* news! James K. Polk was elected, and Henry Clay defeated. Seldom in my life have I passed a more sad and melancholy night. I was a Whig – in 1840 cast my first vote for General Harrison, and holloed myself hoarse hurrahing for Harrison and shouting for "Tippacanoe and Tyler too." And Henry Clay was now my idol, and defeated by such a man as Jim Polk! My Country! Oh, my Country! What are we coming to, when my countrymen can make such a choice! To wait three months for news, and then get *such* news, was more than I could sleep over.

We began talking about future prospects, and what was best to do. To do business, we must have new goods. But with me it was a question how my credit would stand the strain of asking for more until I could pay for the goods I had. On taking account of cash and stock, I found I had cash to pay for my outfit and a part of my indebtedness; but inventorying goods on hand at a fair valuation, I could see no profits beyond my mule, saddle, and bridle, and "Old Blackfoot." The question for me to decide was whether it was better to remain until all my goods were disposed of and lose another year, or to go in and try my luck and credit for another trip. I decided to take the chances and try again, and began preparations for leaving. I had not yet learned to talk much Spanish, but could understand enough; so I thought I could sell my own goods if I had credit enough to buy them.

On March 3, 1845, about 2 o'clock P.M., three of us started for "the States" by way of Taos, the balance of the company going with two wagons by way of Las Vegas. We were to meet them at the Moro river and

take the Ratón route for "the States." We rode to Po-
juaque and stopped for the night at the house of a Mexican, and [had] the usual accommodations at Mexican
houses: *chile colorado, frijoles,*[160] *tortillas,* and *atole,*
using the floor for a table, and the *jerga* [161] (carpet) for
a tablecloth. The *tortillas* [were] brought in on a nap-
kin, and the *atole* in earthen dishes made by the Indians,
and no spoons, forks, or knives, except our own butcher
knives, using fingers for forks, and *tortillas* for spoons.
Our beds were wool matresses, with pillows of the
same; [and there were] no sheets but the common Mexican blanket. Yet we enjoyed our supper and rested
well.

The next morning at breakfast I found myself without much appetite, but supposed the change in rations
and excitement of being on my way to "the States" had
produced the effect. We traveled that day to Embudo
and stopped at the house of an old Frenchman, and
were very cordially received and entertained. The first
thing on entering the house, a bottle of Taos whiskey
and *aguardiente* [162] were set out, of which we all partook with a gusto. And when supper was announced, we

[160] Beans. Kendall wrote: "*Frijoles,* a species of dark beans of large size,
stewed or fried in mutton fat and not too highly seasoned, wind up the
substantial part of a dinner, breakfast, or supper, and seldom is this favourite
and national dish omitted. In fact, *frijoles,* especially to the lower order of
Mexicans, are what *potatoes* are to the Irish – they can live very well so
long as they have them in abundance, and are lost without them. A failure
of the bean crop in Mexico would be looked upon as a national calamity."
Kendall, *op. cit.,* ii, 34. *Frijoles* were boiled a long time, and then fried in
grease and flavored with onions and garlic.

[161] A kind of coarse woolen cloth or stuff, with a shaggy nap on one side.

[162] "*Mezcal,* or *aguardiente,*" according to Bartlett, "is a spirituous liquor
of great strength, much more so than our strongest whiskey. It is obtained
from the bulb or root of the maguay, or *agave mexicana,* and is the common
alcoholic drink throughout the country" [Mexico]. In Paso del Norte *aguardiente,* or brandy, was made from grapes. This brand was of a light color,

all had good appetites and ate heartily — rested well, and breakfasted on a sand-hill crane I had killed the day before and brought along. Crossing the creek, we immediately ascended the mountain — and a long, winding, and steep ascent [it was]. We footed it in Indian file, each driving our [his] mule ahead of him. Arrived at the top, we mounted, rode for some distance by a comparatively level path, and had a good time for rest and reflection.

For some reason I began to think how much better I had relished my breakfast that morning than the morning previous, and to question myself why it was. "Was I sick yesterday, and well today? No, I was not sick, but had no appetite. Why?" Something whispered: "*Aguardiente!* What? Liquor! Can't you breakfast without your grog? Well, Webb, you have got to a pretty pass. If you can't breakfast without your grog, you shall starve, for no more grog do you get till you arrive in 'the States.' "

And I stuck to it. [I] breakfasted light in Taos and Moro and a few days in camp, but crossed the plains without grog; and although for many days all the meals were light, no grog was used by me to stimulate an appetite or as a substitute for short rations of food. . .

We traveled that day to Taos and stopped at the house of that ever hospitable and kind old gentleman, Don Carlos Beaubien, where we spent a couple of days; and then started to meet the company by way of Moro town, and spent the night with Mr. Lucien Maxwell. The next day we joined the company near the Moro

and was known in New Mexico as "Pass whiskey." It was probably the latter kind of *aguardiente* that Webb drank. John Russell Bartlett, *Personal Narrative of Explorations and Incidents in Texas, New Mexico, California, Sonora, and Chihuahua* (New York, 1854), i, 186, 290-291; Gregg, *op. cit.*, xx, 156.

river and started by the Ratón route. E. Leitensdorfer
was the captain, or leader, of the company, and Mr.
C. C. Branham and myself agreed with him to board
us and our mules, and haul our beds and "possible
sacks" for forty dollars each. So we had nothing to do
with laying in provisions or forage for the trip, and
supposed everything was liberally provided.

We found no buffalo and but little game before
reaching Bent's Fort, and rations of meat were getting
short; but [we] supposed we could buy dried meat at
the fort to last us two or three days till we should get to
buffalo. But in this [we] were disappointed. They were
also on short rations, and we made haste to get along.
About fifty miles below the fort we killed a fat cow,
but neglected to take all the meat, as we were sure of
finding plenty farther along as needed. And this was
the last and only chance we had to get meat on the trip,
except a poor old bull near Walnut creek, which we
killed and took the tongue and what little meat there
was. He was so poor he could not run nor hardly walk.
We all did our best at hunting, but not a buffalo, elk,
antelope, or deer could we get; and even the prairie
dogs laughed at our calamity and stayed in their holes.
We had corn which was laid in for the mules, but we
[were] compelled to deny the mules their rations and
use it ourselves. The night guards would boil it. And
we had boiled corn without grease, salt, or other season-
ing, and coffee without sugar, for breakfast, and boiled,
unsifted flour for supper. The ration of flour gradually
lessened along the journey, until the last ten days the
allowance of flour for supper was reduced to three pints
for seventeen men. At Cottonwood creek [163] three men
left the company and went ahead, which gave us a

163 The Santa Fé trail crossed Cottonwood creek, now called Cottonwood

little extra ration, but not enough to be noticed. We did not think of suffering to starvation, but [for] there was but little time; but we were hungry enough not to disdain anything eatable. And we were also very [in]-considerate of the rights and feelings of others, as I think a certain degree of hunger makes a person cross enough to fight on small provocation.

[We] arrived at the Lone Elm,[164] fourteen miles from French's [165] (the first house in Missouri), and camped for the night. The next morning I started ahead of the train by a cut-off and bought provisions for breakfast, and took to camp on the "Blue," [166] waiting for the arrival of the train. I bought a ham [that] weighed about twenty pounds, four and a half dozen eggs, flour, potatoes, and lard for shortening, sugar for our coffee, etc. We ate *all* the ham and eggs, and all of the other provisions we could hold. After a smoke and a short rest Branham, myself, and a man we called Muggins went to the house to settle, and they [Branham and Muggins] wanted to know if we could not get some buttermilk. The woman had just finished churning, and we told her to bring all she had. She brought a large white pitcher full – I think near or quite a gallon – and we passed around the pitcher until it was emptied. [We] settled and rode off – riding slowly. [On account of] the de-

river, near the present town of Durham, Marion county, Kansas. Kansas State Historical Society, *Eighteenth Biennial Report*, 111.

[164] Lone Elm, or Round Grove, was located near the present town of Olathe, Johnson county, Kansas. *Ibid.*, 117.

[165] French's, located in Missouri, was on or near the western boundary of the state and a short distance northwest of the present Martin City, Jackson county, Missouri. *Daily Missouri Republican*, Apr. 27, 1847.

[166] Big Blue river. One branch of the Santa Fé trail crossed this river west of the present village of Hickman Mills, Jackson county, Missouri. Ralph E. Twitchell, *Historical Sketch of Governor William Carr Lane*, Historical Society of New Mexico, *Publications*, no. 20, p. 24.

tention at the house, the train had got some two or three miles ahead of us, and I proposed to Branham to gallop and catch up.

He looked up with a peculiar wink and a don't care and satisfied yet suffering look, and said, "Black Bess can't gallop."

I challenged him to a trial with Dolly. And Muggins began bragging on his pony, until he [Branham] was induced to make the trial, when we found that we all could travel much faster on a walk than on a faster gait, and finally concluded to stop and rest. We could only rest by lying flat on our backs, which we did for an hour or two, and then started for the camp. [We] found all the men resting without cooking supper. And the next morning [we] started for Independence without breakfast, and did not get hungry again for the two days we remained there. We were about fifty days from Santa Fé to Independence.[167]

---

[167] Most of the traders left Santa Fé about March 1, 1845, and arrived at Independence on the following April 16 and 17, making the journey in somewhat less than fifty days. While in Independence they stayed at the Independence House, owned by F. F. Hansford. *Daily Missouri Republican*, Apr. 28, 1845.

SECOND JOURNEY ACROSS THE PLAINS

SECOND JOURNEY ACROSS THE PLAINS

Arrived in St. Louis, I found that those whom I owed felt somewhat encouraged by receiving a part of what I owed, and on hearing an account of the condition of trade, were willing to trust me again on the hope which we all entertained of better luck next time. I settled with Colonel Owens for my outfit and got the promise of another if I wanted it. [I] commenced buying all I could, and wherever I could get credit (by getting my life insured and assigning the policy as security), from one hundred and fifty to six hundred dollars in a place, of such goods as were suited to the market; and with cheek and brass finally succeeded in buying about eighteen hundred dollars' worth of goods, and had them nearly packed.

I had asked Messrs. Doan, King and Company [168] for credit and [had] been refused. They very kindly offered to trust me a reasonable amount to do business in Missouri, Illinois, Iowa, or Arkansas, but they declined selling goods on credit to that trade. When nearly ready to ship the goods bought, Mr. Smith, of Smith and Blackwood,[169] told me that Mr. Doan's son, George,

---

[168] J. Parker Doan and Wyllys King were the principal members of the firm of Doan, King & Co., then located at 131 Main street, St. Louis. They were wholesale dealers in English, French, German, and American dry goods. *St. Louis Directory, 1845*, p. 51; *St. Louis Directory, 1848*, pp. 72, 132; *Daily Missouri Republican*, June 18, 1844.

[169] Charles L. Smith and J. H. P. Blackwood constituted the firm of Smith & Blackwood, then located at 69 Main street, St. Louis. They were whole-

had arrived from the plains, and he had met Mr. Doan
on the street that morning, who asked him [Smith] to
have me call at their store. Mr. Smith said he thought
the invitation meant business, and I went immediately –
wondering, guessing, doubting, yet hoping something
would turn up to my advantage. On entering the store,
I was met by Mr. King, who informed me that Mr.
Doan would like to see me in the counting-room up-
stairs. I was there met by Mr. Doan, who said that he
had sent for me to talk about business. George had
come home from Mexico and wanted to go into the
trade but was not conversant with commercial business;
and he had talked the matter over with Mr. King, and
if I would form a copartnership with George under the
firm name of Webb and Doan, they would give the firm
credit for an equal amount of goods to what I had
bought, thus doubling the amount of the adventure. I
immediately assented to the proposition, and Mr. Doan
said he would have the articles of copartnership drawn
up for our signatures that afternoon, and we could
immediately go to selecting goods.[170]

This was a very advantageous arrangement for me, as
I had been compelled to get credit wherever I could,

sale dealers in English, French, German, and American dry goods. Smith &
Blackwood, Invoice, July 8, 1844, Webb MSS.; *St. Louis Directory, 1845*, pp.
23, 161.

[170] The merchandise purchased by Webb & Doan cost $6267.22, and con-
sisted mainly of dry goods, clothing, notions, hardware, and jewelry. The
following is a partial list of the goods bought: fancy, black, white, pink, and
mourning prints; brown, and bleached sheeting; striped, and checked muslins; blue, and linen drillings; scarlet, and zebra cloth; blue, black, and green
alpaca; red, and white flannel; black cambric; striped, plaid, and black
cashmere; bleached domestics; French lawns; Irish linens; white, and fancy
edgings; cotton flags; bandana, black silk, cotton, and red pongee handkerchiefs; German shawls; white cotton hose; hickory shirts; blue denims;
buck gloves; black silk ties; suspenders; green shoe thread; fine ivory combs;
beads; necklaces; gold rings; fancy, and gilt hair pins; pearl shirt buttons;

and not always for such goods as I desired or at prices as low as I could have bought with a better credit. The goods bought of Doan, King and Company were fresh and in all respects desirable – as good and as well adapted to the trade as I could have bought for cash. At that time and ever since I have felt the deepest gratitude and respect for the confidence then manifested, and always [manifested] during my continuance in that trade.

It was but a few days before we were ready to leave St. Louis on my second trip, and under circumstances far more encouraging than I had any reason to hope or expect when I left Santa Fé. Arriving at Independence, we commenced buying our outfit, and bought fifteen yoke of oxen (two teams of six yoke each and three yoke for [the] kitchen wagon), and sufficient goods to make two good loads to pay duties on. We bought three new wagons, loading the large wagons [with] 5,500 pounds and the small one with about 1,500, besides provisions, etc. Solomon Houck [171] had bought a lot of wagons in Pittsburg,[172] and among them were two heavy wagons with iron axles – a new experiment for freight wagons and one looked upon as

gilded vest buttons; gilded coat buttons; needles; scissors; razors; strops; coffee mills; sadirons; log chains; shovels; spades; hoes; axes; percussion caps; cork inkstands; shaving soap; and candlewick. Webb & Doan, Account of Goods as Baled, 1845, Webb MSS.

[171] Solomon Houck, of Boonville, Missouri, began his career as a Santa Fé trader in the early twenties. By 1849 he had made sixteen journeys across the plains to New Mexico. He was still engaged in this trade in 1852. Benjamin Hayes, Emigrant Notes, 410-412, MS., Bancroft Library; *Daily Missouri Republican*, Aug. 17, Sept. 27, 1852.

[172] At this time most of the wagons used by Santa Fé traders were manufactured in Pittsburg. A number of prairie schooners were also made in Independence, Missouri, where, by 1845, there were seven wagonwright's establishments. *Daily Evening Gazette*, Mar. 24, 1840; *Weston Journal*, Mar. 1, 1845; *Daily Missouri Republican*, Apr. 9, 1846.

quite hazardous. What if an axle should break or get badly sprung on the plains? No chance of fitting a wooden axle to the box for an iron one, or straightening the iron one if badly bent. Wagons were scarce, and Houck proposed selling one of these; and after due consideration I made up my mind to take the risk. This, I believe, was the first freight wagon with iron axles that ever went over the plains, and Mr. Houck followed some weeks after with the second – the mate to it. Gradually they came into use for the Santa Fé trade, but not for the low country.

As near as I remember, it was about the middle of June before we were ready to start for the plains. And we concluded to start when ready, and on reaching Council Grove wait for enough to make up a train. The first night from the state line we camped at the Lone Elm; and there came up a violent storm in the night, and being [too] short-handed to form a guard to herd the cattle, [we] concluded to go to bed, keep dry, and trust to luck. Awaking in the morning, we found every animal gone, and on hunting the tracks found they had started for "the States." There was no way but to follow them on foot, and I started alone, leaving Mr. Doan to look after things in camp and see that the men did not leave, taking [an] outfit for which they owed and as much more as they might be able to carry. Arriving at the [state] line, I found the oxen had been taken up and corralled by Mr. Magoffin's [173] major domo at his camp, and the mules yarded at French's.

There had been a great deal of rain, and the roads

---

173 James Wiley Magoffin was born in Harrodsburg, Kentucky, in 1799. In March, 1825, he was appointed United States consul at Saltillo, Mexico. Later he removed to Chihuahua, where he was in business until the Mexican war. In August, 1846, according to his own statement, he "went into Santa

were very muddy, and the prairie very soft. I went to the camp of Mr. Noland,[174] who had hitched up to start, and found him putting a new tongue to one of his wagons. [It had been] the first [wagon] to make the start over the prairie [and had] mired down. And doubling teams to pull [it] out, the cattle took a short turn [and] brought the wagon "on the lock" and broke off the tongue. I was expecting him to join us, and we would travel together, and expressed my sorrow at his bad luck on the start, when he made a very philosophical reply which I have often repeated when under discouraging circumstances:

"Well, don't despair! Keep a good heart! 'Twill all come right in the spring."

I got the cattle under way for camp, and about half way met one of the men come to assist me. We did not arrive in time to start that evening, but managed to secure the cattle; so the experience was not repeated the next morning.

Fé ahead of Genl. Kearny and smoothed the way to his bloodless conquest of New Mexico." Susan Shelby Magoffin, *Down the Santa Fé Trail and into Mexico* (Stella M. Drumm, ed.), xviii-xix; Ralph E. Twitchell, *The Story of the Conquest of Santa Fé, New Mexico, and the Building of Old Fort Marcy, A.D. 1846*, Historical Society of New Mexico, *Publications*, no. 24, pp. 16, 46, 51.

[174] Probably Smallwood V. Noland, of Independence, Missouri. Noland was one of the pioneer settlers in Jackson county, Missouri, and for a number of years was a representative from that district in the State legislature. In 1838 he became proprietor of the Washington Hotel in Independence. This building was destroyed by fire on the night of February 19, 1845; but he soon erected another and larger structure and called it the Noland House. Noland's hotel, or tavern, was widely known throughout the West and was patronized by Santa Fé traders. James Aull, Independence Ledger, 1827-1828, Aull MSS., Lexington Historical Society, Lexington, Mo.; Waugh, Desultory Wanderings, 1845-1846, pp. 47, 120, MS., Missouri Historical Society; *Weston Journal*, Mar. 1, 1845; *Weekly Reveille*, May 26, 1845; *Daily Missouri Republican*, July 3, 1846; *History of Jackson County, Missouri* (Kansas City, 1881), 181, 643-644.

We hoped to reach Council Grove in fifteen days at farthest, but the rains continued almost daily, and the roads were almost impassable. [We] would have to unload and double teams almost every day, and frequently two or three times a day; and several days [we] would move one wagon at a time with double teams, and then sometimes mire down and have to unload. We were thirty days to Council Grove, rain almost every day, sleeping on the wet ground, clothes hardly dry and blankets wet, and so little chance to dry them that they two or three times became flyblown and maggoty. At Willow springs [175] we mired down a wagon and broke a pair of hounds, and were unable to get out before dark [and] left the wagon standing in the mud and water. In the night it rained and raised the water so it came very near running into the wagon. In the morning we unloaded the kitchen wagon and ran it alongside, and by taking out a few goods at a time and drawing them to the high ground, succeeded in getting out.

While thus engaged, who should come up but Uncle Nick. He had gone to Chihuahua with Colonel Owens, and getting into some difficulty was arrested and kept in the calaboose for some time; but through the influence of friends [he] succeeded in getting allowed the freedom of the city, with the understanding that if he was smart and willing to take his chances he might run away and get out of the country. So the old man started with one man and came to New Mexico, [and] thence by way of Bent's Fort to "the States." His first inquiry was for whiskey and something to eat, and while breakfasting, gave us an account of his trip and adventures. When he left, in crossing the slough, his mule mired

---

[175] Willow springs is about ten miles southwest of Lawrence, Kansas.

down, and in her efforts to get out threw the old man over her head into the mud and water; so we had to assist both in getting ashore. Mounting, he bade us good-bye, and with advice to keep up our courage, as we would find plenty of the same sort ahead, rode off. We found the advice good and the assurance true.

After much labor and difficulty we arrived at the Grove, and found a few wagons there waiting for enough more to come up to make up a train. In three or four days Mr. Hicks, of the old firm of Hicks and Marney, came up with, I think, eight wagons loaded for a cousin of his, Bethel Hicks, who was doing business at about 150 miles below Chihuahua. In two or three days enough wagons arrived to make up a train, and we organized by electing Mr. Hicks captain, and arranged the usual four guards, all hands standing guard two hours every night and the morning guard of each day standing day guard. Leaving Council Grove, we traveled on, the roads improving as we began to get to the high buffalo grass prairie, and I recollect but little of interest or adventure except a little excitement not far from the Little Arkansas.

Three men went from camp hunting, as we were approaching the buffalo range: Mr. Barclay, of Barclay and Doyle,[176] Indian traders; and John Sims, a young man from Georgia; and another whose name I don't recollect. They had not been out more than two or three hours when we saw three men, one on horseback in the lead and two on mules following at

---

[176] Alexander Barclay and Joseph B. Doyle. In 1849 Barclay & Doyle built an adobe trading post on the south bank of the Mora river near the present village of Watrous, Mora county, New Mexico. This post, which was still standing in 1857, was known as Barclay's Fort. The firm of Barclay & Doyle was dissolved in 1856. *House Reports*, 36 cong., 1 sess., no. 321, pp. 175-176; *Santa Fé Weekly Gazette*, Feb. 9, 1856; Davis, *El Gringo*, 51.

the best rate of speed they could make under the circumstances. And on their arriving near enough to identify them, [we saw that they] were our friends the hunters. On inquiring the reason for so much hurry, they said they had discovered a party of Indians stealthily endeavoring to approach them, and thought it the safest policy to make the best time they could to the train. The Indians finding they were discovered, gave chase, and our men finding them gaining upon them, began to think a fight unavoidable. But Barclay said he took command, and called Sims to the lead on his horse, and the other two on their mules found they (their mules) would run much faster. But Sims did not know the country, and in the excitement had lost the direction of the trail from where they were. So Barclay gave the word of command by hallooing, "Right! Left! Ahead! *Faster!*" according to the urgency of the case. When they came up, both men and animals were pretty well fagged by the excitement and the race.

Mr. Barclay took them to be Osage; and I have no doubt they were, as they were frequently met in that section. And if the party was strong they were good Indians, but a weak party or one or two hunters would be treated pretty roughly if caught and allowed to escape with their lives. I have heard of two or three parties being stopped by them, and robbed of nearly everything worth taking, and thankful to get off with their lives. These were, of course, good Indians under missionary instruction, and receiving annuities from our government.

Before arriving at the crossing of [the] Arkansas, we had concluded to take the Bent's Fort route instead of the Cimarrón, thinking we might possibly encounter Texans on the Cimarrón, and began making preparations to go ahead and arrange for duties. Mr. Colburn, Bethel Hicks, Mr. Noland, Tom Otobus, myself, and one other started ahead and traveled at the rate of forty to fifty miles a day, and spending one night at the fort took the same route of the year before by way of [the] Huérfano and [the] Sangre de Cristo pass. We learned that Governor Martínez had agreed to allow the Americans to retail goods, and [that] the prospects of a good trade were more encouraging than we had found them last year, but that the danger from Indians was greater, as the Ute had visited the governor to learn what he intended to do, whether to allow trade and friendly intercourse or not. During the interview the Indians made some demands which the governor saw fit to resent, and a row occurred, and the Indians left, declaring war against Mexicans as well as Americans. So we traveled cautiously on approaching the mountains, and from there on Tom Otobus was the guide and captain of the company and generally rode ahead, the rest following, Indian file.

We had got to within half a day's ride of Río Colorado, and passing through a grove of *piñones* to the open plain and thence a mile or so to the cottonwood timber skirting the Río Culebra, when all at once Tom stooped in his saddle and looking earnestly towards the timber, called out, "People! Indians!" and turned his mule around, taking the path for the grove which we had just left. We all followed in order, getting our arms in hand ready for use, and soon heard a volley of musketry from the grove behind us, and saw a good many people dodging among the trees; but [they] soon came out and saluted us with another volley and a yell of all sorts of sounds and voices. Tom took another look and commenced laughing.

"They are Mexicans," [he said], "and will have a good laugh at us for running."

We turned and met them, and the first to salute him with a shake of the hand was his brother-in-law. The Ute had run off some stock from Río Colorado and killed one or two herders, and these men had been out all night in pursuit, but concluded they had gone as far as was prudent, or they had any chance of proceeding safely.

We left Tom at Turley's and proceeded direct to Santa Fé, only staying in Taos over night. Arriving in Santa Fé, [we] called on the governor [177] and found we would have to pay the same duties as last year, but would be permitted to retail, and there would be some unusual restrictions in regard to contraband goods.[178] Candlewick, powder, and some other goods would be stored and held subject to the decisions of the authorities in Mexico. There were some merchants from El

---

[177] José Chávez y Castillo. Mariano Martínez de Lejanza was removed from office early in 1845. His successor was José Chávez y Castillo, who served as provisional-governor from May 1 to November 16, 1845. On the latter date Manuel Armijo again became governor, though his appointment was dated, July 24, 1845. Bloom, "New Mexico under Mexican Administration," *Old Santa Fé*, ii, 235, 239, 249.

[178] Chávez, the provisional-governor, probably stated that the import duties would not be changed and that the merchants would be permitted to retail. But this policy was altered when General Francisco García Conde came to New Mexico. Appointed military head of the Fifth division of the Federal army, General Conde arrived in Santa Fé in August or September, 1845, and for a time superseded the provisional-governor as actual ruler of New Mexico. Conde prohibited the introduction of contraband, increased the import duties to about nine hundred and fifty dollars a wagon load, and enforced the non-retail decree of September 23, 1843. *Daily Missouri Republican*, Sept. 4, Nov. 3, 1845; Bloom, "New Mexico under Mexican Administration," *Old Santa Fé*, ii, 241.

Paso in town, waiting the arrival of the train, and some were expected from Chihuahua; and things looked fair for a brisk trade. We remained some two weeks, rented stores, and made arrangements for business on the arrival of the train. Mr. Colburn formed a copartnership with W. T. Smith, which he considered a good arrangement, as Smith had spent several years in the country and had an extensive acquaintance.

When we learned the train was passed Las Vegas, Colburn and myself left one afternoon, intending to meet it at San Miguel sometime the next day. When we got beyond the Arroyo Hondo, Colburn began to talk about business prospects, and about dark asked me if I would sell out if I had a chance and return in the fall ready to bring out another stock in the spring. I replied I would, if I could do so on terms to suit. He wanted me to make him a proposition, and after reflecting a few moments, I told him how I would sell. He should pay all expenses of freight, insurance, and passage for myself and partner to Independence, take the outfit, teams, and everything at cost, pay all wages and expenses to Santa Fé, and we would turn everything over to him; and [he was to] give us three thousand dollars net profit. He thought the proposition preposterous, as it was too much. We talked and dickered, and camped in the woods some four or five miles beyond Pecos. [We] picketed our mules and talked till near twelve o'clock and finally went to sleep.

In the morning we started pretty early, and Colburn again began to talk trade. Finally, he offered twenty-eight hundred dollars on my terms, the cost of adventure to be paid in cash, so Mr. Doan could return with the wagons going back, and the profit to be paid in gold dust, so I could return with the men coming out with Wethered and Caldwell. This proposition I accepted, and on arrival at San Miguel met the train and advised my partner, Mr. Doan, what I had done; and he was satisfied and delighted.

Colburn bought out another man with two wagons, on what terms I never knew. [He] also [bought] goods from other parties, and made some quite large sales to low country merchants, and had a very good retail stock on hand. He did very well, and I thought we had. The wagons entered Santa Fé the eighty-third day from Independence.

Messrs. Colburn and Smith took possession of the goods and wagons at San Miguel and entered them and passed through the custom-house without any trouble beyond the usual small annoyances from the custom-house officers, which were usually satisfied by small loans of money which were never paid or expected to be, and small presents of some kind to which they would take a fancy, generally amounting to twenty-five to one hundred dollars according to circumstances and number of wagons entered.[179]

About two weeks after our arrival Mr. Doan took an opportunity to return with a return train, and was paid the amount of the adventure and expenses according to contract, and paying export duties on [the] amount, leaving me to collect the profits and follow about the middle of October. I made my headquarters at E. Lei-

179 The Santa Fé correspondent of the *Daily Missouri Republican* stated that in 1845 the total cost of merchandise transported from Independence to Santa Fé was $342,530, and that the import duties amounted to $105,757. He asserted that the caravans which transported these goods consisted of one hundred and forty-one wagons, twenty-one carriages, two hundred and three men, one thousand seventy-eight oxen, seven hundred and sixteen mules, and thirty-nine horses. *Daily Missouri Republican*, Mar. 19, 1846.

tensdorfer and Company and had a settlement with them of the last year's adventure, which, when closed up, varied but little from [the] estimate made in the spring – profits: mule (Dolly Spanker), saddle, bridle, blankets, etc., and rifle gun ("Old Blackfoot").

About October 10, I received the balance due from C. and S., and began preparations for leaving. B. Pruett [180] had sold out his goods and wanted to return; and [Pruett] having a small wagon and six sets of harness, I agreed to join him and bear an equal share of the expense of mules and outfit and leave as soon as we could get a sufficient company. Wethered and Caldwell's train was expected, and we calculated on a few of the drivers wishing to return.

While getting ready, Uncle Nick came ahead from the train and proposed returning, and told me what day we might expect to meet them at the Río Moro. I had heard that Smith had been bragging a good deal about his business. And from his habit of telling everything he knew and his intimacy with the officers of the customs, [I] thought (as the exportation of gold dust was forbidden by law and subject to confiscation if found) [181] it would be well to get it to the frontier in some way without taking it with me. So I got Uncle Nick to take it out and deliver it to me when we met. Pruett also had some gold dust, but also had some specie on which he paid export duty [182] and would consequently not be suspected as a contrabandist.

---

[180] Benjamin Pruett, of Jackson county, Missouri. In 1846 Pruett returned to Santa Fé and settled there. During the Taos Revolt of the following year he was killed at Mora, New Mexico, about January 20. *Weekly Reveille*, Apr. 12, 1847.

[181] See the Mexican tariff of April 30, 1842. *House Ex. Docs.*, 27 cong., 3 sess., no. 29, p. 251.

[182] The Mexican tariff of September 26, 1843, provided for a duty of six

The afternoon before I intended to start, Don Agustín Durán came in and began talking with Eugene, and from the expression and manner I judged they were talking about me. Very soon Eugene told me that the officers of [the] customs were after me, as we had suspected they would be. As a cover, Colburn had given me a draft on St. Louis, which I produced, and Eugene translated [it] to Don Agustín. And the old man very blandly replied that the cover was well intended and would ordinarily work well, but [that] Smith had inadvertently (while bragging about his business) told the whole story of the trade, and that Colburn had been to the Placer, procured the gold dust, and paid it over; and now here was a bill for the export duties (according to my recollection, two per cent) on twenty-eight hundred dollars, amounting to fifty-six dollars.

"Ask him," [I replied], "how I can be made to pay export duties on specie which I have not got or on gold dust which is contraband, and which I show plainly is not in my possession by producing a draft on St. Louis for the whole amount claimed that I am taking out of the country."

"Tell the young man, Don Eugenio, that he has made his *diligencia* very ingenuously, and indeed I think you must have had a hand in it. The gold dust is but a small package, and we probably could not find it if we hunted ever so earnestly. But the young man is a much larger package, and we shall be very careful that he does not leave town until he pays the $56. And even if he should [leave town], it would be [the] worse for him, as we should denounce him and have all the peo-

per cent upon all gold and silver coin exported from the country. *House Ex. Docs.*, 28 cong., 1 sess., no. 24, p. 113.

ple on the lookout for him, so he could not get out of the country without being arrested. We don't want to make any fuss, but we want the money. Our salary and perquisites are small, and we don't propose to allow this opportunity to get a little ready cash, to pass. So pay the money, take the paper, and do what you please with it, and go in peace."

I paid the money, took the paper, and the next morning left for "the States."

A WINTER TRIP

A WINTER TRIP

On leaving Santa Fe,[183] there were but five: Mr. Pruett and myself, [and] an Irishman and wife who came out with Messrs. Kerford, Jenkins and Gentry, of Zacatecas, as servants of Dr. Jenkins, but [who] for some reason took their discharge in Santa Fé and were anxious to return to "the States" and willing to take the risk of many privations to gain their object. We had hired a Mexican as mule herder, thus making four men and a woman to start, and expecting to wait on the frontier till we could make up a company sufficient to justify us in taking the risk of the trip.

We arrived at Las Vegas about the middle of the afternoon and concluded to stay over night, expecting to meet W. and C.'s [184] train the next day at Moro or Sapello and get returns from Uncle Nick and see what number of men were desirous of returning. But very soon Uncle Nick arrived in town and said the train would camp on the Gallinas about two miles from town that night, and after taking a drink (always the first thing with Uncle Nick), he called me aside to tell me about the gold dust.

"Not meeting you," he said, "I concluded [that] to cache it and tell you where to get it when you came along, would be the safest way. You know as you cross Sapello there are willows along the bank, and some few rods down stream there is a cottonwood tree?"

---

[183] Webb and his companions left Santa Fé on November 2, 1845. *Weekly Reveille*, Jan. 5, 1846.

[184] Wethered & Caldwell.

"Yes."

"Well, you go to that tree and stop and face north or northeast, and go a few rods [and] you will come to a hole, or sink in the ground, and east of that [is] a small bunch of bushes, and in that bunch of bushes you will find the bag containing the gold dust, buried."

"Well, you think I can find it from your description?"

"Why, yes. I can go to it in a dark night."

"And suppose I don't find it; then I shall be at Sapello or Moro and you in Santa Fé, one hundred miles distant. I shall have to hunt you up, and it will necessitate four hundred miles travel to raise the cache."

"Well, you give me another drink and my supper and a fresh mule, and I will go tonight and get it and bring it to you in the morning."

So this plan was agreed on, and after a short rest and refreshments he started off. The next morning he came through with the train and left the bag all right, and I placed it in a pile of shelled corn in the room where we had our harness and baggage, as far into the pile as I could reach.

We found there were but few men who expected to return, and that we should have to wait at least two weeks before there would be any prospect of making up a company; and Pruett concluded to return to Santa Fé and attend to the matter.

A day or two after the departure of the train I went into the living room of our host and found they had company from Santa Fé – a young man named Ortiz, whom I had frequently seen there and rather intimate with the government officers. I had a suspicion that he was after me, but as I could as yet understand but little

Spanish, I could gain no knowledge of his business from his general conversation or by inquiry of other parties. I concluded to keep my eyes and ears open and see if I could learn anything from motions or an occasional word that I could understand which might be dropped in general conversation. I neither saw nor heard anything to increase or confirm my suspicions, except once in the evening I heard the word "*contrabandista*," [185] and I thought he at the same time cast a peculiar look towards me. This suspicion and fear and suspense ([since I was] among enemies in a strange country, and [they] speaking an unknown [unintelligible] language) was very trying to my nerves; but I concluded the only way was to keep cool and keep thinking until some course could be decided on to relieve myself [of] the perplexing anxiety.

The conclusion I finally came to was to raise the cache and find a new one. And as there were many wild geese flying about the cornfields below the town and on the *loma* a short distance east of town, [I] concluded to go a hunting in the morning, taking the gold with me and find a new cache. So very early I started on a hunt, with the gold, which was securely sewed up in a double bag of buckskin. And seeing many geese along the ditch and in the cornfields, I cautiously approached, keeping watch not only of the game but for anyone who might be watching me. Crawling along the ditch towards the flock of geese, I came to a place where an animal had broken through the bank with the foot to the water which had washed under, and I dropped the package into the hole without stopping longer than [necessary], to avoid observation or suspicion of either

[185] Smuggler.

geese or people. I had not gone far (after relieving myself of my load) before a good shot was presented, and I fired and killed a goose, which was very quickly picked up and carried to our quarters and presented to our host. It was a good fat goose, and was very acceptable to all.

I heard nothing of any search; never knew whether my suspicions were well founded or not. And although I afterwards became well acquainted with Ortiz, which continued many years, I never asked him what led him to Las Vegas at that time.

The bag lay in [the] ditch for more than a week, when I began to fear the water might affect the buckskin injuriously, and I concluded to take another hunt and move it to a new place. So I raised it from there and took [it] to the bluff across the meadow and river and cached it in the rocks, where it remained safe and in good order until we left, about a month from the time I received it from Uncle Nick.

In about two weeks after Pruett left for Santa Fé, he returned, bringing with him two or three men from the train, some four thousand dollars in gold dust from Colburn and Smith for me to take to St. Louis, a Mexican shepherd dog, and his arm in a sling, having been badly bitten by the dog. We began preparations for a start, and the married couple concluded to wait for an opportunity to return with a larger train which would afford more protection and comforts. We left Las Vegas with six Americans and two Mexicans – eight in all – one small wagon, about twenty mules, and two horses. The wagon was loaded with about forty bushels of corn, which, with provisions, bedding, etc., made a good load for six mules. On passing my cache, I raised it and put it in the wagon. We had now about eight thousand dollars in gold and specie, which made us feel like keeping a close watch to avoid accidents and enemies.

At the Río Moro we found a family of Americans from Arkansas who had come out in the fall and taken possession of a house built the summer before, bringing some cattle and several good American horses. We remained two or three days and bought half a beef to furnish meat till we got to buffalo, and on November 16 took a final start for "the States."

The first day we drove to a camp a few miles from Wagon Mound and stayed all night. The next morning we started, and on arrival at the Wagon Mound concluded to take a cut-off across the *vega* [186] instead of going around by the road, and it was not long before we found our mistake. We mired down wagon and mules, and finally had to unload the wagon, take off the body, and hitch ropes to the end of the tongue to get the mules on hard ground to pull out the empty wagon. It was dusk before we got onto hard ground, and we were all tired, muddy, and wet and hungry, and no wood within a mile or two; so all but the cook went to gathering weeds, while he tended fire and made coffee and broiled meat. We concluded to take a rest until about midnight, and hitch up and go to Ocate for breakfast.

I told the men to sleep, and I would keep guard and call them when it was time to start. Pruett's dog was a vicious rascal, but I had got somewhat acquainted with him and flattered myself he would not bite me. I had a buffalo-skin overcoat, and leggings coming up to the hips, and as it was pretty cold I put them on. After

---

[186] Open plain.

going around camp and getting the mules on good feeding ground, I returned to the wagon and sat down on
our bed. The dog was lying on the foot, and as I sat
down he began growling. I spoke to him and told him
he knew better than to bite me, but instead of being
pacified, he made a spring for me and caught my left
cheek in his mouth. Under an impulse and hardly knowing what I was doing, I caught him in the mouth by
placing my four fingers on his tongue and my thumb
underside between his jaws. I held him as fast as he
held me. The men arose and took him by the upper
jaw, while I pulled down the under one, and thus drew
the teeth from my face without tearing it.

We concluded to start, as all were aroused and it was
near the time we had intended to start. Pruett was determined on killing the dog, but I begged for his life. And
he was very useful in camp several times, by keeping
the buffalo out. Several times they would walk with the
wind and, partially blinded by the driving snow, be
almost in camp before either we or they were aware
of it. When I got out of the wagon at Ocate, he was
alongside, but on seeing me, ran off into the canyon
and did not again make his appearance until we were
near Red river.

We had pleasant weather and traveled without adventure until we arrived at a camp of W. and C. on
their trip out, where they had dug for water about
seven or eight miles below the Middle Cimarrón
spring.[187] And as there was no water without digging,
we camped for the night. Being so few, we stood no
guard, but picketed all the mules and trusted to luck.

[187] Middle Cimarrón spring was within the present limits of Morton
county, Kansas. Kansas State Historical Society, *Eighteenth Biennial Report*,
114.

About midnight we were awakened by a stampede of the mules, and on jumping from bed I saw every one [of the mules] had pulled up the picket pins and were on the run over a knoll towards the road. Without waiting to call anyone, I started after them just as I had left the bed – in shirt, vest, trousers, and moccasins – supposing, of course, that under the prospect of footing it for five hundred miles and depending upon our rifles for provisions, they [the traders] would feel enough interest to at least get out of bed and make an effort to find them and bring them back. In a few mintues I heard a man behind me (talking to the dog) who proved to be one of my bedfellows (we slept three in our bed), and he said he did not wait to see whether any of the others got up or not. He had his hat but did not stop to put on coat or boots.

It was very cold, and [there was a] clear sky but no moon. We soon struck the road and found they had taken the back track; and we could hear the bell and from the jingle knew they were still on the run, yet a long way off. Whether stampeded by a wolf, buffalo, or Indians, we had no means of knowing, but as they continued running so long a distance we feared the Indians. Yet we determined not to give them up without making every effort in our power for their recovery. Gradually the sound of the bell became more and more faint, until it was lost altogether, and we could no longer follow it as a guide. But when last heard they were still on or near the road; and we now would run some distance and get on our knees and look for their tracks, and if we found ourselves still on their trail, would rise and run again as far as we thought prudent, and [then get] down again hunting tracks. In this way we followed for three or four miles, Haskins complaining that he had stepped on a prickly pear and his foot was full.

"Pull out the thickest," [I retorted], "[and] run on heel [or] toe, or hop, or any way to get along, for remember this may be a life or death race. The chances are against us anyhow, but never give up. I have bruised my heel and run on tiptoe, but that is not half as distressing as it would be to lose the mules and foot it to 'the States'; so keep a good heart, pull out what you can without much delay, and forget the rest in thinking of the lost mules."

Thus we proceeded for a mile or two when, on looking for the tracks, found they had left the road. We crawled back until we found where they had struck off south, and listening could hear no bell, when we felt greater fear that the Indians had them. It was now much slower following, as we had to stop and hunt the tracks much oftener, and in the grass the trail was not so easily followed. But after a while when listening with my ear to the ground, I could hear in the far distance the occasional tinkle of the bell, and in the valley to the west of us. Hope revived, and as they had not left the valley we felt less apprehensive of Indians. Yet it was the part of wisdom to exercise prudence and caution, lest we were among enemies, or by a careless and abrupt approach again stampede the mules. So we followed the bell, stooping as close to the ground as possible, and talking in whispers when necessary to speak, and looking across the prairie in the line of the horizon for any object of interest whether man or beast. The tones of the bell [were] becoming more and more distinct, and the tinkle produced by the motion of the head showed they [the mules] were feeding. Hope increased, and when we approached near enough to take a fair observation and seeing no signs of men, we gradually approached, giving the peculiar whistling call to which they were accustomed in camp, [and] Haskins going for the bell mare, and myself for an old horse belonging to one of the mule boys. We soon had them in hand, Haskins mounting and taking the lead, and myself following the herd, [as] we started for camp.

To describe the feelings of one in such circumstances, is impossible; to have anything like a real appreciation of it without being there, is equally so. But I was there, and I never think of the tones of that bell gradually becoming less and less distinct until at last dying out in the far distance, and hope also dying with the tones of the bell, and the exercise of the will alone keeping the soul from despair; then after an hour or so of almost hopeless endeavor, to again hear those indistinct and doubtful tones, and hope revive as the tones become more and more distinct until the climax of triumph is obtained, is a trying experience, but is a great matter of rejoicing and thanksgiving in all after years.

We mounted and started for camp, and for the first time began to realize how cold it was. But taking a brisk trot, we hoped to get to camp before suffering much from cold. And expecting to find a good fire by which we might warm ourselves on arrival, we proceeded as cheerfully as the circumstances would permit. But success in getting the mules, although a great relief to our despairing hearts, would not furnish clothes to keep us warm, and we soon began to realize that we were a long distance from camp, that the night was excessively cold, and that we were just as we had jumped out of bed.

After proceeding about half way, we met the two Mexican boys who had awaked and missed the mules and taking the tracks, followed as well as they could, but had no idea how far they might be off until they heard the bell. And approaching them, one of them shed his blanket and gave it to Haskins, and the other commenced doubling his for a substitute for a saddle, as the old horse was terribly poor and the backbone very sharp and the distance still three or four miles. But I preferred protection from the cold, and wrapped the blanket around me. Inquiry about the men in camp, found they had left them all snugly tucked up in bed, but awake and watching for an attack from Indians or our return to camp.

Approaching camp, we saw no light or sign to indicate how far we had yet to travel until we got within a few rods, when suddenly a blaze streamed up and we felt – encouraged? Yes, but oh how mad! Pruett heard the stampede and thought it was by Indians, as he heard a noise which he took to be a howl of triumph and defiance, and said he raised the wagon sheet so he could see out, drew his rifle alongside of him, and waited to see what would turn up. Cuniffe [188] and Cassius were bedfellows, and Cassius was deaf and did not hear the noise. But when Cuniffe wakened him and told him the mules had run off, he asked if anybody was after them; and being told that we had gone, re-

[188] Henry J. Cuniffe. This was probably his first year as a Santa Fé trader. He soon settled in New Mexico, where he remained until the later fifties. *Santa Fé Weekly Gazette*, Aug. 13, 1853; *Daily Missouri Republican*, Oct. 28, 1854, Jan. 14, 1859.

plied, "Well, Webb will get them," and rolled over and went to sleep. Our bedfellow had made the fire, and being asked why he had not made it sooner, and my accusing him of having slept, said he could not sleep on account of his anxiety as to what would become of his wife and four babies at home. To sum up the matter, there was a good deal of loud talking, and probably the words used were not the most reverent, but according to my recollection they were expressive; and judging from the conduct of the men the balance of the trip, they made a good impression.

After warming ourselves and taking a smoke, we went to bed. [We] had only time for a short nap before daylight. On rising and looking about to discover the cause of the stampede, we saw the tracks of a buffalo coming down towards the watering place, and when near camp returning towards the hills. And before leaving, [we] saw a buffalo bull grazing in the direction taken by the tracks, and concluded he was the cause of the trouble.

We started at the usual time and proceeded down the river (in which I never saw running water but once between the Lower spring[189] and the Upper crossing),[190] seeing an occasional buffalo and antelope. But as we had meat, the cold increasing, and [there was] no timber for over seventy-five miles, we made the best time we could, stopping over a few hours at Sand creek[191] to prepare for the journey of fifty miles to the Arkansas without water.

[189] Lower spring was on the Cimarrón river near where Zionville, Grant county, Kansas, is now located. Kansas State Historical Society, *Eighteenth Biennial Report*, 113-114.

[190] The Upper crossing of the Arkansas river was near the present town of Hartland, Kearny county, Kansas. *Ibid.*

[191] Sand creek is probably identical with the present North Fork of the Cimarrón river.

[We] started into the *jornada*[192] [at] two or three
o'clock in the afternoon and were soon among buffalo
in herds. [It was] excessively cold, and [there was a]
very high wind, and in the night the buffalo were [seen]
in such numbers that we seemed to be passing through
a continuous herd, and notwithstanding all precautions
we could take, it seemed sometimes as if they would
run over wagon, mules, or men; and we finally concluded to stop for the night. Here the bad dog did us
good service, and all were glad he was spared at the
Wagon Mound and Ocate, when it took all my powers
of persuasion to save his life.

At daylight we started, the cold still increasing, and
although the buffalo were plenty and at no time during
the day were we out of sight of numbers of large herds,
we were able to proceed without annoyance or apprehension on our journey. About eleven o'clock the second
night out, we arrived at the Arkansas and finding some
chips and bits of wood left by W. and C.[193] on their
way out, we made a cup of coffee and went to bed. But
it was too cold to sleep or get much rest. The ice on the
river and the roaring of the wind caused such a chill
and gloom that, although we realized we were in reach
of better shelter and protection in case of a violent
storm than we had been for the last one hundred and
forty or one hundred and fifty miles, it had but little
effect [on] quieting our nerves so we could get comfortable rest.

Early next morning while the cook was preparing
breakfast, we took a look at the river to see what the

---

[192] A day's travel. "The word *Jornada* (journey performed in one day)
is especially applied in Mexico to wide tracts of country without water,
which must for this reason be traversed in one day." Wislizenus, *op. cit.*, 38.

[193] Wethered & Caldwell.

prospects were for crossing. It was frozen over from bank to bank. There was a sand bar near the middle of the river, showing that the water was low and the fording was not as long as usual; but the ice was thick. In some places [it was] thick enough to bear the mules, but where the current was rapid and the water deep, not thick enough; and even if it would [have been thick enough], they were unshod, and it would be almost impossible to get them across without breaking the ice.

After breakfast, [while] discussing the matter with Pruett, he said he feared we were going to have a storm, and he thought we could find shelter on this (south) side of the river near-by, and if we succeeded in crossing that day, it would be some distance before we could find it down the river on the other side. There was, he thought, a cottonwood grove not over two or three miles up the river, and he thought it would be safer to wait a day or two until we had a better prospect for fair weather. I insisted I had rather break the ice, ford the river, and make three miles towards home than to go up the river three miles from home and remain on this side. Finally, he began to bat his eyes, put his hand to his head, and spit, and grunt, and at length announced that he felt the symptoms of sick headache.

"I can do nothing to help," [he said], "but if you can get across without me, go ahead."

Haskins was willing to make the trial, and we each took an ax and went to the river and began breaking the ice and sinking it. I had got into the water some few feet but not yet over my boots, and Haskins being in shoes took wet feet first, and feeling the shock began to complain. I encouraged him to persevere and come on, assuring him that we could get over before night if we would will it, but met [with] the reply that I had boots on, and my feet were not yet wet, and I really had no idea of how cold the water was.

Failing in all my efforts to encourage my companions to effort, I gave up and went to camp, saddled my mule, and went up the river to hunt a camp and perhaps a more favorable place to cross the river. Traveling up the river near the bank, I saw no better crossing. And the river was closed by ice clear across the whole way until I came to an island (or what would be an island in high or a medium stage of water) covered with willows with a luxuriant undergrowth of grass and a good many old cottonwood trees, which afforded a better camp and protection in case of a severe storm than I knew of for many miles down the river. I returned to camp and reported, but still recommended renewing the effort to cross. Pruett was sure we were going to have a storm, and the other men showed no signs of seconding my efforts. So I consented, but told them when I got ready to cross I should make the announcement and take my mules and start, and if any of them chose to accompany me they could do so; otherwise I should go alone, and they could stay till July thawed them out.

We went up to the island and arrived about 2 P. M. Soon after our arrival it commenced snowing – fine, cold-weather snow – accompanied by [a] very high wind, and we all were glad to be in so good a camp. We had good shelter and plenty of wood, and the mules better protection and grass than we found at any other camp on the trip. We started a fire and had got the last meat in the kettle, and the cook was preparing bread and coffee, when Pruett got onto a wagon wheel to see how things looked outside and announced that large gangs of buffalo were coming into the valley for shelter; and [we] soon saw a band coming onto the head of the island where we were camped, and not over two hundred yards off. He took his gun and approached them through the willows, and we soon heard the report and went to him with an ax and butcher knives, and in a short time had plenty of meat in camp.

We began roasting meat on the coals, all in good spirits, and Cassius, the cook, began singing "Home, Sweet Home." The camp and all [the] surroundings tended to place us in good spirits, but this was a little too much. The thought of the comforts of home, and [of] loved friends around the cheerful fireside with no apprehensions of danger from enemies or suffering from cold or hunger, contrasted with our situation (although comfortable compared with what it might have been), [and] was too much. And I called him to order and offered a resolution that any member of the company who, during the balance of the trip, should sing any song of home or speak of the good things of home or of the comforts of home, should be fined a gallon of whiskey payable on our arrival at Westport. To speak of relatives and friends by their names, was admissible, but the word "home," and all endearing references to friends, relatives, or sweethearts, must be left out.

This seems to me now almost as cold and comfortless as the circumstances then surrounding us, but placing myself there (which I can in imagination do in full reality), I would again offer the same resolution, laying aside for the time being all feelings of tenderness or sentimentality as tending to depress the spirits and overcome the will. Tender-heartedness, sentimental love, or even affection strongly manifested have no place in the prairie, unless the object is present with you and under your protection.

The valley on the other side of the river was full of buffalo, as far as we could see up and down the river, and [they] seemed to be moving slowly up the river. And during our two days' stay on the island, it appeared as if a continuous drove was passing along the whole valley, like a drove of cattle which we see passing along the highway.

The river made a turn to the northward just at the head of the island, and the current striking the island seemed to rebound somewhat and take a course diagonally across the river, striking the shore opposite to us near the foot of the island. And the weather was so cold as to freeze the water to the bottom where it was shallow, throwing the running water into a narrow channel; and giving greater depth and a stronger current, kept an open channel from our shore to the other.

The morning of the third day was clear, and we concluded to make an effort to cross; so we gathered camp equipage, harness, etc., and loaded them into the wagons. And as our mules were unshod and unable to stand on the ice, we thought [it] best to run the wagon over by hand below the open channel where the ice was sufficiently strong, and to drive the mules across in the open channel. About ten o'clock we were all ready and ran the wagon over without difficulty to the opposite bank, but were unable to get up the bank onto the land. Leaving it, we returned to the island and mounted a man on the bell mare and started for the head of the island, where we had prepared an entrance (as well as we could) to the water in the channel.

The mules thought the water cold, the way badly prepared, or some other reason led them to be very loth to follow; and we had a good deal of difficulty in starting them. And when all in, the water coming up on their sides, they made the effort to get out, and raising their fore feet upon the ice, would break off large cakes which would float down stream and, lodging against the bank, so obstruct the passage [that] they could not get to shore. Some would succeed in getting upon the ice, but were unable to stand, and after a few struggles would abandon all effort and give up. [The mules] being wet and the weather so cold, we were compelled to give them first attention; so with long ropes thrown around them and men taking hold of each end, we would slide them ashore. Fortunately, there were some willows and bunches of coarse grass, and the mule boys, by running them, would get them warmed up, so that by the willows whipping and brushing their legs, they would in a little time be out of danger. But those in the water were very uneasy and continually breaking off cakes of ice, so we could not get more than one or two out at a time. And we were all, most of the time, in the water waist deep, breaking and sinking the ice, but frequently compelled to get out and slide a mule across.

We were thus occupied till near sundown before we got them all over, and appearances indicating another storm, we concluded to go up the river still farther in search of another camp. When we got out of the water, and before we got hitched up, our clothes were frozen, and it required all our efforts and exercise of will to keep from freezing.

We were just ready to start, when the dog, who had remained in camp while we were crossing but realizing that we were about leaving, appeared upon the ice across the channel but feared to take [to the] water, and set up a melancholy and appealing howl for aid. Cassius said we had been so successful in getting everything across without any disaster that he would go for the poor dog and bring him over. So he again waded the channel, and taking the dog in his arms brought him over, dropping him upon the ground. And all congratulating him for his courage and unselfishness, he raised his head and straightening himself, exclaimed triumphantly:

"We are the six busters, and our labors of this day ought to be printed in the papers."

He was by trade a printer, which I presume suggested the thought.

We started up the river and traveled a couple of miles when we came to a cottonwood grove, where we found a pretty good camp for the mules, and, near-by, as good accommodations for ourselves as we had left. In the night it commenced snowing, and we were storm bound two days more. The third day we concluded to kill and prepare meat enough to last us in, and Pruett killed seven cows, the farthest not half a mile from camp. And we took the best cuts and cut them in convenient pieces for handling and packing in the wagon. And next day we [left], with very cold but pleasant weather, and the snow not deep enough so but what we could make pretty good days' journeys. The first day out we broke our wagon, being heavy loaded and crossing the buffalo paths which were worn deep and frozen; so the jar was more than it could bear. We threw away a part of the meat, and bound up the broken part with buffalo hide, and started again with but little hindrance.

The whole trip down the Arkansas to the crossing of

Coon creek we saw buffalo in great numbers, and frequently saw herds until we passed Walnut creek.[194]
Wolves were numerous, and every night their howlings
and wranglings were so constant and annoying that we
were kept awake a good deal; and I think a novice or
one of delicate nerves would have been unable to sleep
at all. On one occasion [while] coming down the river,
on making a turn around a knoll, we came suddenly
upon a buffalo apparently dead, as there were some half
a dozen wolves feasting upon him. And as we approached, one wolf backed out from the carcass fully
half his length and ran off. On examination [we found
that] the carcass was still warm, and life not extinct,
as was proved by an occasional kick.

To give some idea of the numbers of wolves on the
prairie in the buffalo range, I will give an account of
two men formerly conductors of the mail from Independence to Santa Fé. I think it was in 1854 or 1855 [195]
[that] they went to Walnut creek and built a small
mud fort, and in summer they would sell what few
knicknacks they could to traders and other passing
travelers, and in winter their business was to kill wolves
for the skins. They would kill a buffalo and cut the
meat in small pieces and scatter it about in all directions a half a mile or so from camp, and so bait the

[194] The traders forded Walnut creek a short distance east of the present
site of Great Bend, Barton county, Kansas. Kansas State Historical Society,
Eighteenth Biennial Report, 112.

[195] In the summer of 1855 Allison and Booth, formerly conductors on the
Santa Fé Mail and Stage, established a trading post at the Walnut creek
crossing of the Santa Fé trail. They were especially interested in killing
wolves and in selling supplies to travelers and Santa Fé traders. Their
establishment, which was later called Allison's Ranch, continued to do business until 1860, when it was captured by the Indians. *Daily Missouri Republican*, July 25, 1855, Sept. 18, 1860; *Daily Missouri Democrat* (St. Louis),
Oct. 23, 1858; *Santa Fé Weekly Gazette*, Feb. 21, 1857.

wolves for about two days. Meantime, all hands were preparing meat in pieces about two inches square, cutting a slit in the middle and opening it and putting a quantity of strychnine in the center and closing the parts upon it. When a sufficient amount was prepared, and the wolves were well baited, they would put out the poisoned meat. One morning after putting out the poison, they picked up sixty-four wolves, and none of them over a mile and a half from camp. The proceeds from that winter's hunt were over four thousand dollars.[196]

The weather was excessively cold all the way from the Arkansas to "the States," and we were compelled to break the ice and wade all the large streams. But we traveled as expeditiously as we could, having no occasion to stop to kill meat; and when there were indications of stormy weather, were particular to select well-sheltered camping places by making either longer or shorter daily drives as the occasion demanded.

There were several long and dreary stretches (as from the Little Arkansas to Cottonwood, from Cottonwood to Diamond spring, and from 110 [197] to Willow springs) which were looked forward to with anxiety, as the distances were from twenty-five to forty miles without wood or comfortable shelter either on the road or within several miles of it; so if overtaken by a blizzard we would stand at least an even chance of losing our animals and some of our men. Providentially, we passed these journeys without loss or any great suffer-

---

[196] For another example of killing wolves for their hides, see George Bird Grinnell, *Two Great Scouts and their Pawnee Battalion* (Cleveland, 1928), 28-33.

[197] 110 Mile creek. The traders crossed this creek near the present town of Scranton, Osage county, Kansas. Kansas State Historical Society, *Eighteenth Biennial Report*, 110.

ing, and without laying by until we came to Willow springs, where the appearances so strongly indicated an approaching storm that we left the road and turned south a mile or two to timber, where we found wood and shelter and tolerably fair pasturage for our animals. As we had feared, a severe storm of snow and violent wind came upon us in the night and continued all the next day, but we were in a good camp with plenty of wood to keep us warm and provisions for man and beast. From here to Westport we could see our way without any great risk from cold or storm, as there was no long distance without shelter on the road or near-by, and the day was spent in feasting, rest, and rejoicing. And although we were reckless and wicked traders, we had all heard of a kind Providence, an all-seeing and preserving God, a comforting Spirit, and a guardian angel, and believed in them far enough to *feel* thankful at heart, if not to such a degree as to give expression by the lips to words of thanksgiving.

About eight or nine miles before reaching Council Grove, we camped for the night, and without much shelter but plenty of good grass (for the season). And on rising in the morning and preparing to start, [we] found two of our mules had strayed from camp. Looking in all directions over the prairie and seeing nothing of them, we began circling around camp for tracks leading off, and after some time found them; and making for the road on the back track towards Diamond spring, [we] followed them to the road. And being satisfied they had gone back, I went to camp and saddled Dolly, and was ready to start on the hunt for the mules about the same time the wagon left for the Grove, where they were to remain until I overtook them.

I expected to have a little time with Dolly, but she was more determined than usual not to leave the wagon, and we had a little difference. I had a good, dry, hardwood gad about three feet long, which I applied with all the force I was able, to head, neck, and hips, but all to no purpose. I would pull for the back track until her head was in the direction I wanted her to go, but her will and her body were all the time in the direction of the wagon. I was mad, and Dolly was contrary, and we were both as willful and wicked as we knew how to be. At last, tired of whipping and pounding, I concluded to try what punching would do. And slipping my hand towards the middle of the stick, I raised my hand and with all my strength forced the end upon her loin, and to my surprise felt the end pass through something, and looking at the butt of the stick found it had been cut quite slanting, making a very sharp point. Fearing I had forced it through the skin and flesh into her body, and overcome with shame, remorse, and compassion, I threw away the stick and tried the effect of gentle caresses and kind words: "Whoa, Dolly, now let us compromise. If you will quit, I will"; at the same time patting her on the neck, but not daring to look for the wound. Gradually her ears were raised from her neck, and she looked around kindly, and after a short and reasonable conversation by words, caresses, and signs, we came to an understanding; and Dolly started off on a gallop in the proper direction and seemed to understand, as well as I did, what I was hunting for. I examined to see what damage I had done, and found the stick had penetrated the saddle blanket instead of the body of Dolly, and felt greatly relieved.

We followed the road on the tracks of the mules for

three or four miles until we came to a small ravine, where the grass was tall and some green grass springing up in the bottom, and we both must have discovered the mules at the same time. We turned off the road and soon had them under way for camp. [We] arrived at Council Grove about 2 P. M., and as it was a good camp, and I wanted my dinner, we concluded to spend the balance of the day.

In the afternoon two little boys from the Kaw village came into camp, and after gratifying their curiosity and eating of the best we were able to offer them, they commenced playing around camp and through the timber. Their principal game and diversion appeared to be practicing with the bow and arrow, which were light and adapted to their strength and uses. The arrows were without the iron points used by the men. They showed great skill with the bow, as they would scarcely ever miss any target we would set up for them. And when they were left to themselves, they would select a mark in almost any locality within range of their bow, whether on the ground, on the body, or in the top of a tree. In case one lodged an arrow among the limbs of a tree, they would with extra arrows keep shooting at it until it was detached from its lodgment and fall to the ground. I saw them shoot a small woodpecker in a tall cottonwood tree after but a few shots, and when they had killed him, used him as a target by sticking the bill in the bark of a tree and practicing on him until he was used up. The bow and arrow seems to be the Indian boy's plaything, and the lasso the Mexican boy's, each practicing upon such targets as present themselves, and those requiring the most perseverance and skill, affording the most amusement.

Towards night some Indian men came into camp, and
we learned there was quite a village of them some two
or three miles down the creek. One of them saw a common Mexican blanket belonging to me and proposed a
swap. [He] said he would give me a water pail full of
honey for the blanket; and as we had rather a hanker-
ing after sweets, I concluded to trade. As it was [too]
late to go and return to camp that evening, it was understood that I would go to their village the next morning.

So on the departure of the wagon, two of us proceeded down the stream through the timber to the village, where we found our friend awaiting us and ready
to escort us to his lodge. On entering, we were shown
seats on robes, and as it was about their breakfast time,
we were asked to eat, but declined. They insisted we
should take some honey; and a wooden bowl, or deep
trencher, filled with honey, and a part of a buffalo
horn so shaped that it could be used as a spoon, was set
before us. And we enjoyed a feast, passing the spoon
back and forth, Indian fashion. He brought out a rawhide bag full of honey, and after warming it before the
fire and kneading it occasionally, succeeded in filling
the pail as full as we could conveniently carry it on
horseback to camp at Big John creek.

Arriving, [we] found [a] pleasant and comfortable
camp, and an early supper nearly ready, and all hands
waiting our arrival and anticipating a rich and luxuriant feast of bread, meat, and onions, with coffee and
plenty of sweetening. And although we dined at the
fashionable hour (5 to 7 P. M.), our bill of fare would
be hardly recognized as very high-toned or elaborate.
The table was a blanket spread upon the ground, and the

furniture was a tin plate, an iron spoon, and a butcher knife, with a tin cup for coffee. Our bill of fare was soup, followed by meat with bread and honey. And honey on the plate made the bill of fare: soup and honey, meat and honey, bread and honey, coffee and honey, and honey for dessert. We were all honeyed, but I think I had the most honey and suffered most. That night will be ever remembered as one of suffering. Such a bellyache I never suffered! But the morning brought comfort, and we proceeded on our journey.

As I mentioned before this, we spent one day in a storm at Willow springs (or the timber below it), and about ten o'clock the next day we thought it safe to start, although very cold and the wind blowing very heavy. We had great difficulty in getting the loose mules from the timber. As soon as we would get a short distance into the prairie, they would make a break for the timber regardless of the course taken by the bell mare or the train. Ordinarily, the mules will follow the bell mare regardless of all opposition or danger; and we usually considered our mules safe when separated from the herd (from whatever cause) as long as they were within hearing of the sound of the bell. But this terrible cold and wind was more than they could stand. We caught some and led them, and one which was poor and seemed to suffer more than the rest we covered with a blanket and buffalo robe, when he became more reasonable. And we succeeded in getting to the road, and proceeded on our journey without any further trouble or delay.

From this [point] to Westport [198] we had good camps

---

[198] Westport, Missouri, was founded in 1833. Situated farther west than Independence and just four miles south of the Missouri river, it soon became a starting and outfitting point for trappers, emigrants, explorers, and Santa

and fair shelter, and arrived on December 22. [We] remained one day to arrange for the wintering of the mules and storing of camp equipment, and on the twenty-fourth [199] went to Independence. At the hotel,[200] there was a ball being held, which I looked in on – the first ball I ever witnessed in my native land. *Fandangos* I had seen in New Mexico, and one quadroon ball in New Orleans, but this was the first real American ball I ever witnessed, and – let me think – I do believe it was the *only one*. [I] spent Christmas in Independence, and on the twenty-sixth started by stage for St. Louis.

On my arrival at Independence I met George Peacock,[201] who told me that they had been very anxious about our safety and had made preparations to start out on the prairie to our assistance, as we were so much behind the time we were expected, and the weather had [been] so cold and blustering they feared [that we] were lost or had lost our animals. We had expected to get in a month earlier, and my partner, Mr. Doan, had told them when we might be expected. I felt very grateful that our friends thought enough of us to take the trouble to organize an expedition to go to our relief, and still remember my old friends in Independence

Fé traders. By the early fifties Westport, together with Kansas City, superseded Independence as the point of departure for Santa Fé traders. Westport is now a part of Kansas City, Missouri. *Daily Missouri Republican*, Apr. 12, 1839, June 27, 1840, Aug. 3, 1844, May 10, 1855, Sept. 27, 1860; Theodore S. Case, *History of Kansas City, Missouri* (Syracuse, 1888), 28; *History of Jackson County, Missouri* (Kansas City, 1881), 352, 388.

199 The St. Louis *Weekly Reveille* reported that Webb and his companions arrived at Independence on December 21, 1845. *Weekly Reveille*, Jan. 5, 1846.

200 The Independence House.

201 George Peacock, of Independence, Missouri, was a Santa Fé trader. He was killed at Allison's Ranch in the summer of 1860, when he was scalped and his head split open by a party of Kiowa Indians. *Weekly Reveille*, Nov. 10, 1845; *Daily Missouri Republican*, Sept. 18, 1860.

INDEPENDENCE, MISSOURI, ABOUT 1850

From Charles A. Dana, *The United States Illustrated*, New York, *circa* 1853

with sincere respect and gratitude, not only in this instance but [in] many others when they rendered me efficient service by giving me their confidence and support, when both were so greatly needed as to be of great encouragement and benefit to me. Many, and I suppose most, of my old friends have passed away, but the remembrance of their confidence and kind assistance will ever remain fresh while I live.

Arrived in St. Louis, I found a letter or two which had been long waiting my arrival. And after remaining a few days for rest and to see how the land lay or how good the credit was for a new start, [I] concluded to visit my friends in the East. [I] wrote to Independence ordering four wagons built, and arranging with Colonel Owens for another outfit. I left for Cincinnati by steamboat and had a good long trip. From there [I] took a little stern-wheel boat for Wheeling. Among the passengers was the actor Booth – Junius Brutus Booth – and we traveled together to Baltimore. He had but little to say, and to judge from appearances one would not expect it lay in his power to say or do anything above or hardly equal to an ordinary man. He did not speak or seem to realize that Booth was in any sense entitled to any respect or consideration either as an individual or as an actor. But whenever the name of Charlotte Cushman was mentioned, he warmed up to a state of enthusiasm in the expression of his admiration and respect for her both as an actress and a woman. . . [I traveled] from Wheeling to Cumberland by stage, and thence to Baltimore by railroad – also to New York. From New York [I proceeded] to Bridgeport, I think, by boat, and to Cornwall Bridge by rail, on the old bar rail.

After [a] five years' absence [I] found all well and glad to see me. [I] brought home a Navajo blanket and Mexican saddle as samples of the goods used in the country. The blanket was used by father as a lap and horse blanket during his life, and since [has been] used on the milk wagon, and is still in use, making over thirty-eight years in use and not yet worn out; and I bought it second-hand. I have no doubt it had been used ten years. [I] remained home about a month. [I] visited what friends remained, but found many changes and but few of my old schoolmates and acquaintances remaining in Warren, nearly all, like myself, having left to try their fortunes in new fields. After a good visit I left for St. Louis, and began preparations for another trip with high expectations and, as I thought, good prospects for a prosperous and successful adventure.

There had been a good deal of bickering and ill feeling between our government and Mexico, and I thought I would on my return go through Washington and get a passport. I called at the office of the Secretary of State, and was told the secretary was not yet in, but was invited to sit down and wait his coming. In a short time Mr. Buchanan entered and accosted me in a very pleasant and cordial manner, and on making known my business asked me if I had a certificate or recommendation to show that I was an American citizen. I told him I had not, and did not know that it was necessary. He asked me if I had no acquaintances in Washington; and I answered that I had none but that my father knew Senator Smith, but I could not ask him. Seeing my disappointment and mortification, he in a very fatherly manner told me that he thought I could make myself known sufficiently to him so he would certify me as a citizen. But I thought it better to wait [until] my arrival in St. Louis and get Messrs. Doan, King and Company to apply through the representative from that district. [Mr. Buchanan] very kindly asked me to remain awhile, as he wished to talk with me about the country, its trade and resources; and I did so. My partner was born and lived a few years of his early life in one of the British West Indies, and got a British passport from the consul at New Orleans. Mine arrived before my departure from Independence. But neither anticipated war between the two governments.

TO MEXICO AHEAD OF KEARNY
AND DONIPHAN

TO MEXICO AHEAD OF KEARNY
AND DONIPHAN

On May 9, 1846, we left Independence on my third trip, with high hopes and bright prospects. We had charming weather and good roads, and traveled more rapidly than [on] any trip with a train that I ever made before or since. [We] made up a train sufficiently strong for protection, without any delay. Besides our five wagons, there were three of W. S. McKnight,[202] [Norris] Colburn, Juan Armijo (one of the governor's), J. B. Turley, and some others. Armijo had been reinstated as governor [203] and had a train of wagons ahead of us.

Some ninety or a hundred miles out an express passed us to the California emigrants who were ahead, and we were told a fight had taken place between our troops and the Mexicans somewhere in Texas, and the probabilities were there would be war. We thought we

[202] William S. McKnight, of St. Louis, was an old Santa Fé trader. In 1849 he was appointed postmaster at Santa Fé. Returning to St. Louis in the fifties, he continued to transact business under the name of William S. McKnight & Co. *Daily Missouri Republican*, May 19, 1841, Sept. 3, 1846, Oct. 16, 1849, Sept. 8, 1851, Oct. 6, 1859.

[203] Manuel Armijo was reappointed governor of New Mexico on July 24, 1845, but did not enter upon the duties of his office until the following November 16. Shortly before his inauguration Armijo entertained a number of American traders at the Palace of the Governors. There, in a toast to his guests, he expressed himself in favor of peace between the United States and Mexico, and stated that if war were declared "there would be no fighting by the people of New Mexico." *Daily Missouri Republican*, Jan. 1, 1846. See also Bloom, "New Mexico under Mexican Administration," *Old Santa Fé*, ii, 249.

would be so far in the interior that there would be no danger of trouble, and as the ports would be blockaded there would be a good demand for our goods and at war prices. So we traveled as expeditiously as we could, with good weather and roads and high hopes of profit to encourage us. We got no further news from either way until about half way up the Cimarrón. At the Arkansas a company was made up, and Mr. Doan went ahead, and the captain, or chief man, went with them; and the parties wished me to accept the charge of the train without going through the usual formalities of an election.

This year, having a little capital, good credit, and a fair prospect of business, we thought we could indulge in the luxury of an ambulance, and bought one in St. Louis, and a pair of horses on the frontier of a man named Lewis. Those were the sorrels spoken of previously, and they caused us a good deal of trouble and anxiety, as they got a fright and would quite often break loose, and we would have a hard chase to recover them. Twice we thought them gone, without hope of recovery: once on the Arkansas, when they got frightened and broke loose, and some of the mules followed them; but after a long chase they were brought back. Again, at Sand creek, while staked out grazing, some Comanche Indians came to camp, and they [the sorrels] became frightened and broke loose, when we thought them gone sure; but one of the men, well mounted, overtook them and brought them back. So notwithstanding we got a good price for them, we got no more than paid for the care and anxiety in taking them out.

About half way up the Cimarrón, Albert Speyer overtook us and gave us the certain information that war was declared and that the United States troops had followed him to Pawnee Fork to stop him from entering the country [204] with supplies of goods, as we then supposed, but as I afterwards learned, with arms and ammunition, of which he had two wagon loads in his train to fill an order received the year before from the governor of Chihuahua. He hurried on, and we hurried after him, and although he traveled, as he thought, very fast with mule teams, we with oxen were not far behind at any time and overtook him at Rock creek, between Point of Rocks and Whetstone Branch, and entered Santa Fé but half a day behind him – in forty-five days from Independence.

At Tecolote hill we overtook Armijo's train about noon, and the road was all occupied on the hill and many wagons at the foot. I thought it doubtful whether we would be able to get up that day, as they seemed to be making slow progress; but to be ready at short notice if we should have time to go up, [I] ordered the teams turned out in the yoke and to be kept near camp. We had just got turned out when we heard the noises of an approaching train, and soon George Peacock came up and, from his manner in selecting camp, I thought if he had a chance he would attempt to cut us out and go up ahead of us. Pruett was also in the train, and Rallston, the father-in-law of Jesse James,

[204] On June 5, 1846, Colonel Stephen W. Kearny, then at Fort Leavenworth, despatched two companies of the First regiment of dragoons to detain the caravans of Speyer and Armijo, which he was informed were transporting arms and ammunition, as well as a large amount of merchandise, to New Mexico. Though Captain Benjamin D. Moore, in command of this detachment, traveled with great haste as far as the Cimarrón crossing, he was unable to overtake the caravans. Stephen W. Kearny to Roger Jones, June 5, 1846, Kearny Letter Book, MS., Missouri Historical Society; Stephen W. Kearny to Benjamin D. Moore, June 6, 1846, *ibid.*; *Daily Missouri Republican*, Aug. 3, 1846.

also *his* [Peacock's?] father-in-law. I could hardly see how the two should consent to travel in the same company, as I knew them both well and knew that the old man had very little respect for his son-in-law and had on one or two occasions called my attention to a division fence between them, consisting of two high rail fences and on the land of each, which the old man insisted on, [so] that there should be no cause of difficulty on account of breachy cattle breaking the other's fence without first breaking down their owner's [fence].

After they had turned out, I asked a couple of the boys to go and get up a game of euchre. And having a fiddler along, I asked him to go over and give them a musical entertainment, telling them to report that we should probably order up the cattle to unyoke; and when they heard the order to drive up the oxen, they might come up and take charge of their teams. In an interview with Governor Armijo's wagon master, I told him what might happen, and to keep cool, as [for] if we were the cause of getting him out of the road or so stalled that he was like to be detained, we would all turn in and help him out.

In due time I saw my opportunity and called to the herders to drive up the oxen to unyoke, which they leisurely proceeded to do. And when they arrived at the corral, all hands went to work to prepare [the] teams to start, as fast as possible, three or four men to a team for the first eight or ten wagons. And as soon as geared they formed in lines to block the road; so there were in a very short time four lines of wagons abreast at the foot of the hill, so completely blocking the road that it was impossible to pass us. Peacock was, however, very persistent, and in his efforts to pass us got two wagons so far off the road among the rocks that he had to unload them. The old man sitting [sat] on a rock and looking [looked] on like the wife in the bear fight, [and exclaimed]:

"Go it, husband! Go it, bear! I don't care which whips."

After the affair was over, he congratulated me and said he told them it was a mean trick, and he hoped Webb would be soon enough for them, and he guessed they had found he was. They got up the hill the next morning and again overtook us, but made no attempt to pass us.

On the plains or where the road is in good condition it was allowable to pass each other, but at a bad slough or in narrow or difficult passes in the mountains it was considered mean to take any undue advantage of each other in taking the road.

The Mexican soldiers did not meet us until we were near San Miguel. And one of our party had some doubt what might be done with his candlewick and powder, and was advised by one of the custom-house officers to take it from the wagons in the night and pack it on mules some three or four miles to a settlement on the river between Pecos and San José, and leave it with a person there until he could take it to the Placer where he was living. So one night when camped in the woods not far from Pajarito spring, we called on our fiddler to furnish music for a dance, and while the dance was going [on], on one side of the train, Noland and his men were busy on the other side taking out the goods and packing them for transportation to a place considered safe. He succeeded in accomplishing his object without suspicion or interruption, but he finally lost

the goods, which would have been in no danger of confiscation if he had taken them along and made no attempt at concealment. Colburn also thought it best to
take out a lot of the same class of goods at the Arroyo
Hondo, six miles from Santa Fé, and take them in by
night on pack mules. But the trick was discovered, and
his men arrested, and goods and mules held by the
authorities for some days; and he finally settled by paying a fine, and the goods were restored.

Perhaps both the cases were put up by old Durán,
the custom-house officer, to make a little raise from his
friends which he could get in no other way. It was by
his advice the goods were unloaded and the concealment attempted, and very likely, knowing just when
and how to operate, he got some outside parties to
catch Colburn and divide the funds obtained by the
compromise. The goods of Noland were confiscated by
old Durán himself, but he made a show of necessity,
and Mr. Noland had no recourse. Durán was a notorious gambler; and not long after the arrival of the
train he went to San Miguel and got to gambling and
lost all the money he had, pawned his mule and lost the
proceeds, and confiscated Mr. Noland's contraband
goods to redeem his mule and enable him to leave town.

Several years after, I met him [Durán] in Algodones, and he told me he had been there some days
and did not know when he should be able to leave.

"What business detains you so long?" [I asked].

"Oh, I am in pawn."

"In pawn? What do you mean, Don Agustín?"

"Why I am *in pawn*."

"A man in pawn, how?"

"Well, the night of my arrival they got up a *fandan-*

go, and I went, took a little too much *aguardiente*, got to gambling, lost all the money I had, pawned the mule I rode, borrowed from a friend, lost that, and borrowed more money, giving my obligation not to leave town until I could redeem myself and mule from pawn. I have notified my friends of my circumstances, and expect to receive the money in a day or two to enable me to leave."

Don Agustín Durán, under the Mexican government, was a leading man in New Mexico, among the best educated and most talented men in the territory, and was much respected by, and had a great deal of influence with, the Mexicans. But owing to his vicious habits in drinking and gambling, [he] was liable at any time to get himself "in pawn," or to compromise the interests of his best friends, as well as his own.

On meeting my partner, he informed [me that] the United States troops were advancing on New Mexico under command of General Kearny [205] and that the

[205] Stephen Watts Kearny was born near Newark, New Jersey, August 30, 1794. At the age of sixteen he became an ensign in the New York City and County Militia. On March 12, 1812, he was commissioned first lieutenant in the Thirteenth regiment of infantry, and served with credit during the War of 1812. He remained in the army after the close of the war. His first experience as a soldier on the frontier was in 1820, when he accompanied an expedition that attempted to open a road from Council Bluffs to the mouth of the Minnesota river. During the next twenty-six years he performed military service in many parts of the Far West. He accompanied General Atkinson to the Upper Missouri in 1825; he rebuilt Cantonment Towson on the Red river in 1831; and he commanded an expedition to the South pass in 1845. On July 4, 1836, he was commissioned colonel of the First regiment of dragoons, which was his rank at the outbreak of the Mexican war. Placed in command of the "Army of the West" on May 14, 1846, he marched westward over the Santa Fé trail and occupied New Mexico without firing a gun. He then proceeded to California and engaged the Mexicans in the Battle of San Pascual, December 6, 1846. On June 30, 1846, he was commissioned Brigadier-general, and on the following December 6, Major-general. He died in St. Louis, October 31, 1848. Roger Jones to Stephen W.

advance guard were at the Rayado, and [that] spies
had been sent to Taos and Santa Fé and conferred with
Don Manuel Álvarez, the American consul, and had
left for the Rayado only the day before. Talking over
matters, we thought (as we should have to pay duties at
the rate of seven hundred and fifty dollars [206] a wagon
load, and free goods [207] being so near) that we would
be at a great disadvantage to attempt to remain in New
Mexico. And our goods [208] being adapted to the interior
market, we concluded to go to Chihuahua, and on arrival in Santa Fé commenced making our arrangements. We had two mule teams and two ox teams. We
sold our oxen to Mr. John Scolly and bought some
mules of him or through him, and on his credit, but
not enough to make up the two teams, and borrowed
money of him to buy the balance in the Río Abajo.
Some days were spent in making arrangements, taking
out *guías*, or manifests, arranging teams, etc. Mr. Speyer
had bought out General Armijo's goods; from which I
infer the general, if not knowing the troops were on the
way to New Mexico, thought they soon would be, and

Kearny, May 14, 1846, MS., Adjutant-general's Office, War Department;
Eudora Smith, Stephen Watts Kearny as a Factor in the Westward Move-
ment, 1812-1834, MS., M. A. thesis, Washington University; *Daily Missouri
Republican*, Nov. 1, 2, 1848; Francis B. Heitman, *Historical Register and
Dictionary of the United States Army* (Washington, 1903), i, 586; Louis
Pelzer, *Marches of the Dragoons in the Mississippi Valley* (Iowa City,
1917), 14, 49-60, 120-160.

[206] This is an error. Webb paid a duty of five hundred dollars for each
wagon load of merchandise brought to New Mexico. Webb & Doan, Daybook, 1846-1847, Webb MSS.

[207] The Independence correspondent of the *Daily Missouri Republican*
estimated that the caravans which left Independence for Santa Fé in 1846
consisted of three hundred and sixty-three wagons, fifty carriages, and seven
hundred and fifty men, and transported 9,588 bales of merchandise valued
at about $1,000,000. *Daily Missouri Republican*, Sept. 3, 1846.

[208] Webb & Doan's merchandise cost about $15,000. Webb & Doan, Day-
book, 1846-1847, Webb MSS.

[that] his safest course would be to have as little property under his official guardianship as possible. We
prepared to join him [Speyer] and travel together.

The night before the train was to start, Mr. Doan
went to a *fandango* on the hill across the Río Chiquito;
and on his return to Mr. Leitensdorfer's where we were
stopping, immediately on turning a corner but a few
yards from the home, was struck by a heavy stone on
the face just below the forehead with such force as to
fell him to the ground, insensible and his nose mashed
flat. He was carried to the house and after some time revived sufficiently to tell in whose company he was and
how the affair happened. The friends who were with
him had no idea who committed the deed or the motive
inducing it. But there was an old French doctor there
from Chihuahua who was called, and on examination
pronounced the wound, although serious, not necessar-
ily dangerous, but [it] would render it impossible for
him to proceed with the train. So I had to make such
arrangements as I could under the circumstances for
procuring teams and securing protection for our interests.

I consulted with Mr. Speyer, and he offered to take
our wagons under his protection, as he traveled under
the protection of a Prussian passport, and had also an
English one if circumstances should arise making it
more desirable. E. Leitensdorfer procured a Mexican
who understood English to accompany me as interpreter and assistant, and we went on mule back, leaving
the ambulance for Mr. Doan when he should recover
sufficiently to follow. Dolly Spanker had been stolen
from the herd at Agua Fría, and I left under rather
discouraging circumstances on a new adventure, a new

market, and doubtful about the reception I should meet among enemies. Our drivers were Americans, but the temptation of an enemy's goods for confiscation did not apply to them; and I had some doubts how effectual the cover of Mr. Speyer's passport might prove to be.

We started in the morning and traveled to the canyon below Cerillos, where we stopped and took a lunch and rested. This man [the Mexican interpreter and assistant] accompanied me to Albuquerque and assisted me faithfully, and I traveled with him alone for several days with considerable money in specie which could not be concealed. And I never suspected but what he was honest and reliable until my return to Santa Fé the following year, when I saw him in the chain gang on the square, and inquiring what he was there for, and was informed that he was charged with murder and robbery. Why did he allow me to escape and so soon after avail himself of an opportunity by no means superior to the one afforded by me?

I bought mules enough to make up teams, by retaining a yoke of oxen on each of two wagons as wheelers, and joined the train a short distance below Bernalillo. The train numbered thirty-eight wagons, about four hundred and fifty mules, and about fifty men. A Frenchman, named John Devoe, with two wagons took freight for Mr. Speyer, and acted as guide and assistant major domo, as he knew the country well to Chihuahua and through all the low country. Another man with three wagons, named Harmony, took freight for Mr. S. Mr. S. had a clerk named Oliver, a Spaniard who talked English and was a very agreeable and interesting gentleman. [There was] another man named Phoenix, a brother of J. Phillips Phoenix, a former Mayor of New York, traveling for health, as I understood.

The rainy season came upon us about this time, and we traveled under great difficulties from bad roads and the number of wagons in the train. The way down the river to Fray Cristóbal was so bad that we could not travel more than two to ten miles a day with all day travel and very hard work.[209] We bought a few mules as opportunity offered. And I bought a mule one day of a stranger, and the following night it was lost and I had good reason to believe [that it] was stolen by the same parties who sold it to me. At Parida,[210] Mr. Speyer bought an old picture which he claimed was by one of the old masters and brought from Spain by the ancestors of the man from whom he bought it, and which, he afterwards informed me, proved a very fortunate speculation. So much for being a Jew and a judge of property and knowing a good thing wherever they see it. Parida hill [211] we had heard a good deal about as the worst piece of road between Santa Fé and Chihuahua, except a few miles of road of the same character through the sand hills below El Paso del Norte. And we had not yet concluded whether to take that as the shortest route or to follow down the river on a hard road and travel a longer distance and through two *jornadas*, one of fifty and one of seventy miles.

At Fray Cristóbal we lay by a day to rest and put everything in order to pass through the Jornada del Muerto,[212] ninety miles without water. Sometimes water

---

[209] See Wislizenus, *op. cit.*, 33-37.

[210] The caravan camped near Parida on the night of July 26, 1846. *Ibid.*, 36.

[211] Some of the wagons were upset while ascending this steep, sandy hill. *Ibid.*

[212] "Jornada del Muerto means, literally, the day's journey of the dead

is found at the *laguna* [213] (being a depression in the prairie where surface water gathers and remains for some time), but as yet there had not been sufficient rain to fill it, and we found none and drove on, and on arriving opposite the Gallego spring,[214] concluded to drive off and water. The spring is at the right of the road, and the road is so bad and the water so poor and limited in quantity that we were almost sorry we had stopped, as it was almost as fatiguing to the animals as it would have been to have gone through without water.

Fray Cristóbal takes its name from a peak at the end of a mountain on the east bank of the del Norte where the river enters a gorge and passes for a long distance through a narrow valley; and the valley being much wider above this point and suddenly contracting, makes the end of the mountain quite prominent for a long distance up the valley. And it is claimed by the Mexicans that [because of] the resemblance to the hand and face of an old friar living among them in early times, they named the mountain for him. It requires but little imagination to see a resemblance to the face of an old man.

Socorro was the last settlement on the river on the west side and Parida on the east, until we came to Doña Ana.[215] We made the *jornada* through without any loss of animals, but both men and animals appeared greatly

man, and refers to an old tradition that the first traveller who attempted to cross it in one day perished in it." *Ibid.*, 38.

[213] Pond. This pond, or lake, was usually called Laguna del Muerto, or Dead Man's lake. Gregg, *op. cit.*, xx, 153.

[214] This is an error. Webb refers to Ojo del Muerto, or Dead Man's spring. *Ibid.*

[215] Doña Ana was founded in 1842. Its houses were mostly *jacals*, or huts, which were built of upright sticks chinked with mud. By 1847 it had a population of about five hundred. Bartlett, *op. cit.*, i, 211-212; Ruxton, *op. cit.*, 171; Bloom, "New Mexico under Mexican Administration," *Old Santa Fé*, i, 13.

relieved when we got to the river and had plenty of water and a day's rest.

After a day's rest we proceeded on our journey down the river without passing any house or settlement (except Doña Ana) on either side of the river until we arrived at El Paso.[216] We crossed from the bottom, where the town of Franklin now is, to the west side, a little above the mill, where we camped. And a good many people from the town came to our camp to sell provisions, fruits, etc., to gratify curiosity, and others to show their hatred of the Texans and heretics, and still others to do a little legal work in the mule line.

This was a great trade in El Paso. The Apache Indians would steal mules in the state of Chihuahua and sell them in New Mexico, and they [the mules] would get into the hands of the traders, and on arriving in El Paso would be reclaimed by agents who held the brands of many haciendas to prove the ownership. No doubt many were reclaimed which had been sold by the

---

[216] Paso del Norte, the modern Ciudad Juárez, Mexico, was founded by the Spaniards in the seventeenth century. Wislizenus, who traveled with Speyer and Webb, described the settlement as it appeared in August, 1846: "The Río del Norte, having escaped the mountain pass, runs here into an open, fertile plain, at the beginning of which el Paso is situated. The town is principally built on the right bank of the river; but few houses are on the left. Stretched out along the river to the length of many miles, all the houses surrounded by gardens, orchards, and vineyards, and rich settlements, with cornfields, as far as the eye can trace the stream, lining its green bank— such a scenery will always be attractive; but to a traveller, who has passed over the lonesome plains and through the dreary Jornada del Muerto, it appears like an oasis in the desert. . . The valley of el Paso is the most fertile country that we have seen along the river. Besides maize and wheat, they raise a large quantity of fruits, as apples, pears, figs, quinces, peaches, etc., but especially an excellent grape, from which they prepare the celebrated 'el Paso wine,' and a liquor called by the Americans 'Pass whiskey.' . . The population of the town proper, which is but a small place, and of the long line of settlements that extend for twenty miles down the river, is estimated at from 10 to 12,000." Wislizenus, *op. cit.*, 40-41.

parties reclaiming them. The stock of each hacienda was marked by a brand which signified ownership of the animal, and when stock was sold it was to be marked by another brand which signified that the animal had been legally disposed of. And all animals not having the sale brand were liable to be reclaimed by the owner or his agent wherever found.[217] The animals stolen by Indians, strayed from the owners, unlawfully disposed of by the Mexican servants and laid to Indians or other thieves, and those sold by the owners away from the hacienda without the means of fixing the sale brand on the animals, combined [to] make a large portion of the mules in New Mexico rather insecure property, especially when taken to the state of Chihuahua.

While crossing and arranging camp and turning out, there appeared a man with what appeared a load of old iron behind him, riding around camp and carefully examining every team as it arrived and was turned out. And when we had got all over and settled, he came up and informed us that he claimed four mules as stolen property, and we were notified to take them before the prefect's court for trial. Mr. Speyer asked the favor of a delay until the next day when we should pass through town with the train, and we could take them along, and he would appear before the court with the property and his witnesses. This was consented to, and we thought we were getting along very well if no more mules were

---

[217] Gregg wrote: "No matter how many proprietors a horse or mule may have had, every one marks him with a huge hieroglyphic brand, which is called the *fierro*, and again, upon selling him, with his *venta*, or sale-brand; until at last these scars become so multiplied as to render it impossible for persons not versed in this species of 'heraldry,' to determine whether the animal has been properly *vented* or not: yet any *fierro* without its corresponding *venta* lays the beast liable to the claim of the brander." Gregg, *op. cit.*, xix, 320.

reclaimed than these, as the man left camp, and we saw no other persons whom we suspected of being there for the same business.

During the afternoon I wandered around and visited the old mill, which appeared to be in a very dilapidated condition; but the dam across the river was used to afford a sufficient head of water for purposes of irrigating the large valley below. In this old mill I saw the first sample of that ancient instrument of punishment and sometimes of torture – the stocks. . . Following down the main *acequia* [218] for some distance towards the town, I was surprised to see beaver signs so near a large town. The bank was set with cottonwood trees, and many of them were completely girdled by the beaver, others cut entirely down, and others only partially girdled, but the sign of their presence and labor was plainly visible to within a quarter of a mile of the town.

The next day we drove through town and [to a point] some three or four miles below to camp, as we wanted to remain long enough to lay in some stores, attend court, and I wanted to exchange two yoke of oxen for mules. The trial was short, and all the mules were taken. And before we were through the first trial, there was another arrival from the new camp, and it was short work to produce the iron to fit the brand, and turn the mule over to the claimant. And the new arrivals were so frequent that the court and all interested were transacting business with despatch, if not to the satisfaction of all parties. At last Mr. Speyer, disgusted and alarmed, gave orders to stop the game.

---

[218] A ditch, or canal, which diverted water from the Río Grande through the settlements along the river for purposes of irrigation. *Ibid.*, xx, 155-156; John T. Hughes, *Doniphan's Expedition* (Cincinnati, 1848), 284.

"Tell White," said he, "to gear up and travel, and allow no more mules to be brought away, even if he has to fight. Keep traveling till we overtake you."

We finally cleaned the docket, and they had taken fifteen mules from Mr. Speyer and three from me. I swapped the two yoke of oxen for two mules, and bought one or two; so I kept the number good, and under the circumstances was glad to get off so. We started and overtook the train.

Mr. Speyer concluded to take the route through the sand hills,[219] being shorter and not so long a journey without water as following down the river and by Cantarecio. The sand was very deep, and the hills steep, for some six or eight miles, and it was with great difficulty and labor that we passed them. This route was but little traveled by wagon trains, and I should not like to make more than one trip over that route.[220] The first town we

---

[219] Wislizenus stated that Speyer took the river route. Wislizenus, *op. cit.*, 42-43.

[220] "Ahead of us were the much-dreaded sand hills," wrote Wislizenus on August 16, 1846, "an immense field of steep sand ridges, without shrub or vegetation of any kind, looking like a piece of Arabian desert transplanted into this plain, or like the bottom of the sea uplifted from the deep. . . Having arrived at the foot of the sand hills, we commenced travelling very slow. There was nothing around us but the deepest and purest sand, and the animals could only get along in the slowest walk, and by resting at short intervals. At last my animals were exhausted; they would move no more, and we had not yet reached half our way. In this dilemma I put my own riding horse to the wagon. Mr. Jacquez lent me some additional mules, and forward we moved again. In the meanwhile dark night had come on, illuminated only by lightning, that showed us for awhile the most appalling night-scene – our wagons moving along as slow and solemn as a funeral procession; ghastly riders on horseback, wrapped in blankets or cloaks; some tired travellers stretched out on the sand, others walking ahead, and tracing the road with the fire of their *cigarritos* [*cigarrillos*]; and the deepest silence interrupted only by the yelling exclamations of the drivers, and the rolling of distant thunder. . . About midnight, at last we reached the southern end of the sand hills, and encamped without water." *Ibid.*, 43-44.

came to was Carrizal,[221] which we passed without annoyance of any kind. A few miles below we came to the Warm spring,[222] where we camped, and all took a bath and had a good time. This is a very bold spring at the foot of a small mound apparently of volcanic origin, the water boiling up through the sand over a large space some two or three rods across, and apparently walled up, raising the water to some four feet in depth, the temperature [223] being just right for a comfortable warm bath, and a stream of water flowing from it sufficient to run a mill.

The next drive was to a dry creek in which I never saw running water except this trip. The road was very bad, and although we had no rain that day near us, we saw clouds overhanging the mountains to the west which indicated heavy showers in that direction. The first wagons arrived in camp about eleven o'clock in the forenoon, and camped without crossing, on the north side of the creek. The last wagons did not get in camp until near dark on account of delays by miring down. The drivers arriving in camp first, had large and almost incredible stories to tell about the rattlesnakes which they commenced killing when they first arrived in camp. And as the wagons arrived they would stir them up in the grass while driving in and unharnessing, and

---

[221] Carrizal, the only town on the trail between Paso del Norte and Chihuahua, was the site of a *presidio*, or fort, where a number of soldiers were stationed to protect the inhabitants from the Indians. Formerly it had been a place of some size, but by 1846 it had a population of only three or four hundred. *Ibid.*, 45; Gregg, *op. cit.*, xx, 158; Kendall, *op. cit.*, ii, 60; Bartlett, *op. cit.*, ii, 409-410.

[222] Ojo Caliente. "It is a clear, pure water, in a large basin of porphyritic rocks, with sandy bottom, out of which many warm springs come to the surface." Wislizenus, *op. cit.*, 45.

[223] Wislizenus placed a thermometer in the spring and found that the temperature was 82° Fahrenheit. *Ibid.*

they said by honest count they had killed over fifteen within the circle of the camp fires. During the night the water rose to such a depth that we were unable to cross, and had to lay by three days for it to fall so we could ford.

A doctor from St. Louis, named Wislizenus,[224] [who] was traveling with Mr. Speyer for health, pleasure, and, I think, with a view to some scientific explorations,[225] concluded to leave us here and proceed to Chihuahua. As soon as the water fell so we could get his

---

[224] Dr. Adolph Wislizenus was born in Königsee, Schwarzburg-Rudolstadt, Germany, May 21, 1810. He studied medicine at the universities of Jena, Göttingen, and Tübingen, but in 1833 was forced to flee from Germany to Switzerland because of his liberal political opinions. He received the degree of doctor of medicine at the University of Zurich, and then removed to Paris. Coming to the United States in 1835, he settled in New York City, but a year later moved west to Mascoutah, St. Clair county, Illinois. After practicing there as a country physician for three years, he made his first journey to the Rocky mountains, traveling with a party of trappers from Westport, Missouri, to Fort Hall on the Snake river. On his return he made his home in St. Louis, where he resumed the practice of medicine. His avocation was the study of botany, geology, and meteorology. On May 14, 1846, he left Independence, Missouri, on a scientific tour of northern Mexico, and traveled most of the way with the trading caravan of Albert Speyer. He came back to St. Louis in July, 1847. After several years of travel in the United States and Europe, he returned to his medical practice in St. Louis, where he died, September 23, 1889. Wislizenus, *Memoir of a Tour to Northern Mexico*; Wislizenus, *A Journey to the Rocky Mountains in the Year 1839* (Frederick A. Wislizenus, editor and translator, St. Louis, 1912).

[225] "The principal object of my expedition was scientific," wrote Wislizenus. "I desired to examine the geography, natural history, and statistics of that country [northern Mexico], by taking directions on the road with the compass, and by determining the principal points by astronomical observations. I made a rich collection of quite new and undescribed plants. I examined the character of the rocks, to gain insight into the geological formations of the whole country. I visited as many mines as possible, and analyzed some of the ores. I made barometrical observations, to ascertain the elevations above the sea. I kept meteorological tables, to draw general results from them for the climate, its salubrity and fitness for agriculture, and took memoranda in relation to the people – their number, industry, manners, previous history, etc." Wislizenus, *Memoir of a Tour to Northern Mexico*, 3.

ambulance across, he left us with his servant and arrived in Chihuahua ten or fifteen days ahead of us. The morning after his arrival, his servant took all their arms to a corral near the hotel to fire them off and clean them up. They had several repeating arms, rifles, and pistols, and of course the firing was rapid and continued for some time. Very soon a crowd gathered about the hotel, and continued increasing in numbers and violent demonstrations until the Americans in town were compelled to close their stores, and such as could do so sought shelter in the hotel for mutual defense and protection. Those too far away secreted themselves from the excited mob as best they could. The Americans knew no cause for such an excitement, and as soon as they could get a confidential interview with a Mexican friend, they learned that the Battle of Monterrey had been fought, the Mexicans defeated, and the city taken, and it was supposed the Americans were rejoicing over the news and firing a salute.[226] The mob was prevented from doing any especial damage by the cool and determined manner of the Americans in showing their determination to defend themselves to the last extremity.[227] In a day or two, an order was issued that all the Americans of influence in town, except A. C. Anderson,[228] should leave and go to Cosuhuiriachi, a

[226] This is an error. The Mexicans thought that Wislizenus was celebrating the capture of Santa Fé by General Kearny, news of which had just arrived in Chihuahua. *Ibid.*, 49.

[227] For a somewhat different version of this affair, see *ibid.*, 48-50.

[228] Alfonso C. Anderson engaged in the Santa Fé trade at least as early as 1840. In 1848 he was vice-commercial agent of the United States at Chihuahua. American Merchants in Santa Fé to Manuel Álvarez, Dec. 8, 1840, Álvarez mss., Benjamin M. Read Collection, Santa Fé; Twitchell, *The Story of the Conquest of Santa Fé*, Historical Society of New Mexico, *Publications*, no. 24, p. 60.

small mining town in the mountains, and there remain
during the pleasure of the governor, Don Angel
Trias.[229]

---

[229] On September 6, 1846, six American merchants – Messervy, East,
Wethered, Stevenson, Douglas, and Litzleiter – left Chihuahua for Cosuhuiriachi under an escort of Mexican troops. A week later Wislizenus also
departed for Cosuhuiriachi. All of them returned to Chihuahua, March 5,
1847, after the Battle of Sacramento. Wislizenus, *Memoir of a Tour to
Northern Mexico*, 50-54.

A PRISONER IN CHIHUAHUA

A PRISONER IN CHIHUAHUA

As soon as the water subsided we proceeded on our journey, unaware of any new [or] exciting cause of apprehension. Arriving at the head of the *laguna*,[230] we were approaching the hacienda of Encinillas on the west side of the *laguna*, and Peñol [231] on the east side, about forty miles from Chihuahua. We were anxious to arrive at Peñol to camp, but the road was bad, and we were much delayed, and at nine o'clock we were still two or three miles from our intended camp. While making our way slowly in the dark, we were overtaken by a company of people who seemed to be traveling lightly loaded and as expeditiously as possible.[232] We learned that New Mexico had been taken by our troops, [that] Armijo had abandoned the territory and was on the run for safety in the low country. They passed us, and we understood they were expecting to camp at Peñol.

I was riding in the lead wagon driven by a man named Vaughn, who had driven for me the year before, [and] who had been in the country several years and talked Spanish almost as well as the natives. We were rejoicing over the news and about the speed Armijo was making, when we arrived opposite the hacienda,[233]

---

[230] Laguna de Encinillas, or Lake of Live-Oaks.

[231] The haciendas of Peñol and Encinillas were the property of Don Angel Trias, governor of Chihuahua. Bartlett, *op. cit.*, ii, 418.

[232] This company probably included Manuel Armijo, who was fleeing from New Mexico.

[233] Peñol.

and the roof appeared covered with people watching our approach and to see the train pass. There were many more people than we expected to see, and could account for it in no other way than it was Armijo's people. A few of the wagons of the train had passed the house when the door of the corral in the rear of the house suddenly opened, and a company of soldiers filed out and in double-quick time approached. And the officer placed himself in front of Vaughn's leaders and commanded, "Halt!"

"Why halt?" said Vaughn.

"Because the commanding officer orders you."

Vaughn immediately dismounted from his mule, and with several cracks of his whip as he passed to his leaders, in ringing and defiant tones said, "Halt, hell! You Kit! Boys, jerk your guns! Here's music!" and keeping his whip popping.

Kit laid her ears back and charged. There was no stop for even a moment. Officer and soldiers made way, and every wagon moved until the wagon master appeared and ordered the lead wagons to take their positions to form the corral, when there was no stopping the advance of the teams until each had taken its proper position in the corral, and the word "whoa" was given by the drivers. The intention evidently was to halt us strung out in line, so we should have less means of defense, if we saw fit to resort to extreme measures, than we would have by forming a corral. But hungry and tired mules nearing camp, under the lead of an energetic and brave driver and a good and wicked Kit, spoiled their well-laid plans.

Mr. Speyer went to the house to learn the cause of the trouble, and found that two companies of infantry

CHIHUAHUA ABOUT 1850

From *Album Pintoresco de la República Mexicana*, Mexico, *circa* 1850

and one of dragoons were present with orders to disarm us all and march us into Chihuahua, prisoners. There were some three or four of us in consultation, and we concluded [that] the boys, if they became aware of the demand, would mount themselves and fight their way back to New Mexico. They could easily have done it, but such a course would have given us great trouble and imperiled our pecuniary interests. Mr. S. was also in a position to get correct information through Governor Armijo, as he had the goods the governor had sold him; and if any great danger overhung the interests of Speyer, his [Armijo's] interests would also become involved, and if he [Armijo] should attempt to play a grab game, the governments under whose protection he [Speyer] traveled would demand reparation for all damages. The Lion and the Unicorn commanded unquestionable respect throughout all Mexico in those days; but the American Eagle might soar aloft and screech and threaten to his full capacity, and would command no more attention than the cackling of an old hen.

After talking the matter over, we thought the most prudent way would be to send the mules as far away from camp as we could do with prudence under all the circumstances (at least one or two miles), and wait till morning before telling the boys the news. There was but little sleep in camp that night, those knowing the demands of course feeling very suspicious in regard to personal safety, as well as anxious in regard to the pecuniary interests involved. And the men who did not know the demand, knew that something was up and possibly their personal safety might be involved. I have always felt confident that if the whole truth had been communicated to them that night, and the mules left near camp, they would have mounted and left.

The next morning word was given out that we would not start until afternoon, and [that] they could get breakfast and attend to any repairs required about harness or wagons, and as soon as we became fully aware of the true condition of affairs, we would call them together and make it known to them. Mr. Speyer, in conversation with the officers and also with Armijo, thought we might feel assured that no treachery was intended or was likely to be practiced upon us, and about ten o'clock the boys were called together and the true state of affairs made known to them. A good deal was said about the Texan prisoners and their sufferings, and many of them were much opposed to submitting to the demand. But appeals were made to them to forego all self-will and stubbornness, as we felt sure there was no cause to apprehend personal harm to any of them by submission, and resistance would be pretty sure to imperil our interests, both personal and pecuniary.

"You may succeed," [we said], "in fighting your way back to New Mexico, but it will be at the risk of great privation and suffering, and sure to bring disaster upon us. Is it not at least as safe to submit to the demand with apparent confidence and cheerfulness, as to take the chances of resistance with the certainty of much trouble to follow?"

I suggested that they should, by taking some important spring from every lock of their guns, render them so useless that they could not be used against us or our countrymen, and [then] there would be no inducement to keep them. Again:

"You see those two wagons which have never been

allowed to be corralled with the other wagons, but [have] always been stationed at some distance from camp? They are loaded with Mississippi Yugers and ammunition for them. Let every man have some weapon at hand, a stretcher stick, a hatchet, an ax, or something that can be used in defense for a few minutes, and we can arm ourselves from those wagons and defend ourselves, destroy what arms we cannot use, and take whatever course may be deemed best under the circumstances."

After a considerable [amount] of arguing, they consented to the demand. And it was arranged that a few of the officers should come to camp about 2 P. M. and receive the arms, entering them all on a book with the name of each owner; and no soldiers [were] to be allowed around our camp at the time to create suspicion of bad faith.

Before the hour arrived, I told the boys I would keep a strict watch of all the proceedings, and if I saw anything wrong I would give the alarm, and we would proceed to defend ourselves. Certain individuals were designated to make a charge for the two wagons, while the balance surrounded them and defended them as best they might until the cases were opened, and they were supplied with arms. At the appointed hour the officers appeared and commenced to receive the arms and take an account of them, but were unable to finish up the whole business so as to get an early start the next morning. Everything, however, was done according to agreement, and nothing occurred to impair the confidence of good faith on the part of the Mexicans. "Old Blackfoot" was here again allowed to fall into the hands of enemies.

The next day we started as prisoners for Chihuahua,

under an escort of the two companies of infantry and one of dragoons, and traveled to near Sacramento and camped for the night. It was but a short time before the boys were visiting each other in their wagons, and a soldier was acting as driver, as they preferred riding to walking; and the road [being] pretty good, the teams required but little attention except occasionally. And the mutual relief soon brought about a good understanding between prisoners and guard. There was, I think, but one solitary exception. One of my drivers, named Squire Rains, stuck to his team and would submit to no compromise. Seeing him still driving his team while all the rest were enjoying themselves under the relief afforded by a substitute, I said to him:

"Squire, why don't you let this man drive, and you go a-visiting like the rest of the boys?"

Manifesting great humiliation and anger, he replied, "I never expected to see the day when I should be taken prisoner and disarmed by such a damned set of greasy thieves and blackguards as these. And I tell you what 'tis: if one of them ever seats himself in this saddle, 'twill be when I'm dead, and he'll grow fast to it."

There was no use in talking to him. He was too mad to be reasonable, and too stubborn to take a little pleasure when he had the chance.

The third day as prisoners brought [us] to the bank of the river running along the northern limits of the city of Chihuahua,[234] and we were brought to a halt

---

[234] In 1833 Chihuahua had a population of 10,602. Wislizenus described the city as it appeared in 1846: "Chihuahua has a most beautiful situation in a valley, open towards the north, and surrounded on the other sides by the projecting mountains of the Sierra Madre. The city is regularly built; has wide and clean streets—in some of them quite handsome and convenient houses; plenty of water from the Chihuahua creek, and from an aqueduct; fine gardens around the town; and a delightful public walk (Alameda),

and showed where to camp, no one being permitted to
enter town that night except Mr. Speyer and his clerk,
Mr. Oliver, who was a native of Spain. There were
several who were not Americans in the company, and
after a day or two were allowed to go in when they
desired. But all Americans were under strict guard and
not permitted to leave the camp even to go to the river
for a pail of water without being accompanied by an
armed soldier. People were permitted to visit the camp
from town to sell us provisions, etc., but we had but
little communication except from those who came to
supply us with necessaries.

I think the day of our arrival a detail was made from
camp to go to the prefect's court and make what was
called our "declaration" (which appeared to be an
examination of each individual separately), where he
was called upon to reply to numerous formal questions
as to his age, nativity, religion, occupation at home,
trade (if he had ever learned one), and why he came
to Mexico; whether he had ever served in the army,
and numerous other questions which I cannot now remember.

shaded with cotton trees. The finest place of the city, as usual in Mexico, is
the Plaza, or public square. It is very spacious; has a public fountain in the
middle, and foot walks on the side, with benches and pillars of a white
porphyry, which is found in the neighborhood. Three sides of the square
are occupied with public buildings and stores; on the fourth stands the
cathedral, a very imposing building. . . Although the style of the building
is not throughout Gothic, it shows nevertheless great finish and elegance
of construction; the two equal and parallel steeples in front of it are ele-
vated fifty-two and one-half *varas* [one hundred and forty-six feet] above
the Plaza. Another expensive work of architecture, erected in Spanish times,
is the aqueduct, built of rocks, with arches; it extends 6,533 *varas* [about
three and one-half miles], and provides the southern part of the city with
water, while on the north side the Chihuahua creek runs, which unites
below with the 'Nombre de Dios,' and falls into the Conchos." Wislizenus,
Memoir of a Tour to Northern Mexico, 60. See also Bartlett, *op. cit.,* ii, 432-
435.

The wagons containing arms were moved into town, and our arms also being in the hands of our enemies, we felt in extreme doubt what notion they might take in regard to us, and the blues prevailed almost universally. And many were very despondent, although there was nothing in the conduct of the Mexicans towards us which led us to suspect any very oppressive measures except to retain us as prisoners until instructions should be received from Santa Anna what to do with us. We remained here about fifteen days, when we were instructed to enter the city and camp at the usual camping place in the southern suburbs near the Bull Pen.[235] Here we remained about fifteen days longer.

During this time Mr. Speyer was considering the prospects for trade in Chihuahua. And there being so much uncertainty whether he would be able to sell out before our troops from either New Mexico or Monterrey should open the trade with free goods (which of course we would be unable to stand after having paid both introduction and *consumos*, or inter-state duties), he concluded to proceed to the Fair of San Juan de los Lagos, which is held the first twelve days of December. Here was a new dilemma for me. What had I to hope or expect, if I should stop with my goods, but persecution and confiscation? And how much better would I be off to take my chances as I then was – my goods in Mr. Speyer's possession, and myself a prisoner and liable to be confined in prison or sent out of the country as the interest or whim of the authorities might dictate? Mr. Speyer began hiring Mexican drivers, so as to be prepared for any emergency; having two sets of drivers, so if the Americans were taken from him he would

---

[235] The Bull Pen, located in the suburbs of Chihuahua, was a large amphitheater where bull fights were held. Hughes, *Doniphan's Expedition*, 329.

have the Mexicans, and if permitted to retain all or a portion of either nationality, he would have men enough to proceed without detention. I also hired four Mexican drivers. So we were both under double expense for hire and board of hands.

After removing camp, we could occasionally get permission to go about town. And one day I called on Mr. John Potts, an Englishman and director of the mint, and a man of a good deal of influence, and who seemed to be well posted in regard to the intentions of the governor towards us. He seemed to understand the difficulties under which I labored, and expressed himself as willing to do anything in his power by advice or influence to promote my interest.

One day he told me that he thought perhaps he had a document which I might be able to use to advantage. Mr. J. Tilghman Hoffman, of Baltimore, had crossed the plains in the same train with us the year before and proceeded to Chihuahua. On leaving, he requested Mr. Potts to procure a letter of security for him, as he expected to go out again and wanted to travel through the country to the Fair of San Juan and the City of Mexico, and leave by way of Vera Cruz. He produced the paper, and it was complete in all respects except the filling in of the personal description and the signature. Mr. Hoffman was a very small and feeble man, [of a] dark complexion, and between us [Potts and Webb] the fact that I should attempt to palm myself off for him, was exceedingly ridiculous. But the Mexicans did not know either of us, and I did not propose to assume Mr. Hoffman's position either abroad or at home. But in great difficulty, I decided to use his paper, hoping that I might be benefited, and he in no way wronged. So we filled in my personal description in-

stead of his, and I placed the signature "J. Josiah
Webb," scrawled as near as I could to appear like the
name "J. Tilghman Hoffman," in the body of the
paper, which I never used but once, and then with all
the benefit I could desire or expect.

While camped at the Bull Pen, my mule herder came
one morning and informed me that there was a man in
the corral lassoing a mule which he claimed belonged
to his master, Don Juan Terrazas, the prefect; and he
notified me to appear at the prefect's office and explain
how I came in possession of the property. In doing so, I
stated that I had bought two mules of the same party
and was sure everything was all right, as he was a man
who would not be likely to have mules in his possession
which were of doubtful ownership. True, the brand was
not vented, but I bought them under circumstances
which rendered it impracticable to fix the sale brand.

"You have two mules with this brand?" [he in-
quired].

"Yes, sir."

"Well, produce the other here in an hour," – which I
did, and *lost them both*.

We were finally ordered to prepare for leaving in
three days for Río Florido, on the southern border of
the state and some eight or ten miles from the boundary
line between Chihuahua and Durango, where we were
to remain as prisoners until some decision was arrived
at, what should be done with us. Although we could see
no improvement in our circumstances after a month's
detention in Chihuahua as prisoners, yet a change was
accepted with gladness, and the hope [?] that something would turn up to relieve us from this terrible
uncertainty. When leaving Chihuahua, Mr. Speyer had

Suburbs of Chihuahua about 1850

all arrangements made to go to the Fair of San Juan by way of Durango, and had written to a German merchant there, named Stahlknecht, to get permission from the governor of Durango to enter the state and proceed to the capital with his train and fifty armed servants, stating that he had hired Mexican drivers. I had made no new arrangement with him and could see no other way but to proceed blindfolded (as it were) and trust in Providence; a prisoner, and all my interests in the hands of a stranger or in the power of enemies to myself and country.

We took the route by San Pablo, Santa Rosalía, Guajuquilla,[236] and Zapata to Florido, in charge of the same companies which met us at Peñuelas and guarded us as prisoners during our journey to, and our stay in, Chihuahua. There were several families [which] traveled with the train, leaving the city under the apprehension that our troops would march on Chihuahua either from the north or south, and perhaps both, and they wanted their families out of the reach of the barbarous heretic gringos when they should come. Among them were the families of the general commanding the department, the collector of customs, and two or three other of the leading families of the city. The two infantry companies were to remain at Florido to guard the prisoners who remained, and the cavalry to proceed with the train to Durango as an escort and guard. We arrived at Florido after a long drive, about 3 P. M., and

---

[236] Guajuquilla, now called Jiménez, was founded in 1752. In 1846 it had a population of six or seven thousand. "Guajuquilla is a pretty, quaint little town, with white-washed adobe houses, and looking clean and neat," wrote Ruxton in October, 1846. Ruxton, *op. cit.*, 130. See also Hubert H. Bancroft, *History of the North Mexican States and Texas* (*Works of H. H. Bancroft*, xv, San Francisco, 1884), i, 585; Wislizenus, *Memoir of a Tour to Northern Mexico*, 65.

corralled our wagons in front of, and quite near, the hacienda.[237]

And while the men were turning out, Mr. Speyer and myself called on the proprietor to see what were the prospects before us. I had told him about the letter of security, and before leaving camp he asked me for it, stating that *perhaps* he could use it to my advantage, but stated no plan; and I don't think either of us had any idea how it should be produced or whether it should be produced at all. On receiving it from me, he looked it over, and as we passed along, it disappeared; and I thought the motion was like putting it up his sleeve instead of into his pocket. Yet I said nothing, and the conversation took another turn.

On entering the house, we were shown into the family room, where were the proprietor and two young ladies whom he introduced to us as his daughters. The room was a front room, and our camp was in full view from the window where the young ladies were sitting. The officer in command of the troops had already reported, and the countenances of all seemed to indicate far more anxiety as to what they could do with their prisoners than pleasure in the prospect of entertaining so many strangers. He very soon handed Mr. Speyer a package of letters, and on opening one, a paper fell to the floor which he picked up and seemed to read with much interest and pleasure, and after reading it handed it to Don —— for his perusal. He read it, and very pleasantly and heartily congratulated me upon my good fortune in having a letter of security which would give

[237] This was "a large hacienda with a colonnade of stone," according to Bartlett, "the capitals of the columns being in the Moorish style. It stands on the margin of the plateau, overlooking the valley of the river, and has a very picturesque appearance." Bartlett, *op. cit.*, ii, 463.

me full permission to travel anywhere in the republic. Another enclosure was permission for Mr. Albert Speyer to enter the state of Durango with his train and proceed to the city of Durango with fifty armed men as drivers and assistants.

Don —— (I very much regret that I have forgotten the name of the gentleman) had formerly held the office of governor of Chihuahua, and occupied a high position in social and political society, and expressed a good deal of surprise that Governor Trias should encumber him with the care and maintenance of so large a number of prisoners, and also with the support of the soldiers sent to guard them, there being no provision made for the support of either. Mr. Speyer suggested that if the burden was too great, and if he was willing to allow us to take them with us, we would be responsible for the good behavior and maintenance of our men while they remained in the country, and as the boundary line was but a few miles off and directly on our line of travel, we could soon put ourselves outside the jurisdiction of the governor of Chihuahua and within the jurisdiction of the governor of Durango, whose permission we already had to proceed to the capital with the full number of men in our company. Don —— replied that while he denied the right of Governor Trias to do as he had, he nevertheless felt it his duty as a good citizen and patriot to do all that lay in his power to protect the government from [any] risk or embarrassment which might occur from the unrestricted travel and intercourse of our people while the two Nations were at war.

During this conversation the men in camp were kindling fires and preparing for a dinner and supper, and having breakfasted early and made a long drive, were hungry. And it took but little to stir up a rumpus in camp, and *providentially* one of quite an exciting character occurred just in the nick of time. The young ladies all at once called to their father to know what was the matter in camp, and on looking out he called upon us to rise and explain. On looking out, the whole camp appeared in an uproar; everything was confusion and excitement. Some were in a fist-fight, and some seemed to [be] threatening each other with drawn knives, billets of wood, [and] frying pans; and the loud and bad words were plainly heard by us, if not understood by all. But few had shaved or had their hair cut since leaving "the States," and many had not washed for weeks, and at that moment it seemed to me the roughest, raggedest, and wickedest crowd I ever saw.[238] But we both kept cool and treated the matter as if it was no uncommon occurrence, and did not move to quiet matters or to interfere in any way.

Don —— wanted to know what kind of men they were, and we told him they were first class – a little rough now, but at home and cleaned up they were many of them of the first class in society (which was true). Don —— said he was instructed to allow some of them the use of their guns to kill game, and wanted to know what they would probably do in case they failed to find sufficient game to supply themselves with meat.

"Game is plenty about here, is it not Don ——?" [we asked].

"Not very abundant, but there are deer and wild fowl. But they will have to hunt almost constantly and

---

[238] On account of the rough appearance of most Santa Fé traders, the lower classes of Mexicans thought the Americans were uncivilized and called them burros. Ruxton, *op. cit.*, 138-139.

for long distances to find sufficient meat to supply so large a crowd. Would they be apt to kill my cattle or take my horses to hunt? Or if I should find it necessary to let a number have their guns to hunt, would they be likely to attempt to escape and join your people at Monclova?"

"There is no telling, Don ——, what they might do. You see from their appearance that they are brave [and] daring men, and not used to going hungry where there is plenty of meat in the *llano*, or to go on foot when there are plenty of horses to be caught; and you may be sure they will not starve while meat of any kind is to be found within reach."

As the conversation proceeded, the young ladies frequently urged their father to adopt some plan to get rid of us. And finally they both arose and approached him, and by tender and almost tearful expressions, said,

"For God's sake, father, let them go!"

The old gentleman looked at us with a smile of doubt, indecision, and affection, as much as to say, "What shall I do?"

And finally, after several appeals in the same words, [he] told us he would think the matter over, and if we could come in at eleven o'clock, when all would be quiet in camp and among his own people, he would decide what he would do. We left, and thought the prospects fair for a compromise of some sort by which the interests of all parties might be promoted.

There were several of the men who had intimated that if any opportunity offered they should mount themselves and cross the prairie and join our people at Monclova; and we tried to get all the information we could (without exciting suspicion) in regard to the country and the distance from different points on our route. We thought the nearest point from which it would be prudent to leave would be somewhere between the hacienda of La Zarca and the town of El Gallo. They could procure mules at some places intermediate, and the distance would be but four or five days' travel, and they would be able to avoid nearly if not all settlements after leaving us. We thought it better for the interest of all parties that the Americans should divide. The risk of trouble from the authorities would be less to us, and we had no doubt but those who left would in a very few days be able to work their way to our people with but little risk of danger from any source.

On returning to camp, we had a talk with the men and found that many of them were determined to avail themselves of the first opportunity that offered to attempt to escape to Monclova, whether they were to remain in Florido or were permitted to proceed on the journey with us. We told them we were to meet the Don again during the evening and would advise them early the next morning of the result of the conference; and those who had determined on the course mentioned could notify us the next morning, and we would talk over matters, and they could lay their plans according to circumstances.

At eleven o'clock we called on the Don and found him ready with his proposition. He said he was very anxious to get rid of the men, and his daughters were almost beside themselves with fear of what the consequences would be of their remaining. [He continued]:

"I have this proposition to make you. You two gentlemen give me your bond for the good behavior of these men during their stay in the country. This, of course, is not to be used except in certain emergencies. You will require tomorrow to make any arrangements you may deem necessary with the men, and I will by tomorrow evening find some excuse to send the two companies of infantry back to Chihuahua. And sometime the day after tomorrow, you must gear up and start for Durango against my earnest protestations and denunciations for the bad faith you are manifesting after your assurances that there should be no advantage taken of my returning your arms into your possession. Make haste and cross the line into Durango and out of our care and responsibility, and we will thank God for the riddance."

We returned to camp, feeling that we had a good prospect of release from one difficulty, but from the experiences [we] already had we could form no opinion of how soon new difficulties might arise. However, we went directly to bed, and I was soon sound asleep.

In the morning we arose early, and after breakfast called the boys together for consultation and to arrange plans for the future. We had heard a disturbance in the soldiers' camp very early in the morning, but took no notice of it. And as the camp was some little distance from ours, we did not observe any change, and asked no questions about them. It was not long, however, before it was noised about that the two infantry companies had very early broken camp and marched off in the direction of Chihuahua. We directed the men to make their arrangements to leave the next day, as we were near the Durango line and could in a few hours, by prompt and decisive action, release them from the jurisdiction of the Governor Trias of Chihuahua and get into Durango. [We informed them] that Mr.

Speyer had a permit from the governor of Durango to enter the state and pass through to the city of Durango with his train of wagons and fifty armed men; that I had received a letter of security from General government which released me from bondage as prisoner, and I was free to go wherever I pleased throughout the country; that so many Americans in one company would probably excite suspicion and possibly cause further difficulty; that our road for some days would lead us nearer to Monclova, where General Wool was stationed, and we thought by energy, prudence, and caution such of them as desired to do so might supply themselves with [an] outfit and leave the country; that they might retire for consultation, and that all who desired to leave could give us notice as soon as possible, and we would make up their accounts and settle with them, and we would furnish them some mules, and they could buy others at Cerro Gordo or La Zarca (if they thought best to go with us so far), and four or five days would enable them to place themselves under the protection of our army.

After a couple of hours a number of them (either twenty-one or twenty-three)[239] came and requested a settlement, and said they would at the proper time make a break for "the States" by way of Monclova. This was a larger number than we had expected. [There were] two who were then in my employ — Rogers and Dave McCoy — and one who crossed the plains with me but hired to Mr. Speyer in Santa Fé — a blacksmith named Jennett. After a settlement I suggested that under the circumstances, when the war closed, they might have a claim against the Mexican

---

[239] Twenty-one. *Ibid.*, 110, 130.

government, and if they chose to do so they could give Mr. Speyer a power of attorney to prosecute in their interest. They thought well of it and wanted it done. Mr. Speyer wished me to draw [up] the document, and although I had never made the attempt to draw a legal document, yet I thought I was as well qualified to do so as I was to act as physician, which I had done on several occasions. I drew [up] the document, and they all signed and handed it to Mr. Speyer. The document was afterwards read before a military court of inquiry and pronounced to be very good work for a novice.

After finishing our arrangements with the men, we went to the hacienda and informed our friend of what we had done, withholding the information that the men intended going to Monclova, but intimating that they would probably try and get employment as drivers in some of the wagon trains freighting through the interior. He told us how he had ordered the infantry escort to Chihuahua, and the dragoons would proceed with us to Durango as guard to the families traveling with us. He would have to express some surprise and resentment that the men should leave without his permission. But as Governor Trias had given their arms in his (Speyer's) charge, he [the Don] could not help himself if he [Speyer] chose to give them to the men instead of turning them over to him [the Don]. And as the men refused to stay, and we had permission from the governor of Durango to proceed to that city with fifty armed men without any restrictions as to nationality, we must assume all responsibility; and if we allowed the men to go with us, it would be under his protest.

Returning to camp, Mr. S. informed the ladies that

we should leave for Durango the next morning, and they might prepare to start as soon as possible after an early breakfast. The troops were [to act] as an escort to the Mexican families, and subject to their orders. It was their choice to travel with us as an additional protection, and we felt that their desire to do so was a manifestation of their confidence in us, and would have a conciliatory effect upon the authorities of the towns through which we passed. I am confident that their traveling with us did make a favorable impression upon the authorities at Cerro Gordo and Durango, and that our reception and treatment was far better than it would have been if they had not traveled with us.

After breakfast next morning orders were given to "catch up," and all hands were busily engaged in harnessing and arranging camp furniture to proceed on our journey in the hope of comparative freedom from annoyance and vexations through the state of Durango. When nearly ready for a start, our friend came to camp and inquired what we were doing.

"We are about to proceed on our journey to Durango by the permission of the governor of that state in the documents shown you."

"But these men are sent here as prisoners under my care, and are they going also?"

"They have so decided, and they go under our responsibility."

In the presence of several of his dependents, he warned us that they left without his permission and on their own responsibility, and he should immediately advise Governor Trias of the course they had taken. We drove out and proceeded on our way, and everybody in our camp and at the hacienda was happy. Before camping, we passed the boundaries of Chihuahua and felt comparatively safe, feeling that we could fare no worse than we had for the last month.

I want to say a word in regard to the governor, Don Angel Trias. He was an unprincipled tyrant in all his bearing towards his own people in an inferior position, and considered all foreigners (especially Americans) as only worthy of his contempt. His father owned the hacienda of Peñol, about thirty-five miles north of Chihuahua, which in olden times was celebrated for the large herds of cattle upon it; and all were bred and culled to one color, so that there were none but black allowed on the place. At one time, when young, he was at the hacienda, and falling out with the major domo, pushed him into a boiling caldron of tallow, and left him. He was compelled to leave the country, and spent some time in the United States, and also traveled extensively in Europe. [He] could speak English fluently, and (I understood) also French and German. I never heard an American speak of him with respect, and there was no love lost [between them].[240]

[240] Bartlett, who was favorably impressed with Trias, described him as follows: "General Trias . . . is a gentleman of large wealth and fine accomplishments. After receiving his education he went to Europe, where he spent eight years travelling in various parts, although he remained most of the time in England and France. He is well versed in several of the European languages, and speaks English with great correctness. Of English literature he told me he was very fond; and he considered that no native appreciated the beauties of Shakespeare and Milton better than he. . . There is no doubt that General Trias detests the Americans as a people; yet American gentlemen and officers who stop at Chihuahua, are always treated by him with great politeness and attention." Bartlett, *op. cit.*, ii, 426-427.

TO THE FAIR OF SAN JUAN DE LOS LAGOS

TO THE FAIR OF SAN JUAN DE
LOS LAGOS

Cerro Gordo was the frontier town where all trains
passing from one state to the other were compelled to
present their *guías*,[241] or manifests, for inspection. The
custom-house officers were notorious for their rascality
and cunning in drawing strangers into their foils for
the purpose of collecting boodle. Many Americans
had been drawn into the foils of the rascals and skinned.

We, of course, were on our guard, and careful to
give no excuse for them to demand our detention beyond the time necessary to examine our manifests. But
as it was about forty miles to the next water or camping
place (La Zarca), we were compelled to stay over
night, and had to be on the constant watch lest we or
our men should do something to compromise us and
enable the rascals to bleed us. The men were constantly
approached by the people to trade or swap for some
article of wearing apparel, and we were asked, [as] a
special favor to some of the merchants, to sell them
some goods of which they were out, and [were] offered

---

[241] The *guía*, or custom-house permit, was a sort of clearance or passport for goods. It certified that the merchandise had been regularly entered
at the custom-house and the legal duties paid, and enumerated the points
of destination for the commodities listed in the *factura*, or invoice. The *guía*
was not only required on leaving the port of entry, but also in transporting
goods from one state to another, and even from one village or town to another within a state. William S. Messervy to Powhatan Ellis, Sept. 25, 1841,
MS., Despatches from Ministers (Mexico), State Department; Gregg, *op. cit.*,
XX, 147-148.

extravagant prices for them. By selling them we should have made ourselves liable to have our train detained [a] sufficient time for them to examine all our goods in search of contraband articles. This would have caused us sufficient detention, with the expenses of fifty men and five hundred animals, to have enabled them to demand a large sum by way of boodle, or *consideración*, for our release. We were fortunate enough not to be drawn into any compromise either by ourselves or our men, and left the next morning in high spirits, and the boodlers mortified but watching for the next chance, which was on our return presented to them. And they were not slow to avail themselves of it.

I forgot to mention that while in Cerro Gordo one of the men came to camp and told me a man in town claimed two of my mules. I had bought two mules of Mr. Speyer which he had bought from one of the heirs of La Zarca in a lot of some thirty, and these two were the ones claimed. I went to the house of the claimant, Don Juan Sánchez, and was received very gentlemanly and informed that the mules claimed belonged to his wife, who owned a large ranch formerly belonging to La Zarca. I told them how I came by them, and he said his brother-in-law had sold Mr. S. some mules, and if I could prove that these were a part of them, it would be all he would ask. John Devoe, who was traveling with us and well known in the town, stated that he knew the mules were among those sold to Mr. Speyer by his brother-in-law, and there was no further trouble.

Our men bought some mules in Cerro Gordo, and we traveled on to La Zarca [242] in hopes they would get

---

[242] The hacienda of La Zarca, one of the largest ranches in northern Mexico, was famous for the number and quality of its horses and mules. Gregg, *op. cit.*, xx, 163; Kendall, *op. cit.*, ii, 118-121; Bartlett, *op. cit.*, ii, 468-470.

enough to leave our train a few miles beyond for General Wool's camp at Monclova. We arrived at La Zarca before dark and camped, and sent our mules to a stream a mile or so west of the hacienda under escort of some fifteen or twenty men, as the people warned us that within a day or two they had seen Indian signs, and they expected a visit from the Comanche at any time. We detained a few animals in camp to assist in driving in the mules or giving warning of danger in case of the appearance of the Indians. The animals had got to the creek and [were] nearly through drinking, when on the hills to the west of them, but somewhat farther from them than our camp, we saw a large body of Indians pouring over the hills towards our animals. The men saw them about as soon as we did and came towards camp, making the best time possible. The Indians saw they would be unable to overtake them before reinforcements would arrive, [and] turned and disappeared over the hills.

The people were in great dread of the morrow. They said the Comanche frequently made raids upon the hacienda and carried off female prisoners, and would order the men to bring up the herd of horses and select the best; and if they had any tired or poor animals, leave them, making the sign that they must be well cared for, as they should demand them on their return, and they [the horses] must be well rested and fat. This was formerly the richest hacienda in Mexico. It was said of the former proprietor that previous to the revolution of Mexico, the Spanish government sent a regiment of dragoons to Vera Cruz to be mounted there for service. The proprietor sent, as a present to the government, one thousand gray horses of one year's foal, from this hacienda. The property was still in possession of the heirs, but they are comparatively poor. And the Indians from our side of the Río Grande made annual incursions, driving off stock, killing the people, and taking prisoners, producing great impoverishment and demoralization.

Here the men procured mules sufficient to mount the company. And the next day some fifteen or twenty miles from La Zarca, either twenty-one or twenty-three left our train in high spirits, expecting to reach our people in at least four or five days and be again free men in the midst of friends. They chose David McCoy, whom I hired in Westport, Missouri, and [who] crossed the plains with me to Santa Fé and there hired to Mr. Speyer, as their captain. He was a very clever man and a good hand, but the responsibility of the leadership appeared to be too great for his capacity, and they got lost in the desert of Mapimí and separated and wandered about until half of them famished; and the rest succeeded in gaining the settlements in a wretched and famishing condition.[243]

One of them, named Lyman Marsh, came to the Fair of San Juan before we left, and I hired him there, and he continued in my employ until I returned to "the States." He and Rogers, who left my employ, became separated from the crowd and wandered over the desert for days in search of water. Rogers' mule died, and he

[243] Of the twenty-one teamsters who left the caravan near La Zarca, ten or eleven perished in the desert. The survivors reached Guajuquilla in the latter part of October, 1846. "Such miserable, emaciated creatures it has never been my lot to see," wrote Ruxton. "With long hair and beards, and thin cadaverous faces, with the cheek-bones projecting almost through the skin, and their mouths cracked with the drought, they dismounted before my door, weak and scarcely able to stand; most of them had entirely lost their voices, and some were giddy and light-headed with the sufferings they had endured." Ruxton, *op. cit.*, 131. See also Hughes, *Doniphan's Expedition*, 347.

became so exhausted that he was unable to travel, when Marsh left him with instructions to remain where he was, and if he [Marsh] found water he would return for him.

During the day he [Marsh] came in sight of a range of hills, and from the appearances of the country and the many birds flying around a particular location, he thought he should find water. He left his mule at the foot of the hills and by great effort arrived at the point; and looking down into a deep crevice in the rocks, [he] discovered a pool of water which had flown into the crevice from the surrounding surface during the rainy season, and enough remained to relieve all immediate wants. He was so weak that it was [only] by great effort and risk of life even – that it was only the stimulant of relief in sight – that enabled him to get to the water; and then the self-denial! He dipped the water in his boot and drank from it by the single swallow, resting betimes for some time, and then went to the relief of his mule, carrying both boots full and allowing her to drink from the top of the leg; and setting them down on the ground she would press down until all was gone. Thus he continued until the wants of man and beast were satisfied.

He then returned to where he left Rogers, carrying all the water he could, but only to find him gone. He hunted till dark but saw no trace of him, and went to the hills and camped for the night. In the morning he returned and continued the hunt until hope was gone. And the beginning of hunger reminded him that he must use all his remaining strength to get to the settlements, which he reached in about two days.

His description of the suffering for the want of

water – and the description I afterwards heard from "Wash" Train, one of the Mier prisoners who escaped from Santa Anna's forces in Mexico and wandered in the prairie for nine days without water, and [from] a lost soldier from Colonel Sumner's forces who became separated from his comrades after his (Sumner's) battle with the Cheyenne in 1858 or 1859, and who wandered without food or drink for four days until we overtook him – convinces me that the place of the greatest conceivable torment is that where no water is found, and that the parable of Dives calling upon Abraham to send Lazarus with a drop of water to cool his parched tongue, is a picture of the greatest suffering possible for mankind to endure either here or in the hereafter. Want of food is no comparison. After the third day they say there is no suffering from hunger, and when food is procurable it is impossible to eat. But day and night, asleep and awake, the only thought or dream is for water, water, water.

We were not anxious to make the regular drives on the route to the Fair of San Juan de los Lagos for two reasons: first, we were early for the fair; and second, our mules were not sufficiently strong. Our delays and the uncertainty of our course (or rather the uncertainty of our treatment by the Mexican government), and the large expenditures consequent upon our delay compelled us to trust to the nourishment of grass for our animals, with as little expenditure for grain as we could get along with. So instead of making the drive from La Zarca to El Gallo in one day, as was the custom, we took about two and a half or three.

We, of course, sought camp at night where there was

water. And the second night we were traveling late, and just before arriving at camp we had to descend a steep hill with a sharp turn at the bottom and a deep gully on the left, close to the road. One of my teams driven by a Mexican had a very light pair of wheelers, but were quick to obey and when called to hold back would do their best, and the near mule would slide on all fours as long as possible. On making the turn at the bottom of the hill, she was so persistent and determined in her efforts that she brought the wagon to the edge of the ditch and turned it over, wheels up, in the bottom – mules some in the ditch and some out, and all struggling to get out of the entanglement. Here was work for the balance of the night: to get the goods out of the wagon, the wagon out of the ditch, and all set up and in order for starting in the morning. The gully was so deep that the wheels were considerably below the surface of the ground. By hard work we got everything out and loaded ready for starting in the morning. But the load was without form or comeliness – every bow broken in pieces and beyond repair. But it was the dry season, and [there was] no danger of getting our goods wet.

We pursued our journey to El Gallo [244] and arrived a little after noon, and made a short stop for the purpose of obtaining provisions. It was impossible, in the small towns through which we were to pass, to get flour in sufficient quantity to last but a day or two, and here we could get but a very small quantity. But the people said it was baking day for several families, and the bread was some in the oven and some ready to go in, and they would sell us what they could spare, and we could leave

---

[244] San Pedro del Gallo, or St. Peter of the Cock.

a man to bring it to camp when ready. We bargained for the amount and paid for it, and thought it better to leave two men with an extra mule to bring it to camp.

While there, I asked if anyone had any mules to sell, and one man had some in the prairie and could bring them up in a few hours if we could agree on the price. He showed me about such as he had in selecting from our drove, and gave me his price, but we could not agree on the price by about three dollars a head, and we drove on. General Armijo was encamped near town and said he would break camp and follow us, and travel with us until we left the main road south and struck off for Durango. We traveled some four or five miles and camped, and General Armijo followed and camped some distance in the rear.

The men [who had been] left for the bread did not arrive as soon as we expected, but we felt no alarm for them as we had seen no Indians since leaving La Zarca. But about ten or eleven o'clock General A. sent us word that one of our men had arrived in camp wounded, and said the Indians attacked them but a short distance from town and killed his companion, wounded him, and took the mules and drove them off. He crawled into the chaparral, and as soon as he was satisfied the Indians had left the vicinity, he made the best time he could for camp. We went for him and brought him to camp, [and] found he had a flesh wound in his arm, probably from a lance, but suffering in no other way except from fright. We dressed his wound as well as we could, and early in the morning returned in search of his companion and found his body on the roadside, probably where he fell, but not scalped or mangled according to Indian custom. Probably the mules and their mountings was all they cared for as trophies or reward for the labor of *honest* good Indians, and the bread was probably accepted with thanksgiving as the gift of the Great Spirit. The body was taken to El Gallo and left in charge of the priest, and expenses paid for the burial.[245] This detained us half a day and enabled us to procure a small quantity of bread in place of that taken.

The day after, while traveling in the valley, on the hills to the west and a mile or two from the road we saw the Indians busily engaged in rounding up and driving off a herd of mules. And as this was in the neighborhood where the man said his mules were at pasture, I told the boys he had better have taken my offer, as I thought they were the mules I had tried to buy. On our return from the fair, the man told me that the second day after [our departure], the Indians drove off all his mules.

Two or three days after, we camped, and had to drive the mules nearly a mile through the chaparral to water and sent a strong guard for protection, part of the soldiers remaining [in] camp as guard. It was getting dark, and we heard a great rush towards camp and many voices – some American, some Mexican – and a shouting which we could not recognize, whether civilized or savage, which produced great excitement in camp, the Americans running for their arms, the women leaving their tents and running for the corral, the soldiers in great confusion and consternation, several of them hiding under our wagons. The noise of rushing animals through the brush, and approaching nearer and nearer with such a confusion of voices (and we not knowing whether the animals were stampeded or run-

---

[245] See Ruxton, *op. cit.*, 115-116.

ning from Indians, and if so whether pursued or not)
was very exciting to us all. But if asked whether I was
frightened, I should of course say "No," in reply, but
mentally I should be compelled to acknowledge the
coon. What a relief when we saw the man on the bell
mare in the lead, and the mules following on the run
but in good order, and the men bringing up the rear
somewhat excited but ready for defense both in the
spirit and with arms! They reported that while the
animals were drinking, the Indians appeared within a
short distance and made every possible effort to stampede them, and followed for some distance under shelter of the brush, shouting and shooting arrows but not
exposing themselves to the fire of our men.

In a short time everything became quiet in camp,
supper cooked and eaten, and the mules corralled for
the night. We started next morning without watering,
thinking the Indians might lay in ambush for another
attack. Governor Armijo had left us and gone south,[246]
and we did not see him again until our arrival at the
Fair of San Juan de los Lagos. We saw the Comanche
several times on our route, but they made no attempt to
molest us except on the two occasions mentioned.

Some three or four days before our arrival at Durango, we discovered two men mounted on mules driving a pack mule some distance from the road, traveling
towards the north. One appeared to be a foreigner and
the other a Mexican servant. On discovering us, the
foreigner left his course and came to our train. We
asked him who he was and where he was going, and he
said [that he] was Lieutenant [Ruxton] [247] of the Eng-

---

[246] This is an error. Armijo did not leave Speyer and Webb until after
their meeting with George F. Ruxton. *Ibid.*, 110.

[247] On October 12, 1846, Armijo, Speyer, and Webb met Lieutenant

lish army, and had landed at Vera Cruz and traveled by way of the City of Mexico and all the large cities to Durango, which he left but two or three days since, and intended to go to Chihuahua and thence by way of New Mexico to the United States. We told him we thought he was running [a] great risk, as we had seen the Comanche almost every day for a week or more. But he seemed to think he could go through by keeping a good lookout, and if he was compelled to fight he was well armed and would make the best defense he could. I never met him afterwards, but heard of him in New Mexico, where he was well received by the officers of our army and visited several of the military posts, and afterwards went to St. Louis and back to England. [He] wrote a book giving an account of his travels and adventures.[248] I thought then, and ever since, that no

George F. Ruxton about seventy miles northeast of the city of Durango. Ruxton described their meeting as follows: "A little farther on I saw the long line of waggons, like ships at sea, crossing a plain before me. They were all drawn by teams of eight fine mules, and under the charge and escort of some thirty strapping young Missourians, each with a long heavy rifle across his saddle. I stopped and had a long chat with Armijo, who, a mountain of fat, rolled out of his American dearborn, and inquired the price of cotton goods in Durango, he having some seven waggon-loads with him, and also what they said, in Mexico, of the doings in Santa Fé, alluding to its capture by the Americans without any resistance. I told him that there was but one opinion respecting it expressed all over the country – that General Armijo and the New Mexicans were a pack of arrant cowards; to which he answered, 'Adiós! [A Dios?]. They don't know that I had but seventy-five men to fight 3,000. What could I do?'" *Ibid.*

[248] Ruxton's book, *Adventures in Mexico and the Rocky Mountains*, was first published in 1847. Garrard, who met Ruxton at Bent's Fort in the spring of 1847, described him as "a quiet, good-looking man, with a handsome moustache. He conversed well, but sparingly, speaking little of himself. He has passed over the burning sands of Africa, penetrated the jungles of India, jogged on patient mule through the Tierra Caliente of Mexico, and laid down amid the snowdrifts of the Rocky mountains." Ruxton died in St. Louis in the late summer of 1848. *Weekly Reveille*, Sept. 4, 1848; Garrard, *Wah-To-Yah*, 290.

man of common sense who had any knowledge of Indian character, would think of taking such a trip, with such an outfit, for pleasure.

[After] arriving at a hacienda some twelve or fifteen miles from Durango, [and] soon after turning out, two men came to us with a letter from Mr. Stahlknecht, notifying Mr. Speyer that the governor of Durango wanted an explanation of the use he was making of his passport, which was permission for him to "proceed to Durango with fifty armed men" under his (Speyer's) representation that he had "hired Mexican drivers," and he (the governor) had information that the majority of his company were Americans. This created another sensation in camp, and of course we were all anxious about our reception and whether we were again to be taken prisoners and disarmed. We lay by one day, and Mr. Speyer proceeded to Durango to negotiate. The people at the hacienda were very much excited about the Indian news we brought; as [for] if they were on a raid, they would be sure to visit the place as soon as we left. . .

We proceeded on our way and entered Durango, unloaded our wagons in the warehouses of Mr. Stahlknecht, and sent our wagons and men out of the city to a hacienda about a league distant, and also about a league from a hacienda through which we had passed, the two haciendas and the city forming the three points of a triangle. Three or four days after, we heard the Comanche were raiding the ranches about the city and driving off stock. The authorities embargoed [commandeered] several of our wagons to transport troops and provisions to the battleground, and retained them for three days. Our men, from the tops of the houses where they were, could see the Indians in large numbers rounding up stock (horses and mules), while another portion of the band were threatening and attacking the soldiers who remained behind their barricades on the defensive. The Indians made no attack upon the ranch where our men were, and not an animal was lost, either of our own or belonging to the hacienda. And the proprietor offered to support our men and animals free of cost for provisions and forage, if we would remain a month.

Durango [249] at that time had from 15,000 to 20,000 inhabitants, and could not raise [a] force [large] enough to defend themselves and their stock from a raid of Indians of a nation two hundred or more miles distant. It was estimated that the loss of animals to the people of the state by this raid was 25,000 head, besides many men killed and many women carried into captivity. Lo, the poor Indian! In speaking of the loss of animals, it is not to be understood that the Indians secured that number or the half of it, but many were killed, many tired out by the way, many [were] lost in the desert, and many escaped and were lost in other ranches; so that the total loss to the different owners was the number stated. And from the accounts of the raid at the time and on our return, I thought the estimate a fair one. Lyman Marsh told me that several

---

[249] The city of Durango was founded by Francisco de Ibarra about 1563. Situated on a plateau nearly seven thousand feet high, it was one of the most beautiful cities in northern Mexico. "It presents two or three handsome squares," wrote Gregg, "with many fine edifices and some really splendid churches. The town is supplied with water for irrigating the gardens, and for many other ordinary purposes, by several open aqueducts, which lead through the streets, from a large spring, a mile or two distant." Gregg, *op. cit.*, xx, 164. See also J. Lloyd Mecham, *Francisco de Ibarra and Nueva Vizcaya* (Durham, 1927), 123-124.

times in their wanderings they crossed the trail, and the number of dead animals they saw was to them appalling. They felt sure that by following the trail they would ultimately find water, but in their exhausted condition the risk of famishing was great, and if they should come upon the Indians their death was sure.

We had our goods examined by the custom-house officers, and they were passed without any unnecessary delay or expense, and [we] sold quite an amount to Mr. Stahlknecht and other merchants. After remaining some ten days, we loaded up and started on our journey, gratified to our host for his hospitality and to the authorities for not subjecting us to the persecutions we had suffered under while traveling through Chihuahua.

We traveled by short journeys through the state of Zacatecas to Aguascalientes, leaving the city of Zacatecas [250] several miles to our right and stopping over a day at the little town of Refugio, on the frontier of Aguascalientes, to wait for Mr. Speyer, who went to the city to get what information he could from the foreign merchants in regard to the prospects for sales at the fair. On the night of his arrival, after having partaken of the hospitalities of a merchant to whom he carried letters from Mr. Stahlknecht, he was aroused from his bed by a message from the governor to appear and give an account of himself. His friend becoming responsible for his appearance the next day, he was allowed to return to his rest. The next day he was subjected to a severe questioning in regard to his commercial adventure while our governments were at war,

---

[250] The city of Zacatecas was founded about 1548. It was located near extensive silver mines, which were the cause for its origin and growth. By 1846 it had a population of thirty or forty thousand. Mecham, *op. cit.*, 44-46; Ruxton, *op. cit.*, 75.

PLAZA OF AGUASCALIENTES ABOUT 1850

From *Album Pintoresco de la República Mexicana*, Mexico, *circa* 1850

how many Americans were in his train, and what news he had from the invading army. Mr. S. had two passports – one from the Prussian government and one from the English, using the English [passport] on nearly all occasions. He thought the intention of the governor was, if he could get him entangled in some way, to demand a large sum for [his] release. But on learning that the train must by this time have arrived within the limits of another state and was beyond his jurisdiction, he released him with politeness and compliments. But the matter caused a day's delay and much anxiety in camp.

Again we proceeded on our journey, and without further molestation arrived at Aguascalientes,[251] where we proposed to remain a few days until the time arrived to proceed and get ready for the opening of the fair. During our stay Mr. Speyer took a room at the hotel, where we spent most of the day. And occasionally some of the city people would come in to see what the *Tejanos* were about, and we would entertain them with refreshments and do all we could to avoid molestation during our stay.

One day a monk from a monastery near-by entered the room with his contribution box and the picture of the Saint, to solicit alms. Without kissing the Saint or inquiring the object, we each put a dollar in the box, when the monk drew a paper from his pocket and placed [it] before Mr. Speyer for his perusal. It was a sheet of Mexican paper but little different in size from

[251] "The city of Aguascalientes is beautifully situated in a level plain," wrote Gregg, "and would appear to contain about twenty thousand inhabitants, who are principally engaged in the manufacture of *rebozos* and other textures mostly of cotton. As soon as I found myself sufficiently at leisure, I visited the famous warm spring (*ojo caliente*) in the suburbs, from which the city derives its euphonious name." Gregg, *op. cit.*, xx, 169.

our foolscap paper, with a heading showing it to be for a lottery, and below the heading two columns of names and a few on the other side. Mr. S. took his pen to put down our names, supposing our donations entitled us to chances. The monk immediately placed his hand upon the paper with the exclamation,

"No, no, sir! You aren't dead! You don't understand. I don't want your names. These are the names of persons who have died without confession and whose souls are in purgatory. We solicit donations from christian sympathizers, and when we get a sufficient amount subscribed to pay for mass for the release of one, these names are placed in a box, and it is decided by lot which soul shall have the benefit of the first mass."

The explanation was satisfactory. The monk seated himself and joined us in eating some fruit, and after a pleasant social chat of a half hour or so, left us with many thanks and low bows, inviting Mr. Speyer to visit the institution in the afternoon; which he did and said he had a pleasant and interesting visit.

A day or two after, we were visited by some of the authorities of the city and requested to leave and go to a ranch some distance on our road to San Juan, as they feared if any bad news should come from the seat of war, the populace might become excited, and our interests and perhaps our lives imperiled. At this suggestion we raised camp, and traveled some ten or twelve miles to a ranch where we could obtain pasturage, grain, and provisions for men and animals until the time arrived to proceed to the fair. I think we remained here some six or seven days. And the time drawing near for the opening of the fair, Mr. S. went ahead to hire rooms and secure accommodations for the men and animals during the fair.

The Fair of San Juan de los Lagos [252] was at that time the largest and most important fair in Mexico or on the continent. There must have been from 50,000 to 75,000 people present every day during the fair, and visitors were constantly coming and going. We hoped and expected that the ports being blockaded, goods would be very scarce and command high prices. Mr. S. hired a house sufficiently large for the storage of our goods. And as all sales were made in original packages and sold by samples, we did not require a regularly fitted store. He paid four hundred and seventy-five dollars rent for the house during the fair of twelve or fourteen days, when it was rented for the balance of the year for the nominal rent of twenty-five dollars; the object being to keep the property in order during the year and vacated for rent at fair time, and produce a rent of five hundred dollars a year.

We entered the town on November 27 or 28,[253] and unloaded our goods and prepared for examination by the customs officers. Guards were stationed at the door that day and night, and next day the examining officers came and began work. The laws of Mexico rendered all domestics and prints coarser than a certain number of threads to the square inch, contraband, also many goods of foreign manufacture without distinction of texture or quality – a protective tariff in its broadest sense. The advantage to merchants in attending this fair was that all goods sold there were free from *consumos*, or inter-

---

[252] The Fair of San Juan de los Lagos appears to have had a religious origin. Ever since 1623 pilgrims made annual visits to the town in order to venerate an image of the Virgin Mary. This custom attracted traders. In 1797 Charles IV ordered that the fair be held during the first fifteen days of December. Hubert H. Bancroft, *History of Mexico* (*Works of H. H. Bancroft*, xi, San Francisco, 1883), iii, 640.

[253] Webb arrived in San Juan de los Lagos at least as early as November 26. Webb & Doan, Daybook, 1846-1847, Webb MSS.

state duties, which were one-third the introduction duties, and to us would amount to about as much as we had paid.

This was the place appointed for the meeting of people for the exchange of products of the different sections and states of the republic, as well as of foreign countries. Here we came with about one hundred tons of goods, the products of English and American factories. The English goods [were] transported across the ocean 3,000 miles, thence with the American goods to Independence, Missouri, some 1,200 miles, thence by wagons to the fair about 2,500 miles – in all about 6,700 miles for the English goods and 3,700 miles for the American. We had been on the road from Independence, Missouri, from May 9 to November 27.

About noon on the second day of the examination, labor was suddenly suspended, and Mr. Speyer and the officers left, and we saw no more of them until late at night. Mr. S. returned and reported the situation of affairs. They had examined a bale of one lot of prints which "did not count" – were too coarse in texture and subject to confiscation. Instead of disputing or appealing to higher authority, he invited them out to dinner and wine, and after a liberal indulgence in the refreshments, the subject of compromise was introduced and discussed, and continued amid smoke and wine at intervals until late at night, when terms were agreed upon. The officers were to discontinue further examination and certify to [the] correctness of the manifests and that all the goods were legal in kind and quality, and at the close of the fair they were to receive $1,800 as a consideration.

On December 1 [254] we began selling, and the prices

---

[254] Webb's first sale was made on November 26. *Ibid.*

were such as to justify the hope of a profitable trip. Prints and bleached domestics sold the first day for 28 to 31 cents per *vara* (33 inches), and other goods in proportion. But soon news of fresh arrivals of goods and others on the way depressed the market from day to day, until the last sales were made at 18 to 22 cents.[255] And Mr. S. made a large sale at the close to a gambler from the City of Mexico for pearls, jewelry, and silver ornaments and trinkets, which he had taken in pawn in the way of business.

Trains of pack mules arrived from Monterrey and Tampico (which we had supposed were blockaded by our armies), and from Vera Cruz, Mazatlán, and other seaports – one day 3,000 pack mules from Mazatlán loaded with English dry goods. And about the tenth day of the fair, [there] arrived a German commission merchant from Guadalajara with samples [of goods] from two vessels which had run the blockade at San Blas, and offered to merchants from the large cities at low prices, the goods to be invoiced as sold at the fair and delivered direct to the business place of the purchasers.

About the eighth or ninth day of the fair, the chief customs officer came in for a call and asked how we were getting along, and during the interview advised us that in his opinion it would be well to hurry sales, as it was somewhat uncertain whether the time would be extended till the fourteenth, as had sometimes been done. The legal time of the fair was twelve days, but the military commander appointed by the government

---

[255] Webb sold the following goods at the fair: striped, black, blue, and plaid satinet; brown, and blue cloth; bleached domestics; plaid cashmere; cambric; calico; muslin; prints; *lienzo* [linen cloth]; balzarine; printed lawn; lace; muslin dresses; cotton hose; crêpe shawls; bracelets; buttons; scissors; hooks and eyes; and dress patterns. *Ibid.*

had discretionary power to extend the time two days when he thought it advisable.

About this time my partner arrived from Santa Fé, having recovered from his wound. [He had] traveled to Chihuahua with Dr. Connelly and Francis Macmanus, merchants on their way with trains. But not being allowed to pass by our troops, [they had] left their trains with Colonel Doniphan's command and went ahead to see what the prospects were [for] trade, and the chances of protection or persecution by the authorities in case the troops were defeated or victorious in battle. And [the troops] were afterwards ordered to join General Taylor at Monclova, leaving them [the traders] exposed to the rabble and to the military and civil authorities, on their return. They [Connelly, Doan, and Macmanus] were all taken prisoners. Dr. Connelly being an American, and a Mexican citizen by naturalization, was looked upon with more suspicion, and suspected if not accused of treasonable designs. Mr. Doan said that he was immediately released on his presentation of the Lion and Unicorn (British passport) and allowed to go where he pleased. The others were held as prisoners, in charge of two of the leading citizens of the city, until after the Battle of Sacramento and [when] Colonel Doniphan entered the city.[256]

---

[256] In October, 1846, Connelly, Macmanus, Doan, and Váldez, Santa Fé traders, were taken prisoners by the Mexicans at Paso del Norte. They were immediately taken to Chihuahua, arriving there on October 18. Doan was released on showing his English passport. Though the others were detained for a longer period, they appear to have obtained their freedom some time before the Battle of Sacramento, February 28, 1847. Edwards, A Journal of an Expedition to New Mexico and the Southern Provinces, 1846-1847, MS., Missouri Historical Society; *Daily Missouri Republican*, Dec. 8, 30, 1846, Feb. 19, 1847; *Weekly Reveille*, Jan. 4, 1847.

What a relief to me when I could confer with a partner whose interest was equal with my own, and *we* could transact our business independently and travel through the country under the protection of a neutral and powerful government which afforded ample protection to her citizens wherever their interests called them, and none of whose lawmakers or executors would offer the prayer in [a] legislative assembly that God in wisdom and justice "would grant that the Mexicans might welcome our armies with open arms to hospitable graves."

Mr. Doan assumed control of our interests, under English protection, and I felt much safer from annoyance and persecution than at any time before. I had, it is true, my letter of security. Yet I never used it but on the one occasion, and felt that it was more prudent to abstain unless it appeared absolutely necessary. I had disposed of a good many goods; yet quite an amount remained on hand. And under the recommendation of the customs officer, we thought best to hurry up. So Mr. Doan consulted the representative of an English house [257] in Zacatecas, and he proposed that we should invoice the goods to them as goods sold, and he would take them there and sell them on commission, and he would make returns to us in Chihuahua. We invoiced the goods and marked them with the name of the consignees. And the very next day the officer in charge came in and announced that he had orders to confiscate the goods of all citizens of the United States, and send the proprietors out of the country by way of Mazatlán. Mr. Doan showed his passport, and pointed to the piles of bales and the marks upon them, when he congrat-

---

[257] William Roxburgh. Webb & Doan, Daybook, 1846-1847, Webb MSS.

ulated him on his good luck, and said he had been informed that probably the goods belonged to an American, and he feared he might have an unpleasant duty
to perform.

RETURNING TO CHIHUAHUA

RETURNING TO CHIHUAHUA

We were now compelled to consider the propriety
of a new adventure. We had our teams and did not
know when we would be permitted to leave the country; so [we] concluded to load with Mexican goods and
start home by way of Chihuahua. Our Zacatecas friend
advised us where we could best purchase the goods we
wanted, and we loaded our four wagons with sugar and
piloncillo [258] principally, and a few *rebozos*, [259] shoes,
chocolate, and assorted goods suitable to the Chihuahua
market. There were large stocks of sugar exposed for
sale in the open air on the *loma* (hill) east of the town
and a half mile or so distant from our warehouse. We
bought about ten tons. We could not get to the ground
with our wagons to load, but contracted with a man to
transport it to our wagons by *cargadores*. [260] The sugar
was packed in bales of from one hundred and twenty-
five to one hundred and seventy-five pounds for transportation on mules and donkeys – two bales to the load,
with two hundred and fifty pounds for a donkey, and
three hundred and fifty for a mule, load. . .

While at the fair, a good many Mexican troops
passed through, as we understood on their way to San
Luis Potosí, where Santa Anna was organizing an army
to attack General Taylor. We took our meals at a
restaurant; and one day there were several officers there

[258] A small loaf of unrefined sugar.
[259] Women's shawls.
[260] Carriers.

at dinner, two of whom sat opposite me. After they were through eating and [while] waiting for their coffee, one of them took from his pocket a silver toothpick shaped like a sword sheathed in a scabbard. Unsheathing the sword, he began picking his teeth, when his companion asked him if [he] proposed to use the same weapon for picking his teeth and fighting the gringos.

"Oh yes," he replied, holding it before him. "It is handsome and convenient as a toothpick; and if with the enemy, it will be sufficient as a weapon of attack or defense" – both looking at me as if the conversation was for my especial benefit.

I carefully avoided any demonstration, either by word or look, to lead them to suppose I could understand the conversation. I thought, however, that if they met our army they would have reason to believe they would need more effective weapons and greater skill and courage in the use of them than they had displayed in the past, or they would return in greater haste than they were advancing.

We desired to be safe from the persecutions of the customs officers, and got our friend from Zacatecas to make our *guías* (manifests) ; and not knowing where our troops might be, we took them for Zacatecas, Durango, or Chihuahua, thinking possibly [our] troops might be on the route from the north or from Monclova to Durango, and we would not be permitted to pass to the protection of our armies. Mr. Speyer had sold all his wagons except one, and many of his drivers had consented to go with the wagons; so our train was made up of four wagons and an ambulance of our own, one wagon of Mr. Speyer's, and one of John Devoe. And about the middle of December we started on our return, under the protection of a British passport of Mr. Doan. [We] took our old route through Aguascalientes and Zacatecas. But on reaching the boundary of Durango, we bore east through Juan Pérez and Totonilco to El Gallo, thence to La Zarca and Cerro Gordo, a place approached with dreadful forebodings [on] account of the meanness and dishonesty of the custom-house officers.

We arrived about eleven at night, having made the long drive from La Zarca of forty-five miles; and I asked Mr. Doan to take our *guías* to the custom-house and leave them there for examination. He thought it would be just as well to present them in the morning, as it was so late and probably all [were] in bed, and we were also tired and sleepy. So we lay down and rested till morning. Our *guías* were placed in his trunk at San Juan, and we had no occasion to look at them until we arrived at this place. No officer on the borders of either Zacatecas or Durango had asked to look at them. But we felt perfectly safe that they were all right and that there could be no reason for delay; so we began "catching up," and Mr. Doan went to the custom-house with the papers. The officer said he would look them over, and he could call for them in an hour. Mr. D. remonstrated and said they were all right, and he could assure him that however anxious he might be to find some reason to bleed us, he would find we were beyond his power of persecution. He coolly replied that he could leave them for an hour, and [then] call for them. At the expiration of the time, he went and demanded the *guías*, and was very coolly informed that the time for presenting them in Chihuahua had expired the night before, when, if he had presented

them [to him] and asked [for] an extension of time to
reach Chihuahua, he [the officer] would have been
compelled to have granted it; but the delay had rendered the goods contraband and liable to confiscation.
Mr. Doan examined the papers and found he was correct, and that we were in the hands of an unscrupulous
and unmitigated scoundrel.

Returning to camp, we consulted what it was best
to do, and as there was a Chihuahua lawyer on the road
somewhere, and probably within two or three days'
travel, we concluded to send a man back to meet him
and hurry him up. We "turned out," and sent Old Ramon, our mule herder, on [an] express. And we held
council upon expedients to be tried to release ourselves
from the difficulty. Mr. Doan called several times during the day with several propositions, but all were declined. Expostulation, and appeal for leniency, as our
violation of the law was only technical and not from
any willful evasion, received no consideration, although
met with cold politeness and promise that possibly some
compromise might be effected.

Mr. Doan made a remark (during these anxious
hours of consultation between ourselves) which I shall
never forget, [and] which shows that it is a very important part of a lawyer's education to try projects. He
was educated a lawyer and licensed to practice. I don't
recollect the proposition, but it was one from which I
could see no ground for indulging a hope of its being
accepted; and [I] so expressed myself.

"Well," said he, "I am going to try it on; and if I
fail, there is nothing lost. And if accepted, there is
everything gained."

He tried it on, and failed.

The day passed in great anxiety, with frequent visits by Mr. Doan to the custom-house, but with no ground for the hope of relief. The next morning Mr. Doan was informed that there was one way the matter might be arranged. Mr. D. could pay the *consumos* duties, and he [the officer] would accept the *guías* as all right. And he [Mr. Doan] would [then] get bills from one of the clerks for the same goods, as [having been] bought in Cerro Gordo; and he [the officer] would issue *guías* for presentation in Chihuahua. But this, [he said], would be attended with considerable labor, and of course they [the officials] would be entitled to some *consideración* in the way of money. We concluded to accept the proposition, and Mr. Doan returned to the office and told them to make out the papers and all the necessary entries, and he would go in the afternoon and settle and take the papers and be ready for an early start the next morning.

About four or five o'clock he took a bag of $1,000, as he was told the duties would amount to some seven hundred dollars which he would [have to] pay, leaving about three hundred dollars for [a] consideration. On calling for the *guías*, he found the duties amounted to about seven hundred and fifty dollars, and inquired what the amount of consideration would be.

"In view of the labor and responsibility we take," [replied the officials], "we think $1,000 is as little as we can accept."

"Then I am to understand that your demand is seven hundred and fifty dollars [for] duties and $1,000 [for a] consideration, making $1,750 you require me to pay?"

"That is the amount, sir."

Mr. D. took the bag of money in his hand, bade them good afternoon, and bowed himself out of the door. We were still on the anxious seat, and could see no way but to wait for the arrival of the lawyer to turn up something to help us out.

The next morning, a little after breakfast, one of our men beckoned me to one side. And walking behind a wagon, and looking around to be sure that no person was within hearing, [he] drew a paper from his pocket and handed [it to] me, saying that the gentleman who claimed the two mules as we went down, Don Juan Sánchez, called him into his store and told him to hand this paper to us. And [Sánchez said] that it was the form of an appeal to him [Sánchez], who was the judge before whom the case would be tried if it came to trial; but [declared] that our first step would be to go to the custom-house and make tender of the amount of duties and demand the *guías*. He was very sure he [the officer] would not dare refuse them, but if he did we must get a sheet of paper like the sample, and copy the writing verbatim and present it to him [Sánchez], and he would see us out. The officer spent the evening with him [Sánchez] the night before, and bragged a good deal about having the gringos in his power, and [declared] he was going to skin them. The duties they must pay, [said Sánchez], but not a cent for consideration unless they chose; and from his [the officer's] treatment of them he was not entitled to any.

Mr. Doan immediately went and demanded the *guías*, which were handed him; and then the boot was changed, and they became the suppliants. After "catching up," we gave them one hundred dollars, with the understanding that it was a present.[261] We gave the

---

[261] Webb made the following entry in his daybook: "Paid cash for duties

order to drive out, went on our way without further molestation from the customs officers, and that night camped within the boundaries of the state of Chihuahua.

Mr. Speyer did not travel with us on our return, but spent some days in Zacatecas and Durango on [the] way back, and returned at his leisure. We took the road direct to Chihuahua and arrived without adventure at the Plaza de Toros, the usual camping ground.[262] [We] presented our *guías* at the custom-house and proceeded direct to a store we had rented on the public square west of the main plaza, the name of which I have forgotten.

After we had unloaded, and while our teams were yet standing in front of the store, a Mexican came in and inquired if I was Don Santiago. Receiving an affirmative answer, he said the prefect ordered me to proceed to his office immediately. On my arrival, the prefect was in his judicial seat, and inquired in a very authoritative tone if I was Don Santiago. To my reply that I was, he responded:

"You are fined ten dollars."

"What for?" said I.

"Your teams on entering the city took a street not open to public travel by wagons, and crossed the *acequia* at a forbidden point and soiled the water so it was unfit for drinking."

To my protest that I had done it ignorantly, and that the offense should not be repeated, he ordered me to pay the money without further words, and leave. I paid the money and left.

on goods in Cerro Gordo and bribes to custom-house officers, three hundred and twenty-five dollars." Webb & Doan, Daybook, 1846-1847, Webb MSS.

[262] Webb arrived in the city of Chihuahua early in February, 1847. *Ibid.*

On returning to the store, I found the wagons had returned to the camp, and being busy in arranging the goods and preparing to settle down for a while, I made no inquiries of their route of return. In a short time the former messenger entered and inquired if I was Don Santiago. On my reply that I was, he ordered me to appear at the prefect's office immediately. I went, and on entering, the former inquiry was repeated, the same response given, and the same fine imposed. The reason assigned was that the teams had returned by the same route they entered, contaminating the water [and] making it unfit for drinking purposes. I paid the fine without protest, and left the court.

The next day the messenger again entered and inquired if I was Don Santiago. An affirmative response elicited the third order to appear at the prefect's office. On entering court, the former inquiries were repeated, the same reply made, and a fine of twenty dollars imposed. The reason assigned for the fine was that I had failed to report myself at the prefect's court, as required by law, within twenty-four hours of my arrival in the city. I informed the court that I had twice appeared in court within the last twenty-four hours, and [had] twice been fined ten dollars, and I thought the court [should] accept them as a sufficient compliance with the law and remit the fine.

The response of the court was, "Shut your mouth and pay the money."

While this was going on, Mr. Doan appeared in response to a similar summons, and was ordered to pay the same amount of fine. He showed his English passport and requested the privilege of sending for Mr. John Potts, the director of the mint (whose acquaintance he had made while in the city on his way to the fair), to explain matters and use his influence for the remission of the fines. Permission was granted; and Mr. Potts soon appeared and explained that it was through ignorance of the law and not from any wish to defy or evade it, that we had failed to report, and he hoped, as a personal favor to him, the court would consider the case with clemency and remit the fines. He finally concluded, in consideration of Mr. Doan's being an English subject and fellow countryman of Mr. Potts, [that] he would reduce his fine to the nominal sum of five dollars; but that the American gringo should pay the full amount. We paid the fines and left the court.

American citizens had been subject to these and like abuses for many years. Our consul in Santa Fé, Don Manuel Álvarez, had been insulted, abused, and his life threatened, in his official capacity and office, several years previous.[263] And all over the republic an American passport simply exposed the holder to abuse and insult, while an English, French, or German passport was respected, and guaranteed to the holder the protection of the State and National governments whenever presented. Dr. Connelly and Mr. Macmanus entered Chihuahua from New Mexico at the same time with Mr. Doan. They were taken prisoners, subjected to much trouble and abuse, and compelled to submit to being placed in the custody of two citizens of the city, while Mr. Doan was released and permitted to travel wherever he pleased on presenting his passport with the seal of the Lion and the Unicorn. I myself kept my American passport secreted in the bottom of my trunk, and traveled as assistant wagon master, with myself and

[263] In 1841. See Read, *Illustrated History of New Mexico*, 400.

goods under the protection of a Prussian passport held by Mr. Albert Speyer, a Prussian Jew. It may well be argued, in justification of the Mexican government, that it was in time of war between the two nations. . .

After remaining some days in Chihuahua, and the governor declining to permit us to leave the country, we began to look around for occupation for our men and teams [in order] to pay expenses. We heard of a lot of cotton in San Pablo (below Chihuahua) which the owner desired freighted to Querétaro, and made arrangements to freight five loads – our four wagons, and John Devoe with his one. I remained in Chihuahua to dispose of the goods brought from the fair; and Mr. Doan, our Englishman, [was] to take the freight to the low country, and purchase goods likely to pay freight to a northern market.

The cotton was packed in large sacks, but the only means of compression was by the stamping in of a man. The freight was very bulky, and they could not load full loads in weight. And a load of four thousand to forty-five hundred pounds would be as bulky as a load of loose hay with us (of equal weight). The wagon bows were taken off, and the cotton loaded as far over the sides as was safe, and bales packed as compact as possible and bound fast by wet rawhide straps, which, as they dried, would shrink enough to hold the load strong and firm upon the wagon. Great caution was necessary in transporting loads so bulky on the roads of that country, where no repairs had been made in the memory of man, except by the trains as they passed. On sidling places, it took all hands with ropes to hold the wagons from upsetting, and in miry places many expedients became necessary to avoid unloading. On one occasion they put eighteen mules to pull upon the load, and all the spare men on the lower side to lift, and six mules pulling upon the rope thrown over the wagon and tied to the body on the lower side; and by digging to loosen the wheels, and all exerting their utmost strength in lifting, pulling, and yelling, succeeded in getting out without unloading.

The cotton was delivered at Querétaro, and the train proceeded to Guadalajara, where Mexican goods, principally sugar and *rebozos*, returned north in search of a market and a home or place of security and rest. Mr. Doan met with no special adventure or annoyance on the whole trip.

I very soon moved onto the main plaza, into a store (near the church) owned by Padre Terrazas, a brother of Don Juan, the prefect. Several Americans had arrived in the city during our absence, and by keeping themselves pretty closely in their rooms were getting along without much annoyance. News began to arrive of an expedition from New Mexico and marching towards Chihuahua. "Volunteer" companies were formed (by impressment), and Mr. Potts was employed to cast several cannon, and quite a large force of laborers employed to proceed to Sacramento and build defenses against the approach of our army. The priests were holding mass and preaching to the christian population, exhorting them to organize in every possible way to annoy the gringos, *Tejanos*, heretics, and enemies as they approached the city. It was a very exciting time, and the excitement increased daily after our army left El Paso.[264] The priests told the people that the Ameri-

---

[264] The United States troops in command of Colonel Doniphan left Paso del Norte on the evening of February 8, 1847. Hughes, *Doniphan's Expedition*, 317.

can general, to stimulate his soldiers to greater energy and courage, had promised them (in case they won the battle and entered the city) [that] they [would have] one hour to sack the city, one hour to ravish, and one hour to kill.[265]

It was soon known that our people, including soldiers, teamsters connected with the army, and men belonging to the merchants' trains (Connelly, Owens and Aull, and Macmanus), numbered less than 1,000 [266] men in all. The artillery consisted, I think, of six pieces – four twelve-pound howitzers and two small cannon carrying solid ball. The Mexican organized forces consisted of full 3,000 [267] men with ten pieces of artillery protected by defenses which they were two or three weeks in building. The difference in numbers between the two armies was so great that the Americans were at times quite despondent, as in addition to the inducements to defend their people and city from the invaders, they [the Mexican authorities] had promised free appropriation of all the property and goods belonging to the merchants by soldiers or citizens who would be upon the ground ready to avail themselves of the advantages of the expected victory.

Some ten days before the battle an order was issued by Governor Trias sending all Americans to a town sixty or seventy miles south of Chihuahua. But some

[265] See *Daily Missouri Republican*, May 18, 1847.

[266] "Our force was nine hundred and twenty-four effective men, at least one hundred of whom were engaged in holding horses and driving teams," wrote Colonel Doniphan, March 4, 1847. Hughes, *Doniphan's Expedition*, 317. This number did not include the battalion of one hundred and fifty Santa Fé traders and their teamsters in command of Major Samuel C. Owens, only a few of whom participated in the battle.

[267] Colonel Doniphan estimated that the Mexican forces consisted of about 4,000 men, though the Mexicans represented their numbers as considerably less. *Ibid.*, 320; *Daily Missouri Republican*, Apr. 19, 1847.

ten of us succeeded in escaping from the execution of the order. We kept ourselves pretty close for some time, but I think they were not very earnest in the search for all of us. But some fifteen or twenty were marched off on foot and were not seen until after the battle, when they returned to the city.

Mr. Potts and his brother asked several of us to take refuge in the mint when the battle occurred, as most of [the] citizens and officers would go out to the battle-ground either to witness the battle or [to] participate in the scramble for the spoils, and it was uncertain what the feeling might be at its close. They might attack us in our quarters either in revenge for defeat or to complete their triumph by exterminating all of the gringos they could lay their hands on. Another motive was for the protection of the mint. All the prisoners in the jails had been set free and might take a notion to sack the mint. We took all our arms there and prepared a large quantity of ammunition, and they were placed on top of the building; and ladders [were] provided so we could ascend at the first alarm to a position commanding the entrance. A few could defend themselves against greatly superior numbers. If driven from that position, we could retreat to a second, taking our arms with us. And we had other weapons of defense provided in the shape of several leaden tubs filled with acid and provided with dippers for throwing the acid, if our ammunition gave out or we had no time for reloading. The report of the first cannon from the battleground was to be the signal for making all haste to the rendezvous.

We were in suspense for a day or so after [we had] news of our troops near the battleground – the time occupied in reconnoitering the position and defenses of the Mexicans and [in] disposing of the merchants' and quartermaster's trains in such [a] manner as they could best defend themselves from attack and not require too many of the small force of soldiers for protection. About 11 A. M. Mr. Anderson knocked at my door and asked why I was not at the rendezvous.

"I have heard no guns," [I replied].

"They have been firing some time."

We took a by-street and on arrival found all there – six or eight – the two brothers Potts, Francis Macmanus, Alfonso Anderson, George Carter, myself, and, I think, one or two others, but I do not recollect.

The hacienda of Sacramento is some ten or twelve miles [268] north of Chihuahua, and the hacienda and battleground would have been in view of our position but for a small peak or butte a short distance this side. We all went to our position of defense on the building, facing the main entrance to the courtyard, where we also had [a] full view over the plain to the butte near the field of battle. We hoped, and had wrought our courage and confidence to a point that we expected, to see a race between our people and the Mexicans – the latter retreating, and the former pursuing. After some time the firing of cannon ceased, and we excitedly watched for signs of victory by our troops. An hour or so passed, and [there was] no sign of retreat or report of cannon.

"What is the matter?" [we asked]. "Are our people defeated? Or is the battle still waged with small arms?"

Minutes became hours. Hope gave place to doubt, doubt to despond, and despond to despair, and each in

_____

[268] About fourteen or fifteen miles.

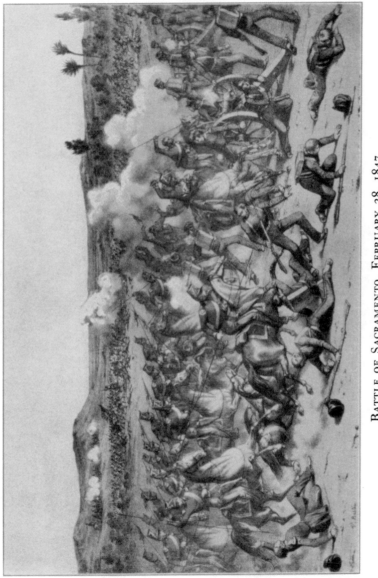

BATTLE OF SACRAMENTO, FEBRUARY 28, 1847
From *Álbum Pintoresco de la República Mexicana*, Mexico, *circa* 1850

turn becoming possessed by one or the other of these emotions. Macmanus was very hopeful and I think held out the longest of any of us, but he at last broke down, and walking back and forth on the roof, wrapped in his cloth Spanish cloak, his hat drawn over his eyes, his head bowed, a complete picture of despair, finally expressed his feelings as follows:

"Have I got to live to see the day when I shall see the women – prostitutes of this town – walking the streets, dressed in goods from my wagons after all the risk and anxiety I have had to get this far? And *de locos* [269] – for nothing! I hope the boys will set every wagon on fire first." Again: "Hark! Did you hear a cannon? No, nothing." Again: "Look! Do you see anyone coming? No, there's no one on the road." Again: "Do you think we've lost, and they're pillaging the wagons? I don't think anything – I don't know what to think." Bang! Bang! Bang! – Macmanus jumping at least three feet from the ground. Bang! Bang! Bang! "Do you hear that? *I tell you*, they're giving them hell now! Hurah-h-h!"

Mr. Potts [warned]: "Keep cool, Mac. They'll hear you on the street, and you may raise a row."

The emotions of such a moment – can anyone realize them who has not felt them?

The firing after a time ceased, but it was dark before we got news from the battleground. At length we heard the rattling of hoofs at a running gate on the pavement down the street and nearing our position, and while passing, the rider was accosted by a man on the sidewalk with the inquiry:

"*Qué novedades?*" (What news?).

[269] Foolishly.

"*Ya perdimos!*" (We've lost!)[270]

Macmanus' tone was changed: "I knew it. I'll bet a hundred – yes, I'll bet five hundred – dollars we've not lost forty – thirty – twenty men. Yes, I'll bet a hundred dollars we've not lost ten men! Pshaw! I don't believe we've lost five men. These people can't shoot anyhow."

We could distinguish the reports of our cannon from those of the enemy (even at that distance) with much certainty. The reports were as different as those of a rifle and musket, owing to the difference in the powder. Our guns gave a sharp short report, not so deep and prolonged as those of the enemy.

About seven o'clock the Mexicans began to come into town in large numbers and prepare for their departure south, and great was the excitement (relating incidents of the battle and hairbreadth escapes) and anxiety to get out of the city with their families before the heretic gringos arrived and began the promised indulgence in their propensities "*de saquear, de florear y matar.*" There was little if any sleep for either Mexicans or Americans that night.

The next morning as soon as it was light I went onto the plaza, and such excitement and wailing I never before witnessed and hope never to see again. The plaza was filled with women and children (but few men) with bundles of clothes, blankets, etc., upon their

[270] General José Heredia, commander of the Mexican forces, attributed his defeat to the following causes: "The disasters of the battle . . . are owing to the greater part of my forces being raw recruits, to its being the first time of their meeting an enemy, and to the inexperience of most of the officers, who, deficient in that military energy so necessary in such emergencies, could not control their men in the moment of danger, and such is generally the case when a hastily collected mass of men have no regular troops to support them." *El Republicano*, Mar. 22, 1847, in *Daily Missouri Republican*, Apr. 19, 1847.

backs, and those who could raise a donkey or any other animal capable of bearing the least burden, had them packed. And all were excitedly discussing what they should do or where they should go to escape violence, which the priests had told them they must expect from our soldiers. Many whom I knew came to me for advice.

"Will your people be so brutal," [they asked], "as to abuse poor and helpless women and children?"

I advised them to go to their homes, put their houses in order, and be assured that they would be as safe from persecution and violence from the Americans as they would from their own people. A good many returned to their homes, not in confidence I think, but not knowing how they could do better. Many fled to the plains and hills surrounding the city, where they underwent extreme suffering, and a good many perished from hunger and exposure. Those who remained kept themselves in their houses for several days, and it was seldom they appeared on the streets for a week or so.

But by little and little, confidence was restored, and the city was more lively with business and *fandangos* than ever before. In the afternoon the army marched into the city and took possession. Our flag floated in triumph at the head of the army (or regiment) and was raised upon the flagstaff on the plaza, and we felt grateful assurance that we were again free. The banished Americans returned to town [and] opened their places of business. Macmanus and Dr. Connelly opened their stores and began distributing their goods for cash value instead of seeing them flouted on the streets "*de locos.*"

Colonel Doniphan sent couriers to General Taylor at

Saltillo with his report, and asking instructions what to do. His men were enlisted for one year, and the term of their enlistment was drawing to a close, and they had been paid but once or twice.

Notwithstanding I was no longer a prisoner, I was still dancing in doubt between the frying pan and the fire. My whole interests [were] within the Mexican lines, and although under the protection of the English government through the passport of Mr. Doan, it was very uncertain whether he would be permitted to come to Chihuahua while occupied by our troops. And if they should be ordered away, and he be permitted to return, would we be able to proceed to New Mexico and thence home? We owed about $15,000 on a capital of about $3,000, and the risk and expenses, with interest accumulating against us, kept me in almost overwhelming anxiety. So great was it that, although more than forty years have passed, all the circumstances and incidents of the time are as vivid as at the time. . .

Colonel Samuel C. Owens, the friend of the traders, the outfitter who would trust us for wagons, teams, provisions, and all the necessary outfit for the trip, who trusted and advised us as if we were his children, and whom we respected as our most trusted friend, was killed in the battle. One of his men told me that he shaved and dressed himself with care, saying he did not know what might happen. If killed in the battle, he wanted to be clean shaved and fitly dressed. He [one of his men] thought that owing to family troubles, he [Owens] courted death, as he told him he "knew of no more honorable or desirable death than to die in battle." Colonel Owens and [Henry] Skillman, an old plainsman, led the charge of the dragoons upon the Mexican redoubts, and getting as the commander thought too far in the advance, they were ordered to halt. Skillman, looking back, saw the dragoons halted [and] returned and joined them, but Colonel Owens kept on, charged a redoubt alone, and with his pistol fired on the Mexicans, who returned the fire, killing the Colonel's horse, which fell on him. And the Mexicans left their defenses and killed and stripped him of his valuables, and returned and got ready to run at the next charge of our troops. The body was found not a rod from the embankment thrown up for defense.[271]

A day or two after the troops entered Chihuahua, the Lieutenant-colonel under Doniphan asked me about Mr. Speyer – what he did with the arms and ammunition he brought in, and also about his treatment of his men at Río Florido. I explained matters as well as I could, and after listening for some time he interrupted me with the remark,

"Well, if you and his other friends can give any evidence to clear him of what he is accused, all right. If not, we shall hang him in a day or two."

Mr. S. kept "open house" and entertained liberally. Whist parties with wine were held every night in his rooms, and many articles of bric-a-brac which he had bought at the fair, such as silver bridle reins, silver fans, and other Mexican curiosities, disappeared from his shelves. And after a couple of weeks he was tried before a court-martial and honorably acquitted.[272] Who was

---

271 Colonel Doniphan described Owens's death as follows: "Col. Samuel C. Owens lost his life by excessive bravery or rather rashness. He rode up to a redoubt filled with armed men, and continued to fire his pistols into it until himself and his horse fell pierced with balls upon its very brink." *Daily Missouri Republican*, June 18, 1847. Owens was buried in Chihuahua. *Ibid.*, May 19, 1847.

272 On May 18, 1847, the *Daily Missouri Republican* printed the following

hung? And did the silver bridle reins serve as the rope?

I must say here that in this threat and in all the conversation, reports of entertainments, or presents, the name of Colonel Doniphan [273] was never mentioned in any manner which would compromise his honor as an officer or his dignity as a man. And Mr. Speyer, in his course with the arms and ammunition and in the treatment of his men at Río Florido, simply followed the course of an enterprising merchant and yielded to what was thought by all for the best interest of his men. For the Americans to divide, was thought by all to be the best course, in order to avoid suspicion and further arrest and persecution.

Colonel Owens was interested in this commercial adventure with a gentleman named Aull [274] from Lex-

news item: "From one of our private letters we learn, that Mr. Speyer, whose hasty journey across the plain to Santa Fé, last spring, excited so much curiosity, was met at Chihuahua, and arrested by Col. Mitchell. It turns out, that Speyer was innocent of any crime. He had six kegs of powder when he left Independence, and sixty muskets, which the Mexicans took from him. Speyer knew he was pursued, but hastened forward to make some $80,000, by being the first in market with his goods."

[273] Alexander W. Doniphan was born in Mason county, Kentucky, July 9, 1808. Migrating to Missouri in 1830, he settled at Lexington, where he began the practice of law. Three years later he removed to Liberty, Missouri. On June 18, 1846, he was elected Colonel of the First regiment of Missouri Mounted volunteers, which formed a part of the "Army of the West" under the command of Colonel Stephen W. Kearny. On the following September 23, about a month after the capture of Santa Fé, Kearny ordered Doniphan to proceed from New Mexico to Chihuahua and report to Brigadier-general Wool. After fighting the battles of Brazito and Sacramento, Doniphan returned to Missouri, arriving there in the summer of 1847. He died at Richmond, Missouri, August 8, 1887. Alexander W. Doniphan, Autobiography, MS., Missouri Historical Society; Hughes, *Doniphan's Expedition*; Connelley, *Doniphan's Expedition*.

[274] James Aull, one of the leading merchants in western Missouri, was born in Newcastle, Delaware, about 1805. In the twenties he removed to Missouri, where he established general stores at Lexington, Independence, Liberty, and Richmond. Residing at Lexington and entrusting the management of his other establishments to competent assistants, he carried on a

ington, Missouri, under the firm name of Owens and Aull. Mr. Aull opened a store and commenced business, but sold goods slowly, as there were a good many who wished to close out and leave as soon as possible. Trade was limited to Chihuahua and a few near-by settlements. The merchants all were anxious to force sales, the troops were waiting anxiously for orders from General Taylor what to do, and all was anxiety and uncertainty for some time.

At length Squire Collins, the messenger sent to General Taylor, returned with orders to abandon Chihuahua and march to Monterrey as soon as it could be done and afford a limited time for the traders to protect their interests. Connelly and Glasgow, Macmanus, and Mr. Aull concluded to take their chances and await the return of the Mexican authorities. Solomon Houck, C. C. Branham, and others decided to sell at almost any sacrifice and return to "the States" via Santa Fé; and all the Americans who could do so, agreed to join them. I could only wait in suspense and see whether my partner, Mr. Doan, would turn up, and when.

There was a capitalist in Chihuahua who was always ready to avail himself of a bargain, with cash in hand for almost any amount. This was Don José Cordero. On the announcement of the day set for the departure of the troops, Mr. Branham and others went to him and

profitable trade until 1831, when he enlarged his business by joining with his brother, Robert, to found the house of J. & R. Aull. Though this firm closed its doors in 1836, James Aull continued in business in Lexington until the outbreak of the Mexican war. He then formed a partnership with Samuel C. Owens and engaged in the Santa Fé trade. On June 23, 1847, after transacting business in Chihuahua for over three months, Aull was murdered in his store by four Mexicans. He was buried in Chihuahua. "Letters of James and Robert Aull" (Bieber, ed.), Missouri Historical Society, *Collections*, v, 268-270, 296.

accepted his first offer, which was fairly liberal under the circumstances; but Mr. Houck, the old trader who considered himself the smartest of all, declined. A couple of days after, he concluded to accept the offer, but Mr. Cordero offered enough less to make the difference about $1,000, which was declined. The following day he went to accept the offer of the day previous, but was told that the offer was only good for the day, and he could now offer only so much, which was about $1,500 less than the day previous. The offer was accepted, and Mr. Houck was out about $2,500 by his smartness.

HOMEWARD BOUND

HOMEWARD BOUND

In two or three days Houck and others, some thirty
or forty in number, marched north by way of Corralitos
and the copper mines (now Arizona) to Socorro, in
order to avoid going through El Paso. The troops
marched south, several Americans – Magoffin, Speyer,
Messervy, and several others – going with them, leaving me still in suspense.

In about a week Mr. Doan arrived in town, greatly
to the satisfaction of both of us. [He] had made the
round trip without accident or interruption, and had a
good stock of Mexican goods to dispose of. After consultation we decided to take them to New Mexico for
a market; and as the goods consigned to Zacatecas were
yet unsold, Mr. D. would remain in Chihuahua, and I
would take the train in charge and proceed on my
return to the U.S. Mr. Aull was also desirous that he
should remain and assist him in the disposal of his
stock. I think the wagons only remained one day in
Chihuahua and were started off in charge of John
Devoe, who had one wagon, making five wagons in all
and about ten or twelve men. I decided to take the
direct route through El Paso, and if necessary we all
resolved to stand by each other to the last, hoping that
the presence of our troops in New Mexico and the possibility of the retaking of Chihuahua from the south
would deter the authorities from any measures of detention or outrage.

Our teams were strong, and we fed [them] grain

whenever it could be obtained, and made good time to El Paso. [We] camped for the night at the usual camping ground south of the town. In the morning while at breakfast, my mule boy, Antonio, came and informed me that there was a man among the mules with a lot of branding irons and claimed two or three mules. I requested him to come to the camp fire, when I recognized our old acquaintance of the year before and asked him if he expected we would submit to the same treatment as last year. He replied that his brands fitted the brands on the mules and there was no *venta*, or sale brand.

"My friend," [I said] "just look across the river. Do you see those hills? They are, or soon will be, in the U.S. – and even El Paso may be – and you had better look out. We shall not give up the mules without a fight. Tell your officers that if they must have the mules, to prepare to fight for them. We shall, as soon as through breakfast, 'catch up' and proceed on our journey and go directly through El Paso without stopping, unless the attempt is made by the authorities to detain us, when we shall defend ourselves to the last man. Boys, see that your guns are in order and plenty of ammunition in your shot pouches."

He rode off, and the word was soon given to "catch up," and we passed through the town without molestation or annoyance and crossed the river.

My journey to Doña Ana and through the *jornada* was made in good time and without adventure or accident, except when some six or seven miles from Fray Cristóbal. And about ten o'clock at night, word was passed to the lead wagon: "Hold on!"

"What is the matter?"

"Tire run off."

We stopped, took off the wheel, wedged on the tire, and in less than half an hour word was given to go ahead. [We] arrived at Fray Cristóbal and camped for the night. [We] rested a part of the next day and proceeded to Valverde and camped for the night. The night was chilly – dark and cloudy with some sleet. I called Don Juan (Devoe) on guard, and he answered promptly, rose from his bed, took up his gun, wrapped himself in his blanket, and with several grunts and groans followed me to the herd. When I was about to leave, he relieved himself as follows:

"Dese dam Ingens! Dey make me loose a heap sleep."

The time, associations, and dangers surrounding this camp, with [the] mode of expression of this old Frenchman, who never shirked any responsibility or failed in the performance of any known duty, left an impression never to be forgotten. And after a lapse of more than forty years and many experiences of a far more exciting character, I can repeat his exclamation in full sympathy with him.

Here the Navajo Indians ran off one hundred and fifty mules from Mr. Speyer in 1844, and in 1846 a large number from Colonel Doniphan, which led to his delaying his trip to Chihuahua for a time and following them to their country to show them that they could not with impunity depredate on the Americans. Here many depredations and murders have been committed by not only the Navajo, but by the Gila and Mescalero Apache.

This was formerly the headquarters of Don Pedro Armendariz, the former proprietor of the Armendariz Grant. I became acquainted with him while in Chihuahua, and he told me he once made the attempt to occupy it, but the Indians were [so] bad (or perhaps, according [to] the present morbid sentimentality, he was so bad and the Indians so good) that he had to abandon it. Lately it has fallen into the possession of a syndicate, which, for the purpose of advancing civilization and christianity, is about asking a national appropriation for a canal a hundred miles or more long to carry the water from the Río Grande for irrigating and other purposes for the public good, and of course governed by no selfish or personal motives.

We traveled up the Río Grande valley as rapidly as possible for two reasons: in order that we might overtake the company of Houck and Branham, and because the feed was scarce and high, and we were anxious to get rid of our loads and onto the prairie before our animals gave out. I went to Santa Fé in advance of the train and sold our goods, and arranged with Houck's company to overtake them at the Moro river and travel with them to "the States." Here, for once during the trip, we were in luck. No trains could be expected from "the States" for a month or more, and sugar was nearly exhausted from the market. I sold out the first day of my arrival at forty cents a pound, and the Mexican goods, *rebozos*, etc., at a fair profit. The profits on this adventure were sufficient to cover all losses accruing previously, and afforded a small profit on the trip.

It now seems a long way to wagon goods from Guadalajara, Mexico, to Santa Fé in New Mexico, nearly or quite 1,800 miles, and make a profit on them. But that was forty-two years ago, and then there was no railroad or telegraph west of the Mississippi river; and today – well, look at the maps.

When the wagons arrived in Santa Fé, the teams were much exhausted; but we unloaded and sent them forward with but a day's delay. And [we were] unable to procure grain of any kind in Santa Fé, and were assured that we could get no corn or grass till we reached San Miguel, fifty miles [distant]. I overtook the wagons at old Pecos, twenty-five miles [away], and found the teams used up.[275] Several mules [had been] left behind, unable to travel, and the last half day's travel [they] had to change some mules in the teams every mile or so. I had engaged to haul the baggage and provisions for some twenty-five or thirty volunteer dragoons [276] whose time was about expired, and they were going to "the States" to be discharged. And as we had the assurance that all the Indians on our route had "concluded to unite and avenge their wrongs!" we were glad to take some risk of delay through the mountains in order that we might have a stronger force for the protection of our property and scalps in case the much abused Comanche might want them for their personal benefit. . .

From the report of the men and the condition of the stock, I became satisfied that something must be done to get feed for the mules, or many would be lost, and we would be unable to overtake Houck. I went forward about six miles to a ranch (some distance from the road) owned by Señor Ulibarri, and bought about twelve bushels of corn at five dollars per bushel and hired him to pack it to camp. This enabled us to get to Ojo Pajarito (Bird spring), where we sent the mules into the valley for water. They drank freely, but many were so weak they were unable to ascend the hill to

[275] Webb left Santa Fé about June 13, 1847. *Weekly Reveille*, July 19, 1847.
[276] The Laclede Rangers, of St. Louis. *Daily Missouri Republican*, July 19, 1847.

camp, and we were obliged to assist them by having a man walk [on] each side and hold them up while a rope was thrown around their hams, and two men taking hold of each end of the rope would pull them up. A second feed of corn was given them, and they were turned into the *bosque* [277] to pick up what they could find in the way of grass, sprouts, etc. The next morning one was missing, and after quite a search he was found dead in a bunch of brush and nearly eaten up by wolves – not more than a dozen rods from camp. It was asserted by many that if the carcasses of dead animals within four rods of the road were placed in a line, head and tail to meet, it would form a complete line to San José, about forty-five miles from Santa Fé. My opinion was that it was not an extravagant estimate.

Arriving at San José, we got all the men we could, out cutting willows (which were just coming in leaf) and bringing them to camp for the mules. And I saw an old pile of straw (which had lain on the ground all winter) which was brought and fed to the mules before giving them their corn (which was all fed out before leaving for San Miguel, where we secured corn and straw for perhaps half a ration), [and] which, with what we secured at Tecolote and Las Vegas, carried us comfortably to the prairie.

This experience shows the difference between horses and mules for teaming over the arid prairies or mountain regions of the West. Horses require the best of forage and plenty of it, with a long rest, while mules will do good work on short rations and [with] much less time for rest; and when brought to good rations, [the mules] will in a day or two recuperate to the performance of full labor.

[277] Grove.

We found our friends waiting for us at the Río Moro, where we organized by voting Solomon Houck as captain, with the soldiers forming a front and rear guard, and several of the best mounted among us as scouts.[278] I think the first train we met was on the Cimarrón river. They had been much annoyed by the Indians and cautioned us to keep a good lookout, as they [the Indians] were in large numbers and unusually daring. From this [point] on, we met many trains, not one until we passed the Big Bend of [the] Arkansas but what had been attacked, and nearly all had lost one or more men.

Before reaching the Arkansas, we met F. X. Aubry,[279] who warned us of the danger from Indians. He said he had one man killed a few rods ahead of the train. The man was walking along, not apprehending any danger, when an Indian shot an arrow from his ambush in the grass, ran and lanced and scalped him, and escaped before his men could recover from their surprise sufficient to shoot – and this within gunshot of the train. With him were two men (one of whom had crossed the plains as driver for me the year before), who, in attempting to overtake a train in advance of them, were

278 The company consisted of eight wagons, about seventy men, and a number of loose mules. *Weekly Reveille*, July 19, 1847; *Missouri Statesman*, July 23, 1847.

279 François Xavier Aubry, a native of Maskinongé, Canada, was a Santa Fé trader, an explorer, and the fastest long-distance rider the frontier ever produced. His quickest trip on horseback was performed in September, 1848, when he rode about seven hundred and eighty miles over the Santa Fé trail from Santa Fé to Independence in five days and sixteen hours. This record was never equalled or excelled. He was nicknamed "Skimmer of the Plains." On August 18, 1854, after returning to Santa Fé from one of his journeys, he engaged in an argument with Richard H. Weightman, who, in self-defense, stabbed Aubry to death with a bowie knife. *Daily Missouri Republican*, Sept. 10, 1854; "Letters of William Carr Lane, 1852-1854" (Bieber, ed.), *New Mexico Historical Review*, vi, 190.

surprised by Indians and succeeded in getting into Fort Mann [280] and defended themselves for nearly two days until Aubry came up and released them. The Indians could have killed them, but not without the loss of at least an equal number of lives, and there was not sufficient booty (aside from the scalps) to justify the risk. . .

Every train we met, we were warned to look out for the Indian on a white horse. And after crossing the Arkansas, [we] were more cautious in keeping well together, and [had] scouts far enough in advance to give the train sufficient time to corral and secure the animals and form in line for defense. We were all, of course, under considerable excitement and constant apprehension, and often we would discover something to arouse our suspicions, and frequently result in ludicrous mistakes.

While traveling down the river between the crossing and the point of leaving to take the Coon creek route, the scouts (Captain Houck, Lieutenant Elliott,[281] and myself) discovered a suspicious object in the far distance and stopped to ascertain its character. It was a white object with something black upon it, and as we were constantly on the lookout for the "man on a white horse," we felt it to be of the greatest importance to be

[280] Fort Mann was situated near the north bank of the Arkansas river a short distance west of the present Dodge City, Kansas. It was built by Captain Daniel Mann in the spring of 1847, because, according to Garrard, "a station, equidistant from Fort Leavenworth and Santa Fé, was needed by the government, at which to repair the wagons and recruit the animals, by rest, in safety." Garrard, *Wah-To-Yah*, 296-297. See also Philip G. Ferguson, Diary, Aug. 3, 1847, MS., Missouri Historical Society.

[281] Richard S. Elliott was born in Lewistown, Pennsylvania, July 10, 1817. In the forties he moved to St. Louis, where he practiced law. At the outbreak of the Mexican war he enlisted in the company of volunteers known as the Laclede Rangers. Elliott, *Notes Taken in Sixty Years*, 2, 7, 214, 216-220.

assured of its character. The wind was blowing quite fresh, and the dazzling rays of the sun over a slightly depressed surface in the prairie rendered it difficult to decide whether it was large or small, [and] far or near in distance. We examined the object with the naked eye and the spyglass, and for some time were unable to decide its character. At length, on a second or third look through the glass, I thought I had got a sufficiently accurate view to give a decided opinion, and closing up my spyglass and putting it in the case, with perfect assurance and decision, said,

"It's a man on a white horse, or I'm a liar."

My comrades thought the same, but could not hold the instrument sufficiently steady on account of the wind to become fully convinced. At this moment a raven rose from the white object, and we were all convinced that our man on a white horse was only a raven on a buffalo skull, and not over forty or fifty rods off. The joke was a good one and frequently told at my expense. [282] But anyone who has traveled over the plains will admit that it is a mistake easily made, and that one

---

[282] One of Webb's companions sent an account of this incident to the St. Louis *Weekly Reveille*, which published it on July 26, 1847: "By the way, I had almost forgotten one of our adventures on the way. On the second day out from the crossing of the Arkansas, all on the look-out, of course, one of the gentlemen owners of the train saw some objects in the plain rather suspicious in appearance. Men they certainly were, one mounted, the other on foot. He drew a spy-glass on them for a moment – it was enough: 'A man on a white horse, or I'm a liar!' he exclaimed, and galloped off towards them for a closer view. The glass was soon levelled again, and after a long, steady view, the glass was lowered. As it came down the 'man' rose up, accompanied by his companion, and off they 'flew.' The white horse remained quietly in the prairie. The two men were two *crows* – one sitting on an old buffalo head, the other on the ground. An old buffalo head, so white as you know it to be, passes very well for a white horse on the plains; but if you think we hadn't a good joke on the gentleman owner, I advise you not to back your opinion with a wager! I won't tell his name now, as we expect him to come down handsomely on the way to St. Louis."

is liable to overestimate, as well as to underestimate, distance.

While crossing a hill, or break, in going down the river, we saw in the bottom on the other side, a horse, but could see no person about, or anything to indicate whether it was a wild or a stray horse. Again the spy-glass was used, and a close examination convinced us that it was an American horse and picketed. The conclusion we came to was that it was a horse stolen from some train and was picketed there to induce some of us to cross the river to obtain a prize, and instead to lose our hair and whatever other property we might carry with us which a good Comanche would value. As the train drove up, several of the boys saw the horse and claimed him by right of discovery, under the rule of the prairie that to the first discoverer and claimant belongs the property. They all saw the trap, but as we were in a hurry and not spoiling for a fight, [they] decided not to cross either individually or in force.

The next day about ten o'clock, while traveling by way of the cut-off or dry route, we saw two men approaching from the river bottom and soon discovered that they were Americans, and one of them in army dress. They proved to be Lieutenant Love,[283] of the army, and Old Fitzpatrick,[284] an old mountaineer and

---

[283] John Love was born in Virginia. Upon graduation from the United States Military academy in 1841, he was promoted in the army to brevet second lieutenant in the First regiment of dragoons. He served at the frontier posts of Fort Gibson, Fort Scott, and Fort Leavenworth, and in 1845 accompanied Colonel Kearny on his expedition to the South pass. On June 30, 1846, he was commissioned first lieutenant. During the Mexican war he engaged in the Battle of Santa Cruz de Rosales, March 16, 1848. He died on January 29, 1881. George W. Cullum, *Biographical Register of the Officers and Graduates of the U. S. Military Academy, at West Point, N. Y.* (New York, 1868), ii, 13; Heitman, *Historical Register and Dictionary of the United States Army*, i, 643.

[284] Thomas Fitzpatrick was one of the most famous trappers and guides

trapper who was traveling with the lieutenant as guide and scout. They informed us that the caravan consisted of three government trains of about twenty-five wagons each, with a paymaster's outfit with over $100,000 in specie, under escort of two companies of dragoons under [the] command of Lieutenant Love; and that the morning previous the Indians had attacked them and drove off the stock of one train. Traveling with the train was a merchant with two wagons who had lost all his cattle and was unable to move. The officer was unable to render him any assistance. Seeing us passing in, light and with a large number of extra mules, they thought we might make some arrangement to furnish him teams to proceed with the caravan, leaving the teamless train behind until the government could send teams from Fort Leavenworth.

We turned off our road and went to their camp on the river, and found a confused condition of affairs: a trader who was without teams, mourning not only the loss of teams, but unable to get his goods to market, and not only great delay, but bankruptcy in prospect; a government train to be left on the prairie until teams could be sent to move them, which was no great matter

in the Far West. A native of Ireland, he migrated to the United States at the age of sixteen. He was engaged in the fur trade at least by the early twenties, and continued his interest in this business for about twenty years. In the forties he not only led emigrant parties to Oregon, but also guided some of the government expeditions of Frémont, Kearny, and Abert. As trapper and guide, he became well acquainted with the character and wants of the Indians of the Far West. In August, 1846, when the War Department, following the recommendations of Colonel Kearny, created an Indian Agency for the tribes of the Upper Platte and Arkansas, Fitzpatrick was appointed as the first agent. He served the United States government in this capacity until his death, February 7, 1854. *Daily Missouri Republican*, Feb. 13, 1854; LeRoy R. Hafen, "Thomas Fitzpatrick and the First Indian Agency of the Upper Platte and Arkansas," *Mississippi Valley Historical Review*, xv, 374-384.

to the government, but [it was to] the teamsters left on
the prairie for a long and uncertain time and exposed
to be scalped by Indians if they leave the camp to procure fresh meat or cross the river for wood; one or two
of the soldiers killed and several in their tents suffering
from wounds more or less severe, one of them having
been shot through the lungs with an arrow which remained in the body until withdrawn by cutting off the
feathered end and pulling it out. The man was alive
when we left on the night of the day after. So many
Indians appeared across the river that the lieutenant
thought it imprudent to leave the camp without defense, and only sent one company to make the attempt
to recover the stock.

The wagon master of this train told me that before
turning his stock from the corral, he got upon a wagon
wheel and looked over the prairie for a long distance,
as far as he could see up and down the river, and saw
no signs of horses or people, except several of the picket
guards on the hills overlooking the valley. He gave the
order to let the cattle out, and they passed out slowly
and in a string, marching a long distance towards the
hills, when all at once large numbers of Indians sprang
up as if from out of the ground, mounted, yelling,
and with rattles of some kind in their hands and tied
to the tails of their horses. They charged among the
cattle, lancing a few. The immense racket and smell of
the blood so frightened them that none were saved.
After it was all over, he [the wagon master] went out
and found the prints in the grass where the horses and
Indians had lain down during the night, inside the
picket lines, ready to rise and charge at the earliest opportunity.[285]

---

[285] The attack on Lieutenant Love's command occurred at dawn on

We soon began to lay plans to assist the trader (whose name I forget)[286] from Arrow Rock, Missouri, and soon came to the conclusion that we could help him out. A merchant from Taos who had the winter before been broken up in his business, [and who had] saved his [own] life by escaping to the mountains and his money by burying in the ground, [had] asked to join my mess, and [had requested] that I should transport his baggage to "the States" with the purpose of buying a new stock. During the afternoon he [the merchant from Taos] bargained for the goods and wagons [of the trader from Arrow Rock], and we began refitting the wagons from oxen to mule teams, bargaining for mules, harness, etc. And by noon the next day both parties had made arrangements to return to their homes and families very well satisfied with their opportunities and bargain. The buyer was Peter Joseph, father of the delegate in congress from New Mexico.

Having accomplished our object, and in a manner far more satisfactorily and profitably to our friends than any of us had anticipated, we prepared an early supper, and as soon as it was dark left camp, intending

June 26, 1847. The Indians, well armed and mounted, began the attack by stampeding the cattle of one of the trains. "About twenty of the dragoons started to recover the cattle, if possible," wrote an eyewitness. "They followed about a mile, when a regular engagement took place. The Indians appeared to be on the retreat; but this was only done to get the men as far as possible on the prairie. About one hundred Indians had been stationed on the opposite bank of the river, and they now charged across, came up in the rear of the dragoons, and completely surrounded them. They now had it hand to hand – six to ten Indians upon one man at a time. The engagement lasted twenty minutes, and five of our men were killed and six wounded. . . They [the Indians] scalped three of the men. Some of them had as many as twelve to fifteen wounds from the lance, and were horribly mutilated; the throat of one was cut from ear to ear – the ears of another were cut off." *Daily Missouri Republican*, July 17, 1847. See also Thomas Fitzpatrick to T. H. Harvey, Sept. 18, 1847, MS., Missouri Historical Society.

[286] Mr. Miller. *Weekly Reveille*, July 26, 1847.

to travel as far and as long as the mules would stand it
to travel without feed or rest – running from Indians!
Our camp was but a few miles above the mouth of Big
Coon creek, and when we arrived at the crossing but a
short distance from the Arkansas, we discovered tracks
of horses in large numbers where they had crossed the
stream, and the bank on the opposite side still wet with
water shed from their feet in passing out of the creek.
We interpreted this sign to mean that the Indians had
anticipated that we would travel through the night and
stop at Pawnee Fork for breakfast, and they would
precede us and await us in ambush. We, of course, kept
a good lookout for signs and tracks, and by great labor
and caution, dismounting and crawling upon our hands
and knees, we were enabled to keep ourselves posted as
to their course and probable intentions. We found they
had divided into two parties in [on?] the way, and
after crossing Ash creek, six miles from Pawne Fork,
they had taken their course to that stream, so that one
party might strike it some distance above the crossing
and the other some distance below, thinking we would
cross the stream and stop for breakfast, and they could,
while [we were] taking our rest, charge upon our animals and drive them off with comparatively small risk.

Arriving at the west bank a little after daylight, we
found some wagons abandoned, buffalo robes scattered
over the prairie, wagon sheets and everything that a
war-party would desire and could carry off, gone,
[and] one old ox near the wagons, alone and discon-
solate, waiting for some friend to come along [to] take
him in charge and set him to work. An acquaintance
named Coolidge, a native of New Hampshire [who]
had spent the winter in Pueblo trading with the Ute,

Cheyenne, and Arapaho, had here been attacked, his stock driven off, and he and his men compelled to shoulder their blankets and provisions and march three hundred miles to the next house. Perhaps, if still living, he loves the Indians, sympathizes with them, and laments the wrongs and injustice done them by his ancestors; but I don't believe it. We were going in empty, and by stopping a day or two we might have packed the robes and loaded them into our wagons and taken [them] to a shipping point, thus perhaps saving something for him; but the danger we foresaw prevented [this]. And we told the men to gather robes enough for each a good bed, if they so desired, but [they] should not stop a wagon.

We crossed the river, and instead of stopping, traveled on till we came near Pawnee Rock, where we found water in a depression of the prairie, and where we could see an enemy for a long distance and prepare for defense; and [we] concluded to camp for food and rest for ourselves and animals. Our Arrow Rock friend, in relating his late experiences, told us we were still in danger, although out of the usual range of the Comanche. The border Indians sometimes when out in the buffalo range would join the Comanche and have some fun and take some scalps, and return as friendly Indians, having won trophies and honors among their people, under the name of another nation at war with the whites. The Osage (*Wazhazhe*) were frequently suspected of pursuing this course. Mr. [Miller] told us that there were large numbers of Indians – Osage, Sauk and Fox, etc. – not far from the Big Bend on a hunt; and when on their way out, while [they were] camped at Walnut creek, several Osage came to their camp, took dinner, smoked the pipe of peace, and when [they] moved out, the Indians left them, as they said, for their village. Among the Indians who ran off their cattle, he was sure [that] he [saw] some of these same Indians disguised in war dress and paint, but [with] the same horses and trappings; and notwithstanding the change in personal appearance he was sure they were the same Indians. This was a sort of border ground raided by war parties of the Pawnee, occasionally by Comanche and Kiowa, and the hunting grounds of the Kaw, Osage, [and] Sauk and Fox; and I once met the Iowa some forty miles east from here on their return from their hunt.

We took a short rest and traveled to Walnut creek, where we stopped for supper and another short rest, intending to "catch up" and travel in the night to Big Bend. But before we were ready to start, there came up a bad rain, which compelled us to remain over night. The next morning, after stowing away our wet bedding, and firing off, cleaning, and reloading our guns, we renewed our journey, and had not proceeded far before we saw a man on horseback ascend a butte some distance on our right, near the breaks of the Arkansas; and another, and others at short intervals, until the butte was covered with Indians. We immediately corralled securely our riding and loose animals inside the corral, and unhitched the four pair of led mules from the point of the tongue and corralled them, staked the wheelers to the ground; and very soon every man was in line on the south side of the wagons, armed and equipped to receive the Indians, whether friends or enemies. The warning often repeated by our friend was,

"Now boys, you've got to fight. They'll say '*Wazhazhe*,' but don't be fooled."

It was arranged that if they appeared claiming to be friends, Messrs. Houck and Elliott would meet two of the Indians some distance in advance but under protection of our rifles.

Very soon Indians left the butte [and] came towards us on the run, with others following, which appeared as if they meant war. But on our making the sign for them to halt, they halted in line. We signed them to send two men in the advance, while our two would advance and meet them for a parley.

The first sound greeting our ears was *"Wazhazhe."*

The next [sound] was from our own side: "Yes! Dam *Wazhazhe!* Boys, don't be fooled by 'em. We've got to fight. They're treacherous devils."

On the assurance that we would not be fooled by them, but would be ready for them as friends or enemies, he quieted down. The four men soon met and began to talk as well as they could by signs, when an Indian advanced from their line as if to take part in the negotiations. This, he knew, was not in order, and to impress upon the minds of him and his friends that we would not permit it, I advanced a rod or so and signed for him to stop – which he did, but soon started again to advance. I cocked my rifle, raised [it] to my shoulder, and aimed so he could see that if I pulled the trigger he was sure to be hit. He made no more moves to advance, and all parties on both sides remained in their positions until the talk was closed.

These were Osage on a buffalo hunt [we were informed], and the Sauk and Fox were encamped on the Arkansas below the Big Bend, and all were friendly to the whites. They would travel with us as far as Plumb Buttes, and we would be convinced that they were not deceiving us, and we would separate as friends. We consented, but on condition that they should not approach our wagons, but travel at a distance from our wagons.

Everything arranged, we hitched up and started on our route, and had not traveled far before everything indicated that there [were] large parties of Indians on their spring hunt, as they had told us. Many dead carcasses of buffalo were scattered over the prairie on each side of the road as far as we could see for several miles on our way. Soon numbers of Sauk and Fox came from their camp on the Arkansas, and we soon felt assured that there were so many from the frontier tribes they would not presume to attack us under the guise of hostile Comanche or Pawnee, and we permitted nearer approach and greater familiarity. Between Plumb Buttes and Cow creek they left us, and we saw no more Indians or buffalo except a few Kaw. We now breathed free and felt a great relief, as we were so near out of the land of our enemies.

A day or two after passing Council Grove,[287] we met Colonel [Alton R. Easton],[288] who was going out with five companies of troops for New Mexico. They had met the messengers sent by Lieutenant Love to Fort Leavenworth with his report of the attack of the Comanche on his camp, and we camped for dinner but a

---

[287] Webb arrived at Council Grove on July 7, 1847. Since his last visit, several buildings had been constructed at this place. Under a huge oak tree on the western side of the grove was a small blacksmith shop which had been built by the government in the summer of 1846. Near-by stood a trading establishment erected by Boone & Hamilton in the spring of 1847. It consisted of a store and a dwelling constructed of logs and roofed with shingles. Boone & Hamilton, who had a similar establishment at Westport, traded with the Indians and sold supplies to travelers over the Santa Fé trail. *Weekly Reveille*, May 3, July 26, 1847; *Daily Missouri Republican*, July 31, Sept. 25, 1847; Garrard, *Wah-To-Yah*, 8; Ruxton, *op. cit.*, 309.

[288] *Daily Missouri Republican*, July 19, 1847.

short distance apart. While we were eating, some of the men came to interview us and get an account of our adventures. After talking some time and asking many questions about the country and our adventures on the route, one of them, who seemed to have become convinced of our cowardice and our incapacity as prairie men, asked if we thought they would find any Comanche on the road out. I told him I thought, as they were a pretty strong party, they probably would not; but unless they were very cautious, the Indians would find some of them. He, in a low tone, but not so low but what I understood him, said to his friend he "did not see how so cautious and timid a man should ever venture upon the prairies." I made no remark to indicate that I had overheard him, but told him that prudence and caution on the prairies was the most effectual way to carry the hair across them.

Some time after my arrival in St. Louis, I read an account of the loss of several men from Colonel [Easton's] party on the Arkansas. It seems they camped on the bank of the river on the north side, and several of the men went across the river for wood, when the Indians raised from their ambush in the grass and killed and scalped them before assistance could reach them. They found all the bodies but one that night, and carried them to camp.[289] The next morning a party was sent over to make another search, but did not succeed in finding him. After breakfast and as the troops left camp, a large party was sent across to make a last search, and succeeded in finding the man still alive, but badly wounded [and] all the hair scalped from his head. I

[289] On July 21, 1847, the Indians killed eight and wounded four of Colonel Easton's battalion of infantry. *Ibid.*, Aug. 12, 16, 1847; *Weekly Reveille*, Aug. 16, 1847.

afterwards heard that he recovered and for some time remained with the troops in northern New Mexico and about Pueblo.

We reached Independence [290] without further adventure, made arrangements for the care of our stock, and left our wagons with Mr. Stone (the maker) for repair, expecting to make another trip to New Mexico that season. The wagons were a curiosity. The running gear and bodies [were] so dilapidated that repair seemed impossible. They had run eight thousand miles without the repairs of a blacksmith. Many breaks [had been] repaired by extra parts and timber carried for the purpose, and others made secure by wrapping with rawhide in the green state, which, when dried, would shrink so tight as to make them as secure as iron bands for a time; and when they gave out, were renewed with the same material. Mr. S. measured some of the wheels and told me they were three to four inches lower than when new, caused by the tire becoming loose and wedging up, cutting out the fellows, and forcing the spokes into the hub; so that it frequently became necessary to cut them off inside the hub with a chisel. No iron axles were run on the prairie for carrying freight until 1848.

[I] arrived in St. Louis,[291] and settling up our indebtedness, I concluded to take a rest of a month or so and enjoy the freedom from care and anxiety I had so long suffered – anticipating a good time in corresponding with friends at home with whom I had had no communication for fourteen months. But the change was too great, and my anticipations were not realized. A

---

[290] The traders arrived at Independence on July 13, 1847. *Missouri Statesman*, July 23, 1847.

[291] Webb arrived in St. Louis on July 19, 1847. *Daily Missouri Republican*, July 20, 1847.

week or two after my arrival I was attacked with jaundice and suffered extreme depression of bodily and mental infirmity, which continued for a month or more.

I was anxious to make another trip that year, as there appeared to be a fine prospect for trade, and felt willing to take the risk of another trip through the Indian country. Mr. Doan had engaged to remain in Chihuahua and assist Mr. Aull, the partner of Mr. Owens who was killed at the Battle of Sacramento, in selling out his stock, and I was desirous of finding another partner. I made proposals to a young man with whom I had some acquaintance, and whose reputation for steady habits and business capacity was good; and he, after considering the matter, about consented to join me. We were to draw articles of copartnership and commence purchasing goods on Monday. But the mail from Independence on Sunday brought news that a train was attacked by Indians on the Arkansas and sustained a serious loss of men and animals, and that a mail had been cut off and nearly all the men killed — which so discouraged my friend that he declined the adventure. Unable to find a partner, and it getting late in the season for the forming of a strong company, I abandoned the trip for that year.